The War of the Gunboats

By the same author

The Ironclads of Cambrai
North Sea Oil – The Great Gamble
The Buccaneers
PT Boats
Alaska – The Last Frontier
Tank Battles of World War One
A History of Fighter Aircraft
A History of Bomber Aircraft
The E-Boat Threat
The Adventure of North Sea Oil

Novels
Stones of Evil
The Wildcatters

The War of the Gunboats

Bryan Cooper

Pen & Sword
MARITIME

First published in 1970 in Great Britain by
Macdonald & Co. (Publishers) Ltd,
and in the United States by Stein and Day

This edition published in Great Britain in 2009 by
Pen and Sword Military
an imprint of
Pen and Sword Books Ltd
47 Church Street, Barnsley
South Yorkshire S70 2AS

Copyright © Bryan Cooper 1970
SBN 35602941 7

ISBN 978 1 84884 018 8

The right of Bryan Cooper to be identified as Author of this
Work has been asserted by him in accordance with the Copyright,
Designs and Patents Act 1988.

A CIP catalogue record for this book is available from the British Library

Typeset in 10pt Palatino by
Mac Style, Beverley, East Yorkshire

Printed and bound in the UK by
MPG Books Group

Pen and Sword Books Ltd incorporates the Imprints of Pen and Sword
Aviation, Pen and Sword Maritime, Pen and Sword Military,
Wharncliffe Local History, Pen and Sword Select, Pen and Sword
Military Classics and Leo Cooper.

For a complete list of Pen and Sword titles please contact
PEN and SWORD BOOKS LIMITED
47 Church Street, Barnsley, South Yorkshire, S70 2AS, England
E-mail: enquiries@pen-and-sword.co.uk
Website: www.pen-and-sword.co.uk

Contents

Acknowledgements   6
Introduction   7

Chapter 1   Intercept and Attack   11
Chapter 2   The Little Boats   22
Chapter 3   Into Battle   41
Chapter 4   Fight for the Narrow Seas   48
Chapter 5   Disaster in the Far East   56
Chapter 6   The PTs in Action   60
Chapter 7   Battle of the Mediterranean   66
Chapter 8   In the Balance   76
Chapter 9   The Big Raid   93
Chapter 10   The South Pacific Campaign   106
Chapter 11   The South-West Pacific Campaign   118
Chapter 12   The Growing Offensive   127
Chapter 13   Hit and Run in the Aegean   137
Chapter 14   Battle Squadron   146
Chapter 15   With the Partisans   151
Chapter 16   Preparation for the Great Invasion   164
Chapter 17   D-Day and After   178
Chapter 18   The Riviera War   191
Chapter 19   Return to the Philippines   196
Chapter 20   Arakan   203

Epilogue   210
Bibliography   215
Index   217

Acknowledgements

The author would like to thank the Imperial War Museum, the Department of the US Navy, Vosper-Thornycroft (UK) Ltd., and WWII PT Boats Museum and Archives in Germantown, Tennessee, USA, for the photographs used in this book; also John Batchelor for his drawings, and Carol Stuart and Laurence Genin for their computer expertise.

Introduction

The closest-fought sea battles of the Second World War were those of the 'little ships', the highly manoeuvrable motor torpedo boats and gunboats of all the major navies.

Small enough to move unseen over moonlit waters, penetrating minefields and harbour defences to take the war close to an enemy's coast, and fast enough to fire their torpedoes and speed away again before the enemy's guns could be brought to bear on them, they were deadly weapons in coastal waters. Too small and numerous to be given the dignity of individual names, they were known by numbers instead – to the British as MTBs and MGBs; to the Americans as PT boats; to the Germans as S-boats; and to the Italians as MAS boats. They fought in every major theatre of war, in the English Channel and the North Sea, among the dreamy islands of the Aegean, off Burma and Malaya and in the South China Sea, and across the Pacific islands to the final liberation of the Philippines.

Night was the time of their hunting. By day, because weight of armament had to be sacrificed for speed, they were vulnerable to attack by aircraft and other surface warships. But at night they could rely on surprise as their main advantage.

At rest in the water, the boats were squat and beamy. But at speed they were things of beauty, planing over the water at 40 knots and more, with bows lifted, slicing great waves from either side of their hulls and leaving wakes foaming far behind them. The men who rode these night hunters might curse the pounding they got, but they knew an exhilaration of speed that no other kind of ship could give. Their battles, when similar craft of opposing sides met, were fought hand to hand at closer quarters than any other kind of warship.

But paradoxically, speed was not a main requirement in the ideal torpedo attack, which was made by lying in wait with engines cut in the path of a convoy, then idling unseen and silently towards a target, launching torpedoes and slipping away before the enemy knew what hit them. This was not always possible, of course, and once sighted, speed was often the only means of escape. Rapid manoeuvrability, a low silhouette which made them a difficult target and the use of smokescreens, were their primary means of protection. Guns were mounted, but they could only be really effective against craft of their own size, as with the motor gunboats which the Royal Navy developed for the specific purpose of combating German motor torpedo boats.

The main purpose of the little ships was to attack enemy shipping, but they were used in many other ways. Apart from protecting their own convoys, they took part in combined operations raids, transporting troops and supplies, and giving covering fire during beach landings. They raided harbours, dropped secret agents on lonely shores, captured and boarded merchant ships in a manner reminiscent of the buccaneers of old. Their only limitation was range, because of the high fuel consumption of their powerful engines, and their inability to take much punishment in heavy seas.

There were three main areas of conflict in which motor torpedo boats took part, and in broad terms their operations reached a peak at three distinct stages of the war. First, there was the fight for the seas off the east and south coasts of Britain which, with Germany's occupation of France and the whole coastline of Western Europe, became as grim and desperate as the air battle taking place in the skies overhead. This was their greatest arena of operations. Not only were motor torpedo boats of both Britain and Germany used for attacking each other's merchant convoys by mine and torpedo, but there was a direct confrontation between them as they strove to defend as well as attack. Included in the Coastal Forces of Britain were crews and boats from the Dominion and European allies and, at a later date, from America. It was not until the end of 1942 that Britain began to reach equal terms with the German *Schnellboot*, perhaps the most successful of all motor torpedo boats, which were generally called 'E-boats' by the Allied forces, standing for 'Enemy War Motorboat'. The fight grew in intensity in 1943, and again in 1944 with the Normandy landings; it lasted until the very end of the war when the German boats, although by then outnumbered and outclassed, were still harrying Allied shipping.

The second area of conflict was in the Mediterranean, where sea fighting followed the progress of the land battle as it extended from North Africa to Sicily, Italy and the Balkans, and built up to a climax with Italy's surrender. Here also the motor torpedo boats attacked as well as defended convoys as both sides fought to keep open lines of supply to their land forces. Malta figured prominently in this struggle, both as a base for MTBs and as a target for attack by German and Italian boats. But the whole canvas of operations in the Mediterranean was on a larger scale and gave greater scope for the kind of lone role that suited the individual temperament of those who served in small boats. Either singly or in units, craft would set out from their bases for days at a time to attack enemy convoys, take part in commando raids, and cooperate with partisans behind enemy lines, hiding by day amongst the many islands in the region, or sheltering in quiet bays and inlets. As in home waters, British Coastal Forces included Dominion and American crews and boats. For a while, an American PT (patrol torpedo boat) squadron was the sole representative of the US Navy in these waters. The war in the Mediterranean was significant for the large number of Italian MAS boats operating in the early stages, Italy having given more attention to the military application of such craft before the war than the other powers, which tended to concentrate on big ships to the neglect of smaller ones.

The third and last area to come into prominence was the Pacific and Far East. Although British Coastal Forces were employed to a limited extent off the coasts of Malaya and Burma, this was mainly an American area of operations in which the use of PT boats during the island-hopping strategy to liberate Japanese-occupied territories was perhaps the most successful of all. As well as being used to attack coastal supply ships, the PTs took part in some of the great fleet battles in the Pacific and were effective against Japanese warships up to the size of light cruiser. Because of the nature of the Pacific War, they cooperated very closely with the US Army during troop landings. The Japanese, on the other hand, did less than any of the other major powers in the development of motor torpedo boats. One of their main weapons in this type of craft was the *Shinyo* suicide boat, the marine equivalent of the *Kamikaze* plane, which appeared in large numbers during the latter stages of war.

Motor torpedo boats of all the powers depended greatly on the development by private companies between the two world wars of motorboats for sport and pleasure. Men like Sir Malcolm Campbell and Sir Henry Segrave, with their record-breaking achievements over water, provided valuable knowledge for research into fast boat design. Because most of the major navies of the world, including the Royal Navy, had paid so little attention to the possibilities of motor torpedo boats, even though they had been used very successfully during the First World War, particularly by the Italians against the Austrians, there had been much interchange of ideas between countries which were later to find themselves on opposing sides. Also, the smaller nations, perhaps because they were unable to build big ships, were very alive to the possibilities of motor torpedo boats, and firms like Vosper and Thornycroft built MTBs for many foreign navies. At the beginning of the war, there was an extraordinary situation in which the few British MTBs that were in service were powered by Italian Isotta Fraschini engines – perhaps the best of the small-boat petrol engines – which immediately became unavailable; the German *Schnellboot* was based on the design of a motor launch built privately by the Lürssen yard for an American customer; Thornycroft boats built for the Yugoslavian Navy were captured by the Italians and used by them, and later the Germans, against the Allies; an MTB design by the British Power Boat Company was used as the basis of the first American PT boats; the American Packard engine, which became the main power unit for all British and American boats, was itself a development of the Rolls Royce Merlin engine; and a Thornycroft design was the basis for most of the limited number of boats built by the Japanese.

There were similarities, too, in the manning of small craft. Most of the Allied crew were civilian volunteers, often from the ranks of pre-war yachtsmen and motorboat enthusiasts. To a greater or lesser extent they were at first regarded with scepticism by the men of the regular navies. This attitude changed after the small boats had proved their worth, but the tactics involved in fighting in such craft had to be worked out by the volunteers themselves through trial and error.

Diverse as they were, what all the small-boat operations proved is the vital importance of coastal waters. It is not only through such waters that merchant ships must bring supplies from overseas, but very often coastal convoys are the only practical and economic means of transferring materials from one part of a country to another. These convoys must be protected, while at the same time there is the need to attack those of the enemy.

Equally, from the military point of view, coastal waters are a major factor in mounting any expeditionary raid or invasion. This applies to defence as well as attack, whenever it involves the transporting of a large body of men by sea. Germany's plan to invade Britain failed because this vital command of the seas was lacking. The evacuation from Dunkirk was only possible because Britain just held a balance of power in the English Channel.

Small craft are not, of course, the only factor in a consideration of coastal waters, nor for that matter the most important. Other ships are involved – the German S-boat commanders, for instance, feared British destroyers more than they did the motor gunboats that had been designed specifically as weapons to be used against them. But a combination of the two – destroyers and motor gunboats – was even more effective as later operations in the North Sea proved. Air power had an even greater role to play, certainly by day. Its value in attacking enemy warships and merchant shipping was one of the great lessons of the war and it became the predominant weapon in the control of narrow waters. But again, it was most successful when used in cooperation with other forces. By mid-1943, for example, Britain's Coastal Forces were finding it extremely useful to work with Fighter Command groups in offensive sweeps against enemy shipping between the Dutch coast and the Channel approaches. Fighter cover overhead could ward off attacks by enemy aircraft on an MTB returning home in the morning from a night's operations. On the other hand, that same boat might have sunk a 'flak' ship in the North Sea and thereby perhaps saved one of the bombers sent out the following day to attack a German convoy. There was a growing appreciation of the inter-dependence between all the various Services concerned.

Covering as this book does the employment of motor torpedo boats in all the theatres of war, not only by the Allies but by the Axis powers as well, it has not been possible to describe more than a few of the operations in which they took part. The aim has been to select examples that represent the different ways in which these craft were used. A complete list of operations would require a very much lengthier book and would in any case be repetitive, as so many were alike. Many patrols were made, of course, which saw no action at all. As in every activity of war, there were long periods of monotony and sheer misery from the cold and damp of the North Sea, or the sultry heat of the Philippines. Also, there were other areas in which small craft kept up the watchful work of patrolling and seldom, if ever, came into contact with the enemy, such as in the Caribbean, off the North American coast, in the Aleutians, and off the coasts of West and South Africa. But such activities are outside the scope of this book, which is concerned with actual operations and actions as seen against the background of the war at the time.

CHAPTER 1

Intercept and Attack

The night of 8/9 September 1941, clear and calm but with the hint of an early autumn in the air, set the pattern for a new type of warfare at sea: the war of the 'little ships', the motor torpedo boats and motor gunboats of British Coastal Forces.

There had been brushes with the enemy before. A few had been partially successful. But most had been so disappointing that many naval planners were doubting the wisdom of devoting effort and expense to these small craft that seemed so prone to mechanical failure and were so seldom able to make contact with the enemy – and even then the damage they inflicted was usually very slight.

But it took time to learn new tactics for a new kind of war. There were no precedents, no rules to fall back on. In boats that were mostly old and of obsolete design, the coastal force crews on both sides of the Channel, of both the British and German navies, were feeling their way and learning from their mistakes. And on this September night, the first major success was achieved, setting the pattern for small-boat warfare that was to remain for the rest of the war.

In Dover Command, the frustration of past failures was even more keenly felt. Although a Coastal Force unit had been operational from Dover for nearly a year, the results had always been disappointing. Either they failed to intercept the enemy or, if they did, their attacks were beaten off. And now, just entering the third year of the war, it was a matter of vital importance, for the battle of the convoys in the Straits of Dover had become a battle of survival for both sides. Vulnerable as they were by day to aircraft bombing attacks, and to shelling by long-range shore batteries on either side of the narrow Straits, British and German convoys had taken to running the gauntlet by night. And this was the time of the motor torpedo boats – the night hunters.

On the staff of the Flag Officer, Dover Command, was a man who had been a sailing enthusiast before the war and something of an expert on radio navigation. This was Julian Rogers-Coltman. Now, as an acting temporary Lieutenant Commander of the Royal Naval Volunteer Reserve, he had over the months built up a highly efficient system of radio-direction finding. Using twin radio beams to get a bearing on any ships in the area, he had time and again been able to put the MTBs on the track of German convoys. But their indecisive attacks had always been unsuccessful. He feared the same would happen yet again when, at 21.32 hours on the night of 8 September, an RDF signal was sent to him at Command Headquarters in Dover Castle, warning of a German convoy that was just leaving Boulogne and which looked as if it was going to make a dash northwards through the Straits.

Dover harbour in those days of the war sheltered a strange assortment of ships. Instead of the pre-war cross-Channel steamers and pleasure craft, there were sleek, grey-painted destroyers and corvettes. The fishing trawlers and drifters were still there, but mounted on their forward decks were Lewis machine guns, incongruous amongst the nets and fishing gear. And then there were the MTBs: 60- and 70-foot hulls lying low in the water, wheelhouse and mastheads raked back, angry with guns fore and aft, and with cylindrical torpedo tubes snouting out on each side of their decks.

The young crews of the 6th MTB Flotilla, mostly RNVR officers and Hostilities Only ratings, had been out for five nights in succession. They were now on a one-hour stand-by notice – some in fact were at a local variety show, including the Senior Officer, Lieutenant Commander Edward Nigel Pumphrey RN. But within half an hour they had been recalled to base, by which time further RDF reports had shown that the German convoy was indeed going to make a run for it through the Dover Strait. Shortly after 22.00, Pumphrey went over details of the mission with his crews in the briefing room while they waited for the final telephone call from the Castle to get underway.

Pumphrey had already had one encounter with the enemy, after joining the flotilla earlier in the year (a flotilla usually comprised eight boats). Like the others, it had been unsuccessful. The crews lacked experience with this new kind of fighting craft. Too often a wild dash into the night had resulted in failure to contact the enemy. The open sea was a vast and remote place at night, in the days before all boats were equipped with radar, and it was only too easy to pass by the enemy, even within a range of a few hundred yards. But commanders like Pumphrey and their crews were learning fast.

Only three boats were operational: Pumphrey's own, which was *MTB 35; MTB 218,* commanded by Lieutenant C.E. 'Chuck' Bonnell of the Royal Canadian Naval Volunteer Reserve, one of many Canadians, Australians, New Zealanders and South Africans who had joined this navy of little ships; and *MTB 54,* commanded by Lieutenant Per Danielsen of the Royal Norwegian Navy. His was one of several Norwegian-manned boats serving with the MTB flotillas of the Royal Navy; there were also Dutch, Polish and Free French crews.

Interception was planned to take place off Blank Nez. At the same time, a unit of motor gunboats which was on patrol in the vicinity was warned to stand by and join in the attack if the interception was successful. The boats were ready and waiting in the harbour, maintained as they always were in an operational condition. The fuel tanks were filled, torpedoes loaded into the 21-inch cylindrical tubes, one on either side and forward of the wheelhouse, and angled slightly so that the 'tin fish' would clear the bows when fired; ammunition for the .5-inch guns aft had been checked. Within minutes of the order to get under way, the crews had put on oilskins and rubber boots, and clambered onto the boats. It was 22.30.

To the south-east, out to sea, banks of cloud were building up black on the horizon. There was no moon yet but there was some visibility. The first pale stars had appeared. A light wind brushed the waves, but in the harbour the water was glassy smooth, with only an occasional ripple splashing at the boats moored alongside the jetty.

With a splutter, the centre of the three engines which powered each boat broke into life and settled down to a steady drone. Pumphrey was about to give the order to leave harbour when Danielsen signalled from the Norwegian boat that he was having trouble with one of his engines. This kind of hold-up occurred only too often, before more powerful and much-improved American engines began to arrive in large numbers later in the war. Ordering Danielsen to follow when he was ready and meet up at the rendezvous point if he couldn't find them, the two boats, *MTB 35* and *MTB 218*, moved slowly away from the jetty and made for the harbour entrance. With the coxswain at the wheel and the commanding officer of each boat beside him, the crews went to their various stations to secure for sea and prepare for action: the first lieutenant to the small charthouse just forward and below the bridge to plot the course; the gunner to the swivel turret behind the wheelhouse, to crouch over the .5-inch machine guns; the telegraphist to the radio telephone (or wireless telegraph) in the cubby hole behind the bridge to monitor the signals being sent out from Command Headquarters to all the little ships on Dover patrol, and especially to receive new RDF reports on the movements of the German convoy; the motor mechanic and two stokers to the cramped engine room. In Pumphrey's boat, along for the ride, was Lieutenant D.G. Tait, the acting spare commanding officer of the 6th Flotilla. He was helping the first officer, Sub Lieutenant Harwin Sheldrick, to plot their course.

'Ahead port. Ahead starboard.'

At Pumphrey's order, the two wing engines started with a deep roar and the boat moved faster through the water. Now the three engines, each giving over 1,000 horsepower, were being held back and at 15 knots the MTB shuddered with the urge to leap forward. The second boat was following behind on the port quarter.

In the engine room, Acting Chief Motor Mechanic Thomas Gordon thrust the throttle levers forward. The sound was deafening as the engines reached full power, the smell of burning oil pungent and almost overpowering. The bows lifted clear of the water as the speed increased. Long V-shaped trails foamed out in their wake.

Newer MTBs which were coming into service with the Royal Navy by the end of 1941 were capable of even faster speeds – up to 40 knots and more. But even at something around 35 knots, the 70-foot wooden hulls of the two boats seemed to fly as they lifted out of the water, their dark outlines silhouetted sharply against the waves cascading from the bows. The coastline rapidly vanished into the dusk.

At the wheel of *MTB 35*, the coxswain, Petty Officer James Hadley, followed Pumphrey's orders as further RDF reports came through. The German convoy was now steering eastwards through the Straits, within a couple of miles of the French coast. At 23.23, after nearly an hour at top speed and with the engines running very hot, they approached the interception point, just off the French coast and 2 or 3 miles ahead of the convoy. The wing engines were cut and the boats slowed down on centre engines only, to about 10 knots.

This was the worst moment of all, after the breathless ride through the night: waiting for the interception, hoping that the RDF plots had put them in the path of the oncoming convoy. In the early days, MTBs had tried to attack enemy convoys at speed from some distance off, as soon as they had located them. But they themselves had been given away by their wakes and the vital element of surprise had been lost. The small boats had often found themselves outmanoeuvred and shot at before they could get near enough to release their torpedoes with any chance of hitting the targets. Other commands had developed the tactic of 'lying in wait'with engines cut in what they hoped was the convoy's route, so that when the ships were close they could fire their torpedoes and, if lucky, creep away before being seen. If they were seen, then the engines would be crash-started and they would rely on their superior speed and the smallness of the target they made to avoid the enemy's gunfire.

In the narrow waters of Dover Command, covered as they were by RDF, they could rely on the additional advantage of accurate plotting to bring them to the interception point. But there was still the same need to make a surprise attack if they were not to be beaten off by escorting patrol boats before getting close enough to fire their torpedoes. And this was the tactic that Pumphrey had decided upon, of getting just far enough ahead of the convoy to be able to cruise in quietly for the last few miles, preferably with the dark horizon behind them so that the moon, if there was one, would light the enemy's path. That was the theory at least. It was now time for Dover Command to test it in practice.

The crews of both boats waited and watched tensely. And most of all, listened. On such a calm night at sea, sounds could be heard a long way off. A cough, the thud of a hatch closing, a stifled curse – all seemed to echo and intensify in the stillness of open water. The sound of engines would be heard if the convoy came near them. But there were dangers in following such tactics. They might suddenly find themselves a sitting target in the middle of a group of S-boats. Or the convoy might change course at the last minute and sail right on by.

Pumphrey scanned the horizon to the south-east through his night glasses. A chip of moon hung low in the sky, enough to give some visibility for about a mile. Beyond that was darkness, hiding the enemy-occupied coast of France which was less than 2 miles away. In the gun turret, Able Seaman John Carruthers tried to warm his spray-frozen fingers by breathing on them. Jakes, the torpedoman, once again checked the firing mechanism of the torpedoes. If they met the enemy, it was vital that they fired correctly. They were the sole reason for the MTB's existence. The fumes in the engine room had cleared a little by now. Gordon and the two stokers, Mason and Scantlebury, were taking the opportunity of topping up the oil levels. Ordinary Seaman Gillings, the signalman, held his lamp in preparation to flash a signal to Bonnell should they sight the enemy.

At 23.35, a sound was heard on the starboard bow. And then dark shadows were seen, looming out of the mist about 2,000 yards away. Two merchant ships, of around 3,000 tons each, loaded right down in the water and steering a north-easterly course. At Pumphrey's command, the telegraphist signalled to base: 'Two enemy ships sighted 140 degrees South Foreland 15½ miles. Closing.'

The boats crept forward, closing the enemy ships at a 45-degree angle. 1,800 yards, 1,500 yards…and then other shapes became visible. Two with tall masts that looked like armed trawlers; and smaller, more sinister outlines. E-boats (as the S-boats were called by the Royal Navy). At least eight of them, screening the rear and either side of the convoy. In fact, in coming up to the convoy, the MTBs had passed between two S-boats at a range of 1,000 yards without realizing it. But fortunately, they were not seen. The German lookouts were not expecting trouble so close to their own shore.

Now on a parallel course following the convoy, it became apparent that the speed of the German ships was just a few knots faster than the MTBs could make on single engines. The convoy was gradually pulling away. There was no alternative but to start all engines – which would immediately give away their presence to the enemy.

It was 23.42 when Pumphrey ordered: 'Engage enemy'. The wing engines roared into life and the two boats leaped forward, waves spreading out from their bows. The nearest S-boats heeled sideways as their coxswains, caught by surprise, turned away from their path. But other boats had seen the attackers as well. A curtain of green tracer arced towards the MTBs.

Within seconds, the stillness of the night was shattered. The trawlers opened fire with their 37mm guns. Lights flashed in all directions. The German shore batteries joined in. Starshells burst overhead, vividly illuminating the scene, then fading into sparklets of light that came dripping into the sea like spent fireworks. The batteries were not daring to use high explosive for fear of hitting their own ships, but the starshells showed up the MTBs clearly. Streams of tracer bullets, green, red and white phosphor burning like a myriad swarming dragonflies, criss-crossed in midair, their singing sweet until bursts hit a hull with a drum of thunder, sparks flew from tearing metal and long gashes appeared in the deck timbers. The two boats swerved from side to side to avoid the gunfire, much of which was fortunately going over their heads. The sea churned and frothed with falling shells and the smell of smoke and cordite filled the air as the sound of the engines rose to a screaming pitch. The fight had begun.

Fifteen miles away, the gunfire was seen by Lieutenant Stewart Gould from the bridge of *MGB 43*. Together with *MGB 52*, commanded by Lieutenant Barry Leith, this boat was racing towards the interception, having received a bearing from Dover Command Headquarters. The boats altered course slightly to head directly for the lights flashing over the distant horizon.

Four hours previously the two boats under Gould's command, as Senior Officer of the 3rd MGB Flotilla, had left Ramsgate to carry out a routine patrol in the vicinity of the Varne shallows, between Dover and Boulogne. They reached the East Varne buoy at 21.37 and then turned in the direction of the South Varne buoy. It looked as if this patrol was going to be as uneventful as on all the other nights. The first motor gunboats had been brought into service less than a year before, no more than a few converted motor anti-submarine boats to begin with, armed only with .303 machine-guns. The newer 63-foot craft such as Gould and Leith commanded carried more formidable armament: not only an Oerlikon and four twin-mounted Lewis guns, but also a number of depth charges strapped to the deck. These had originally been intended for anti-submarine warfare, but British destroyers and aircraft had kept most of the U-boats out of the narrow seas – they were now concentrated in the Atlantic for attacks against Allied convoys and were therefore out of range of the little ships. So the MGB commanders had devised a new and hair-raising use for the depth charges: dropping them under the hulls of German merchant ships after cutting sharply across their bows.

The MGBs were similar in construction to the MTBs. Gould himself had served in torpedo boats before transferring to gunboats and had taken part in the evacuation from Dunkirk. Like the MTBs they had yet to fight a successful action in this area. As Gould headed for the distant gunfire, he too was wondering if now, at last, they were to have their chance. It would be galling for the MTBs to have it all their own way – at this time there existed a friendly rivalry between the crews serving in the two types of craft.

On giving the command to engage the enemy, Pumphrey had directed *MTB 35* towards the rear merchant vessel from a position about 10 degrees abaft her beam. With enemy gunfire hailing around them, the little boat sped forwards. Pumphrey took careful aim over the torpedo sight, calculated to allow for the speed of the target and the running time of the torpedo. At a range of 800 yards and pointing ahead of the target, Pumphrey pulled the torpedo firing lever, with Jakes standing by to fire the torpedoes from a secondary system in the event of there being a failure. There was a dull clang and a hiss; the boat gave a slight shudder. Pumphrey was vaguely aware that only the starboard torpedo had seemed to splash into the water. But there was no time to find out. He immediately gave the order 'Hard-a-starboard', and the boat turned away.

By now the German fire was more accurate and several bursts hit the MTB, but a moment later there was a tremendous explosion behind them. Pumphrey and the rest of the crew turned. Smoke and flames were billowing up from the merchant vessel. The Dover flotilla had achieved its first success.

MTB 218 hadn't been so fortunate. Her two torpedoes had been fired at the leading merchant ship, but at the last minute, the ship changed course and the torpedoes passed harmlessly by. Then two S-boats came up behind the MTB, their white-painted hulls showing up clearly, and opened rapid fire. Chuck Bonnell ordered a disengaging course at a speed of 32 knots. His torpedoes fired, there was no more he could do. He looked round for the other MTB, but it had disappeared in the darkness. The S-boats were still chasing. Bonnell's gunner returned the fire of one of them, and then, mistaking each other in the darkness, the two S-boats began firing between themselves. By the time they realized their mistake, the MTB had escaped. Assuming that *MTB 35* had also fired her torpedoes – with obvious success, judging from the explosion – and had also broken off the engagement, Bonnell altered course for the rendezvous point north-east of the Varne.

Once there, he waited for half an hour, but Pumphrey's boat failed to appear. So, thinking Pumphrey might have gone straight home, Bonnell set course for Dover and, after an uneventful voyage, arrived back in harbour at 01.39 on the morning of 9 September.

But *MTB 35* hadn't yet started out for home. After disengaging, Pumphrey had taken her clear of the convoy and within five minutes was once again alone in the sheltering darkness. He ordered the engines to be cut and checked for damage. It was not serious. Then Jakes, the torpedoman, reported that the port torpedo had misfired and was still in the tube. The regulations stated that during an attack both torpedoes should always be fired together, so that there was still the chance of a hit if one missed. It was a lucky coincidence that they had hit their target with just one torpedo and still had the other one left for further action. At a cost of several thousand pounds a time, they weren't weapons to be wasted.

It was six minutes past midnight. The convoy had completely disappeared, probably on an altered course to avoid further attack. They couldn't even hear its engines. All was quiet. Suddenly, a boat loomed up on the port side causing an immediate alarm. Could it be one of the S-boats searching the area for just such a sitting target? Pumphrey ordered the challenge signal to be given, a flicker of light from a shaded blue lantern. Carruthers trained his guns on the dark shape that was coming nearer, ready to open fire should it be one of the enemy boats. But the signal that came flashing back across the water was the correct one. As the boat closed, they saw it was Danielsen's *MTB 54*, which had left harbour about half an hour after the other two boats.

Information was exchanged. The Senior Officer learned that *54* had reached the French coastal shipping route at 23.20 and stopped to listen. After fifteen minutes, they heard the sound of firing. Danielsen was about to follow when two boats came near, recognition signals were exchanged and they proved to be the two MGBs heading in the same direction. Danielsen had been lucky; earlier in the war, trigger-happy commanders in such a situation had sometimes fired first and asked questions after. But the crews of the little ships had learnt a lot since then.

Ordering the Norwegian boat to follow, Pumphrey set off to try and find the convoy again, following the easterly course it seemed to be taking. His boat had one torpedo left, *MTB 54* still had both torpedoes intact. The battle was by no means over.

The MGBs in the meantime had failed to make contact with the enemy, the gunfire having ceased before they could arrive on the scene. Gould exchanged signals with Coltman in Dover and also with Pumphrey, and, learning of the general direction the convoy had taken, also set off to intercept. The plan was that the MGBs would attack the S-boats from behind and leave the way clear for the MTBs to make a torpedo attack on the remaining merchant ship.

The MTBs began the long, hard chase, passing inshore of the convoy so they could make an unexpected attack from its starboard beam. Because the enemy coast was so close, they had to run on single engines with speed reduced to 10 knots. Further RDF plots received from Dover showed that the convoy had resumed its previous course. By now, news of the first successful attack and the present hunt was known by all those on duty in Dover Command Headquarters and Coltma's operations room was crowded. Other channels were cleared so as not to interfere with messages to and from the MTBs. For once, after months of nothing to report but negative signals, the little ships were the centre of attention.

Danielsen was the first to see something. At about 00.45, he reported to Pumphrey the sighting of dark shapes to the south that looked like ships. The two boats went to investigate, only to find that the shapes were the buildings and cranes on the pier in Calais harbour. With a red face, Danielsen followed *MTB 35* as the two boats slipped quietly away and went back to their original course.

The first actually to sight the convoy was Gould, in *MGB 43*. He signalled the information to Dover Command and also to Pumphrey: 'Enemy convoy sighted 104 degrees South Foreland 24 miles.' The time was 01.14.

As far as Gould could make out, there was one merchant ship and about six escorts, two of them armed trawlers and the remainder S-boats. He decided to shadow the convoy until the MTBs had time to close for their attack, and took station on the port quarter, about three-quarters of a mile behind. But the minutes passed and there was still no sign that the MTBs had seen the convoy. All Gould knew was that they were several miles to the west. At 01.40, he decided to make a depth-charge attack with the dual purpose of inflicting as much damage to the enemy as he could and also guiding the MTBs to the area. Just at that moment, however, he saw small craft coming up astern of the convoy at high speed. It wasn't where he expected to see the MTBs, but they could have changed their position. 'Thinking they might be our MTBs,' Gould later reported, 'I challenged. This was answered by heavy and accurate fire from shell-firing machine-guns. I then saw that they were German S-boats, four of them, in line abreast.'

Both of Gould's Lewis gunners, Able Seamen S.J. Beckett and E. Fletcher, were severely wounded by fragments of cannon shell, so that they were unable to take any further part in the action. *MGB 52* had one engine and one Lewis gun disabled, but this did not deter Gould. With *52* following, he increased speed to 30 knots and engaged the S-boats with full armament. Turning north, he then raced across the bows of the leading German boat and dropped a depth charge, set to go off at 100 feet. There was a dull explosion and no more was seen of the S-boat. Meanwhile, the other German boats were being repeatedly hit with Oerlikon and Lewis-gun fire, so that after a couple of minutes they broke off the action and turned away to the south at high speed. Gould then set about the rest of the convoy, closing to within 600 yards and engaging with gunfire. The enemy were so demoralized by now that they were firing wildly in all directions, and at one point, as Gould later recalled, the trawlers were firing at their own S-boats.

All this provided an excellent opportunity for the MTBs which were coming up on the starboard beam, while the gunboat action was taking place on the convoy's port quarter. In fact, Danielsen had spotted the convoy only two minutes after Gould. Pumphrey couldn't see the German ships himself so he ordered *MTB 54* to attack first as it was the faster boat. By the time they had got into position to engage, they could hear firing from the rear of the convoy, where the MGBs were taking on the S-boats.

MTB 54 turned northwards and within a few minutes was 1,200 yards from the merchant ship. She fired both torpedoes, then laid a smokescreen and veered round towards the front of the convoy. *MTB 35*, following about 200 yards behind, ran on through the smoke and on emerging found four S-boats closing fast on the starboard bow. Dead ahead was the merchant ship. Pumphrey decided to go in close to make sure of it, thinking that Danielsen's torpedoes had missed, but just as he fired his one remaining torpedo, the vessel blew up in a great billow of black smoke and wreckage. Both of 54's torpedoes had hit amidships.

There was no time to watch this final success, however, for Pumphrey suddenly found himself in a highly dangerous situation, still under fire from the four S-boats. Ahead was the blazing merchant ship and on the port side was one of the armed trawlers. To get past, it meant closing on the trawler at a range of less than 100 yards. Deciding this was the lesser of the evils, Pumphrey turned hard to port in the direction of the trawler.

The trawler's fire was not very accurate, but at that range she could hardly miss. A hail of machine-gun bullets and cannon fire raked the MTB. Pumphrey, Jakes and the telegraphist were all wounded. The two wing engines spluttered and stopped. Half the stern was shot away, taking the steering gear with it, and a fire started in the petrol compartment amidships. Out of control, with only the centre engine to push the boat along at about 5 knots, she began circling slowly to port towards the trawler, still under fire from both the trawler and the S-boats. Pumphrey had no choice but to stop the centre engine to prevent the boat coming even closer to the trawler. She was now a crippled, stationary target. Carruthers kept blazing away at the trawler with the .5-inch guns, so effectively that he managed to keep down the return fire from the German ship. But there were no guns with which to engage the S-boats which were now lined up about 500 yards off. It was a critical situation in which it seemed only a matter of moments before the S-boats came in for the kill.

Meanwhile, unaware of the MTB's difficulties, the MGBs broke off the engagement at 02.55 and set course for home. They had been fighting for just over one hour, during which time they had destroyed an S-boat and put the second of the two trawlers out of action – it was still on fire six hours later when the RAF sent a reconnaissance plane over.

But *MGB 52* was badly damaged, with one engine out of action and a serious manifold leak in one of the others which made her speed very erratic. The water in the engine room was waist high and the motor mechanic, R.J.J. Stanley, and the two stokers, T.R. Harrison and W.E. Jones, had a bad time of it, continuously bailing for six hours. On the way home, a Dornier 17 shadowed the two craft for about twenty minutes at a height of 500 feet. The plane was finally driven off by 43's gunner, Able Seaman Lanfear. *MGB 43* finally arrived at Ramsgate at 09.20, after *MGB 52* had been taken in tow by a destroyer to Sheerness.

MTB 54 also disengaged at 03.00, after passing the sinking merchant ship and the second trawler which was on fire. Two S-boats made an attack, but the MTB escaped by making smoke. Danielsen brought her into Dover harbour at 05.12, undamaged and without casualties.

Pumphrey's boat was now alone and although the convoy had been devastated – two merchant ships, one S-boat sunk, one trawler on fire – there were still one trawler and five S-boats left. But there was no time even to consider the enemy craft. The fire was still blazing in the petrol compartment, the main engines had broken down and there was no means of steering the boat. Incredibly, the S-boats held off. When one of them did nose in to a range of 100 yards and opened fire, Carruthers swung his guns round and returned the fire. Red and green tracer crossed in the air. But Carruthers' was the more accurate, hitting the bridge of the S-boat, which sheered off after a few minutes allowing Carruthers to return his attention to the trawler.

When the stern and one of the rudders had been blasted away by a 3-inch shell, Hadley, the coxswain, had tried to steer the boat away from the trawler by means of a bucket dragged through the water on the port side. This hadn't worked. So now, with the help of Jakes, he set about trying to rig a hand-steering device. It meant they both had to lie flat on the stern deck and hold an improvised tiller in place. Jakes's legs were riddled with splinters from cannon fire, but he didn't mention this until much later. The telegraphist was also badly wounded, having been shot through the kidneys. He was barely conscious but remained at the W/T, sending signals about their situation to Dover Command.

Meanwhile, in an attempt to put out the fire in the petrol compartment where 700 gallons of burning petrol were swilling about in the bilge, Sheldrick, the first lieutenant, operated the fire extinguisher levers in the wheelhouse. At the same time, Ordinary Seaman Gillings seized a hand extinguisher and leaning well over the side of the boat, squirted foam through the shellhole. The methyl-bromide acted quickly and the flames died out, but in error, the chemical had also been released in the engine room, filling it with poisonous fumes. The three crew members from the engine room came stumbling up on to the deck, gasping for air and almost unconscious. They had to be given artificial respiration, which was organized by Lieutenant D.G. Tate, the man who had come 'just for the ride'. After a few minutes, and still retching, they went back to the engine room and continued working on the engines, in spite of the fumes.

Fifteen minutes went by while these feverish attempts to make the boat operational were carried out. The trawler was only firing occasionally, and very inaccurately, her gunners kept down by Carruthers' fire. But the S-boats were still there. They had stopped engines and lain off in a group about 800 yards away. Suddenly, they restarted their engines, formed up in a line and came slowly towards the MTB.

Pumphrey knew that this must be the end. He ordered the life-raft to be cleared and floated alongside. The crew were to abandon ship as soon as the enemy started firing, while Pumphrey himself would remain on board to restart the petrol fire in order to destroy the boat. It would not fall into enemy hands.

But, just as it had been so incredible that the S-boats had left them alone for so long, now they steered slowly past at a range of 400 yards without firing a shot. Pumphrey's only explanation of this extraordinary occurrence was that the Germans must have thought the MTB was one of their own boats, even though they had been firing at her earlier.

Whatever the reason, it saved *MTB 35* and her crew. As soon as the S-boats had gone, Gordon managed to start the starboard engine, Gillings went back to help Jakes with the hand steering and the boat began its erratic course home. But they were not out of trouble yet. As soon as the boat was moving, water came pouring in through the shellholes and it looked as if she was going to sink after all. Then the mechanics got the other engines going again and Pumphrey found that at top speed, the water pouring into the engine room was just as quickly drawn out through the broken stern. So top speed it was, in spite of the steering difficulties and the zig-zag course which would have driven a navigating officer to despair. Even when running into a fog bank while approaching the English coast, they still had to keep up this speed to prevent the boat from sinking. The result was they got lost, came past the Goodwins on the wrong side, and it was 07.30 before they approached Ramsgate.

As soon as they slowed down, the boat began to sink. Pumphrey had hoped that she could be kept dry by pumping until the slipway could be prepared to take her, but there was no time. And so, unceremoniously, *MTB 35* had to be run up onto the sand and was beached.

Not only was this the first successful operation from Dover Command, it set the pattern for MTB operations for the rest of the war. It resulted in the award of the OBE to Coltman, the DSC to Pumphrey, Gould and Danielsen, the Conspicuous Gallantry Medal to Lanfear, the DSM to Gordon, Carruthers and Able Seaman James Tait RNR of *MGB 43*, and Mentions in Despatches for Leith, Sheldrick, Hadley, Ordinary Seaman Nelson, Allen Chaffey of *MGB 52* and Motor Mechanic Ronald John James Stanley of the same craft.

In the spring of the following year, Pumphrey and Gould were transferred to destroyers as Coastal Forces were increasingly taken over by RNVR officers. Pumphrey eventually finished the war as a Commander with the DSO and two bars, in addition to his DSC. Gould later returned to MTBs in the Mediterranean in 1943 and had gained a bar to his DSC before he was killed in a daylight raid on the German-occupied coast of North Africa.

CHAPTER 2

The Little Boats

The motor torpedo boat answered the need for a small, fast craft that could operate in coastal waters and which could also be economically built in large numbers by numerous boatyards, leaving the shipyards free to concentrate on building bigger warships. As with so many modern weapons, it was first developed and used in the First World War, although steam-powered torpedo boats had been in existence for some years before this. And the concept of torpedo boats went back even further, to soon after the invention of the torpedo itself at the end of the eighteenth century, when thought was first given to the means of delivering the new weapon.

It was an American engineer, David Bushnell, who in 1775 invented what he called a torpedo, although in a modern sense it was actually a floating mine. (The torpedo, developed as a kind of mine that could be propelled through the water under its own power, did not appear until a hundred years later.) At the time of Bushnell's invention, it was generally accepted that the force of an underwater explosion would be dissipated through the water and could not harm the hull of a ship, even when detonated close to it. Bushnell proved the contrary, that water in fact acted as a solid barrier which could drive the force of such an explosion against the hull, and that even a small explosive charge could damage or destroy a large ship.

He was unable to raise much interest in the idea, however successful his demonstrations, and eventually with some bitterness, he gave up. Twenty years later another American, Robert Fulton, resurrected the idea. Seeing it was also necessary to deliver the weapon to its target, Fulton invented the first crude submarine, which he called a 'plunging-boat'. He tried to interest first the French and then the British in the idea. But even though the two countries were at war at the time – Fulton's activities were surrounded with cloak-and-dagger intrigue – both refused to support the development of these weapons and showed only the mildest interest in the face of demonstrations that were both dramatic and highly successful, as when Fulton blew up a large ship in the Thames before an invited audience of naval and military leaders. It was not only a reaction against something new that contradicted all previously held theories, as Bushnell had found. It was a realization of the threat that this new type of weapon posed to the large fleets in which the power of the maritime nations lay. They would be at the mercy of any country, however small, which only had to manufacture and lay a few mines in the right places. The mine was regarded as a barbaric invention and certainly not one that a traditional naval power like Britain was going to help to develop. This attitude to mines and torpedoes was still held by many naval leaders before the First World War, and was even evident at the beginning of the Second. It was partly the reason why the major naval powers tended to neglect the development of motor torpedo boats between the wars, whereas they proved so popular with smaller nations.

The first extensive use of mines, still called torpedoes at the time, came during the American Civil War when the Confederates employed them very effectively against the blockading Union ships. ('Full speed ahead and damn the torpedoes,' was the famous command of one Northern Admiral.) A Confederate officer, Captain Hunter Davidson, went one step further. In 1864 he developed the idea of tying an explosive charge on the end of a pole mounted over the bows of a rowing boat, and setting off at night to ram enemy ships. A great deal of damage was caused in this way, but although Davidson himself survived, others were not so fortunate and the attackers were often blown up together with those they attacked. However, in its primitive way, this was the forerunner of the torpedo boat.

This idea was taken up and developed by other nations when the war was over. An Austrian frigate captain, Giovanni Luppis, experimented with a self-propelled boat, driven by a clockwork motor, which carried an explosive charge in its bows; the boat was steered and the charge released by means of remote cable controls. He took the idea to an English engineer, Robert Whitehead, who at the time was manager of a firm of engine builders at Fiume in Yugoslavia. After building a model, Whitehead rejected the idea as impractical, instead turning his own attention to the possibility of making an explosive charge that would travel through the water under its own power. This was the true birth of the modern self-propelled torpedo that was to revolutionize warfare. Whitehead completed his first torpedo in 1877, powered by a compressed-air engine driving a single propeller that gave a speed of 6 knots and a range of 700 yards.

In the meantime, shipbuilders, both in Britain and Germany, had begun building steam-powered torpedo boats fitted with the kind of 'spar torpedo' projecting over the bow that Davidson had developed. Yarrow built one of the first in 1872, using a 30-foot steam-driven launch. Such craft were already in worldwide demand when Whitehead's self-propelled torpedo became available. Within months, all the fleets of the world were clamouring for torpedo boats. Small navies as well as large were determined to have the fastest torpedo-carrying craft that could be devised by such firms as Yarrow. And builders in other countries were soon busy designing craft of their own. It was after seeing some exceptionally fast torpedo boats being built in France in 1892 that Alfred Yarrow suggested to the Admiralty the need for a fast, more heavily armed ship that could chase and destroy such craft. The Admiralty, concerned at the alarming growth in the number of torpedo boats that could threaten the big but relatively slow ships of the Royal Navy, readily agreed. The torpedo gunboat had already been developed as a means of countering the torpedo boat, but had proved to be too slow. What Yarrow did was to put the same machinery as in a 500-ton torpedo gunboat into a 250-ton torpedo boat 'destroyer'. This ship, the *Hornet*, was the first of a new class that was to become known throughout the world as the destroyer.

The original function of destroyers was to fight torpedo boats. But from the start, they themselves were also equipped with torpedoes, so that they operated as torpedo boats as well. In the race during the years leading up to the First World War to achieve superiority over each other in speed and armament, both the torpedo boats on which the Germans concentrated and the destroyers built by Britain and America became rapidly bigger. What started as torpedo-carrying launches became vessels of 1,000 tons and more. But their very size created new problems, not only because they were now larger and easier targets themselves, but because of their vulnerability to mines. There was still a need, although it was only appreciated after the war had started and even then only by some of the major powers, for a small torpedo-carrying craft of the kind originally intended – for a motor torpedo boat in fact. Such craft became possible with the invention of the internal combustion engine and after the first efforts, at the turn of the century, to mount petrol engines into small boats.

The most successful were developed by the Italians. Known as MAS boats (first standing for Motoscafo Armato SVAN, after the yard in Venice that built them, and later, Motoscafo Anti-Sommergibile – motor anti-submarine boats), these were between 50 and 70 feet long, and carried two or four torpedoes at a top speed of 33 knots. A number came into service in 1916 and were used very effectively against Austrian naval units and shipping in Adriatic harbours. Their most notable successes were the sinking of the light cruiser *Wien* at Trieste on 9 December 1917, and the battleship *Szent Istvan* in the Straits of Otranto on 8 June 1918.

In Britain, with the major shipyards concentrating on the building of bigger ships and destroyers, it was left to the firm of John I. Thornycroft to carry out the work of designing and building motor torpedo boats, based on a 40-foot motorboat which they had built some years before the war. Britain had entered the war with little conception of the extent to which the Germans would use mines and submarines. The Royal Navy still thought largely in terms of big warships and it came as a shock to find how vulnerable they were against these weapons – even though the weapons were hardly new, as their earlier history shows. In fact, the Germans laid no less than 10,000 mines in British home waters alone. The Grand Fleet itself was lucky to escape tangling with the first minefield to be laid, in the Southwold area, by steaming northwards only a few days before. Something had to be found to deal with this menace when it became clear that German policy was to fight the war at sea with mines and torpedoes, using submarines, torpedo boats and minelayers, instead of with big ships in the traditional manner. Much of the answer was found in the Auxiliary Patrol, a force which began modestly with a few trawlers and yachts pressed into service to clear minefields, and which grew until by the end of the war it totalled 5,000 yachts, patrol gunboats, trawlers, whalers, motor launches, drifters, motorboats, paddle or screw minesweepers and boom-defence vessels, manned almost entirely by volunteers, including the Royal Naval Volunteer Reserve. At one time or another, craft of nearly all these types were responsible for sinking submarines.

There was also another type of boat, known as the Coastal Motor Boat (CMB), which was the forerunner of the Second World War MTBs. The CMBs first came into service in 1916. Built by Thornycroft, they were torpedo-carrying boats capable of 33 knots, originally 40 feet in length but later increased to 55 feet. Sixty-six of them were in commission by the end of the war. They had been responsible for some dramatic and successful actions off the Belgian coast in the latter stages of the war, particularly during the daring raids on Zeebrugge and Ostend when amongst the many awards for gallantry won by the crews of the CMBs and MLs (motor launches) were three Victoria Crosses. But their most spectacular success was in a post-war operation, when in a raid on Kronstadt in 1919 after the Russian Revolution they sank the cruiser *Oleg* and damaged or disabled two capital ships and two destroyers for the loss of only one CMB.

The MLs, which also came into service in 1916, were literally 'maids of all work', just as they were to be in the Second World War. They were 75-foot motor launches specially designed and built for the Royal Navy by the American Electric Boat Company (ELCO) in Connecticut and shipped across the Atlantic. Powered by two 250-horsepower petrol engines which gave a speed of 20 knots, and armed with quick-firing guns, fifty of them were initially purchased, followed by 500 of a later 80-foot version. They were used for chasing submarines, escorting shipping, exploring minefields and sweeping up and destroying mines, laying smokescreens, and rescuing pilots whose aircraft had crashed into the sea. They only had a sea endurance of two days at the most, but contrary to first expectations they were seaworthy in bad weather, although not to the extent of being suitable for carrying torpedoes.

America's entry into the torpedo-boat field had been in 1908, when ten craft based on a Lewis Nixon design were built for Russia. They proved their seaworthiness when one made the voyage from New York to Sevastopol under its own power, without damage. But in spite of these and the MLs that were later built for Britain, the US Navy, understandably perhaps with a coastline that was well away from any likely war zone and therefore without the same need to be protected, saw little use for small boats. Tentative designs for 115-foot and 150-foot motor torpedo boats were drawn up, largely at the instigation of Franklin D. Roosevelt, who as Assistant Secretary of the Navy at the time, recommended their construction for coastal defence. But they were not built and, like the Germans, the Americans concentrated their efforts on building seagoing torpedo boats and destroyers.

After the war, in spite of the success of CMBs and MLs, and the evident need for such craft, official British interest in motor torpedo boats lapsed. What little work in design and development that did take place was left mainly to motorboat enthusiasts and men like Hubert Scott-Paine and Commander Peter du Cane, who had the foresight to appreciate the importance of small craft in coastal waters. The Royal Navy, as well as the other Services, was certainly hampered by a lack of funds, caused by the euphoric mood of pacifism amongst the general public that was responsible for much of the appeasement policy later blamed on the politicians. But there was also a tendency in the Admiralty once again to think primarily in terms of big ships at the expense of smaller ones, and to neglect the danger that had been so apparent in the First World War of an enemy basing their sea policy on the use of mines and torpedoes.

It was Italy which carried out most of the development work on motor torpedo boats between the wars, so that when the Second World War started, the Italian fleet had a larger number of these craft than any other nation.

Italian Boats

Two Italian boatyards, SVAN in Venice and Baglietto in Varazze, designed all but a few of the hundred or so motor torpedo boats in service with the Italian Navy when Italy entered the war in 1940. The Italian boats were smaller than those built by Britain, America and Germany, having been designed for use in the calmer waters of the Mediterranean and Adriatic rather than the North Sea. They ranged from 48 feet in length, displacing 12 tons, to 60 feet, displacing 26 tons. But the Italians had one great advantage in possessing the Isotta Fraschini marine petrol engine, which gave the Italian craft speeds of up to 45 knots, making them faster than any other boats in service at that time.

Most of the Italian boats were built by Baglietto. But the SVAN yard was first in the field with the 48-foot *MAS 423* commissioned in 1929. This 12.75-ton boat was powered by Isotta Fraschini engines of 1,500 hp which gave a speed of 40 knots, and was armed with two 6.5mm machine-guns and two 17.7-inch torpedoes. It was the basic design for most of the small craft built in the early 1930s, although the speed was later increased by more powerful engines, and depth charges were also carried.

The Baglietto type, built in 1936 with *MAS 502*, was larger – 55 feet in length, 21 tons, powered by Isotta Fraschini engines giving over 42 knots – and was armed with one 13.2mm machine-gun, two 17.7-inch torpedoes and six depth charges. This remained the basis for the *MAS 513*, *MAS 526* and *MAS 536* series that were built up until 1939 and formed the bulk of the Italian motor torpedo boat fleet at the start of the war, although the size of the craft increased to 60 feet and 26 tons. Fast and effective as they were in shallow coastal waters, all these craft were severely limited in their capacity to withstand heavy seas. It was to answer the need to operate further afield that the MS (Motosilurante) boats were developed and built in 1941 by the CRDA, Monfalcone yards.

These boats were built on the pattern of the German *Schnellboot* and resulted from the capture by the Italian Navy in April 1941 of six Yugoslavian boats that had been built in Germany by Lürssen between 1935 and 1939. The first series of eighteen boats, MS *11-MS 36*, were 90 feet overall, 63 tons, powered by three Isotta Fraschini engines of 3,450 hp which gave a top speed of 34 knots, and were armed with two or four 20mm/65 machine-guns, two 21-inch torpedoes in tubes and twelve to twenty depth charges. The second series of eighteen boats, *MS 51-MS 76*, built in 1942 also by CRDA, were basically of the same design, but carried two additional 17.7-inch torpedoes in light staffs aft. Plans had been drawn up by the CRDA yard for further MS series of 105-ton and 120-ton craft, but were cancelled after Italy's surrender in 1943. At that time the boats still in service were either transferred to the Germans, captured by them or scuttled.

Another type of motor torpedo gunboat was developed and built by the Baglietto yard after Italy's entry into the war for the specific purpose of submarine hunting. Known as VAS (Vedette Anti-Sommergibile) boats, the first series of thirty (*VAS 201-VAS 230*) came into service in 1942. They were 90 feet overall, displaced 68 tons, powered by two Fiat engines and an auxiliary Carraro engine which gave a speed of approximately 19 knots, armed with two 20mm/65 machine-guns, four 8mm sub-machine-guns, two 17.7-inch

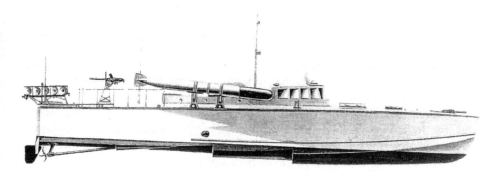

The small, light Italian motor torpedo boats in service early in the war were the fastest of all such craft, some chieving speeds of over 45 knots. They were highly manoeuvrable but less seaworthy om heavy seas. Speeds were reduced as the boats became heavier nd better armed. This Baglietto-built 1941 MAS 526 series was powered by twin Isotta-Fraschini engines giving 42 knots and armed with two torpedoes, six depth charges, and a 13.2mm machine gun.

Italian MAS boat
Displacement: 66 tons
Dimensions: 28 x 4.3 x 1.6
  metres
Engines: 3 Isotta Fraschini,
  total 3,450 hp
Maximum speed: 34 knots
Armament: 2 x 1 21inch
  torpedoes, 2 x 1 17.7inch
  torpedoes aft, 2 to 4
  20mm/65, 12 to 20 depth
  charges
Crew: 19

ITALIAN MAS

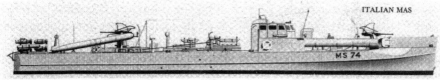

torpedoes and thirty depth charges, and carried a crew of twenty-six. Eighteen boats of a second series *(VAS 231-VAS 248)* came into service in 1943 with similar armament but powered by one Isotta Fraschini and two Carraro engines, which gave approximately the same speed. A third series of 90-ton boats were captured by the Germans while still being built in 1943, and were later commissioned by the German Navy as motor launches and minesweepers.

British Boats

Having scrapped or sold most of the First World War CMBs, it was not until 1935 that the British Admiralty placed its first orders for MTBs, as they were now called, with Scott-Paine's British Power Boat Company. These boats were built to Scott-Paine's design for a 60-foot craft with a hard-chine, planing hull (as distinct from a round bilge displacement hull). The planing hull was more or less mandatory in order to achieve high speed with a short boat, but although it gave inherent lateral stability it did severely restrict speed in rough weather because of slamming of the flat bottom, while another disadvantage was the high plume of water it created astern which could be seen from miles away at night. Nevertheless, this design had a lasting influence on most of the British and American boats built during the war.

The first BPB boats were powered by three 500-hp Napier petrol engines giving up to 33 knots, and were armed with two 18-inch torpedoes and .303 machine-guns fore and aft. The Admiralty purchased six to begin with, which were formed into the 1st MTB Flotilla under the command of Lieutenant Commander G.B. Sayer, and sent to Malta in June 1937. They successfully made the passage under their own power in heavy weather – a considerable feat at that time – and orders were placed for twelve more. Six were shipped to Hong Kong as the 2nd MTB Flotilla. The remaining boats were intended to go to Singapore but as they had only reached the Mediterranean by the summer of 1939, when war seemed inevitable, they were allocated to the 1st Flotilla at Malta to bring its numbers up to twelve.

In the meantime, other British boatbuilders were competing for orders now that the Admiralty was showing more interest in small craft. Two MTBs were built as private ventures, a 68-foot craft by Commander du Cane's Vosper Company, and a larger 70-foot Scott-Paine boat, powered by Rolls Royce engines. As the war clouds gathered, this contest between Vosper and the British Power Boat Company was eventually decided in favour of Vosper. Their designs became the basis of most of the short MTBs used by the Royal Navy during the war (as distinct from the long MTBs which were over 100 feet).

Some 200 Vosper boats were eventually built and commissioned, including a few taken over at the beginning of the war that were being built for Norway and Greece (although an order of three boats for Rumania was allowed to go through). Thornycroft MTBs that were building for the Chinese Navy, Finland and the Philippines, and several other craft building for the Netherlands and France, were also acquired in the same way. The Vosper yards could not by themselves cope with all the numbers required and many of the Vosper boats were built in other British boatyards, as well as in America.

Modifications in design detail were continually being made as new equipment and armament became available. But there were three basic series of Vosper craft. The first was developed from the experimental boat built in 1937 and chosen by the Admiralty after extensive trials the following year; they were 70 feet overall, 36 tons, powered by three Isotta Fraschini engines giving 3.600 bhp and a top speed of just on 40 knots, armed with two twin .5-inch guns and two 21-inch torpedoes in tubes, and carried a crew of ten. The first batch of them was built in 1939 and began to come into service the following year. The biggest problem was with the engines. There was no suitable diesel engine available, and petrol engines exposed the craft to the risk of fire and explosion, a hazard the crews had to cope with throughout the war. But even with petrol engines, Vosper's had been compelled to use the Italian Isotta Fraschini again as no suitable British power units were available. These gave excellent performance but the supply naturally ceased when Italy entered the war. Supercharged Hall Scott engines were used for a time until supplies of Packard engines could be obtained from America, the first arriving in 1941. Thereafter, these were used to power virtually all the British boats, both short and long, as indeed they also powered the American PT (patrol torpedo) boats.

Vosper's second series of MTBs began to come into service in 1942; they were 72.5 feet overall, 47 tons, powered by three Packard engines giving 4,050 bhp and a top speed of 40 knots, armed with one twin .5-inch and two twin .303 machine-guns (the machine-guns were later exchanged for one 20mm gun and a 6-pounder was also added), two 21-inch torpedoes, and carried a crew of twelve (later brought up to thirteen). Although there had been pressure from those serving in Coastal Forces for the very noisy main engines to be fitted with silencers so that a quiet approach could be made when stalking the enemy, this was not done until early 1943. The 1942 boats instead were fitted with two Ford V8s in addition to their main engines, which could be clutched to the outer shafts to drive the boat silently at about 6 knots. This was a laborious process and reversing it in order to get away quickly at top speed, while perhaps under fire, was a hair-raising experience.

The third and last series came into service in 1944; they were powered by the same Packard engines giving a similar speed to series two but were 73 feet overall and armed with one twin 20mm, one twin .5, two twin .303 machine-guns and four 18-inch torpedoes, and carried a crew of thirteen.

These Vosper boats formed the basis on which Light Coastal Forces, as it came to be known, was formed. Together with the twenty Thornycroft boats taken over from other navies, thirty-two J.S. White craft also of 73 feet but powered by Sterling engines, and thirty-eight American boats acquired under lend/lease (twenty-nine Elcos, five Higgins and four US Navy experimental craft), they saw most of the offensive action in home waters and the Mediterranean until the larger boats came into operation in 1942.

Within this class of short boat (under 100 feet) was the MGB, equipped with heavier guns in place of torpedoes, and developed for the specific purpose of fighting the German motor torpedo boats which were threatening British coastal convoys. In 1938 and 1939, the British Power Boat Company had begun to build MA/SBs (motor anti-submarine boats) when it seemed possible that enemy submarines might operate in the English Channel. These boats were a twin-screw version of Scott-Paine's 60-foot MTB design, which sacrificed speed and torpedoes in favour of anti-submarine weapons and Asdic equipment. They were powered by two Napier engines of 1,000 bhp which gave a top speed of 25 knots, and the only armament they carried were .303 machine-guns, one twin mounting on some craft and four twins on others. Six of these craft were in service when war broke out, with another sixteen 70-footers under construction. It soon became apparent, however, that air patrols were sufficient to keep most submarines away from coastal waters, and in any case the submarine-hunting capabilities of the MA/SBs were not found to come up to expectations. And so in 1940, the twenty-two craft then completed were converted into MGBs, armed with two twin .5-inch machine-guns and either one 2-pounder, one 20mm or

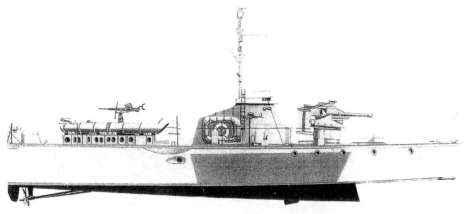

The 73-foot Vosper MTBs which came into service in 1944 in time for the Normandy invasion were the most technically advanced yet produced, including the latest radar, IFF (identification friend or for), and echo-sounding equipment. They were powered by three Packard V12 main engines which gave a speed of 36 knots and two Vosper V8s for cruising and silent running. The torpedo tubes on the Type II boats were reduced from four to two to allow for the heavier armament of a 6-pounder Quick Firing gun in a power-driven turret mounted forward of the bridge.

Vosper 72½ ft MTB
Displacement: 40 tons
Dimensions: 72½ ft x 19¼
ft x 6¼ ft
Engines: 3 supercharged
Packard of 1,400 bhp
each
Maximum speed: 39 knots
Endurance: 400 miles at 20
knots
Armament: 2 x 1 21inch
torpedoes, 2 depth
charges, 1 x 2 .5inch and
2 x 1 .303inch
machine-guns; later
development included 1 x
2 20mm and 1 x 1 2pdr
forward
Crew: 13

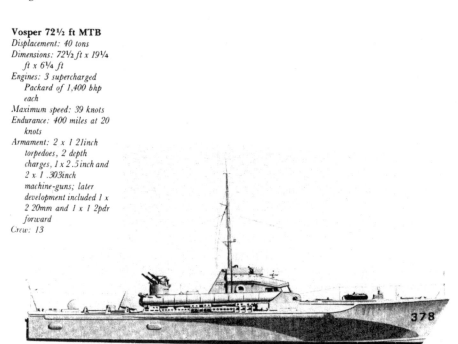

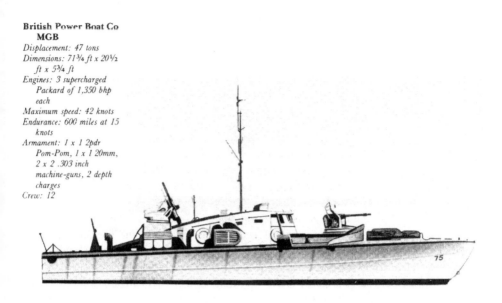

British Power Boat Co MGB

Displacement: 47 tons
Dimensions: 71¾ ft x 20½
  ft x 5¾ ft
Engines: 3 supercharged
  Packard of 1,350 bhp
  each
Maximum speed: 42 knots
Endurance: 600 miles at 15
  knots
Armament: 1 x 1 2pdr
  Pom-Pom, 1 x 1 20mm,
  2 x 2 .303 inch
  machine-guns, 2 depth
  charges
Crew: 12

four .303s. All MA/SBs that were also under construction or ordered were completed as MGBs.

The urgent need for motor gunboats required more than these converted anti-submarine boats, so the British Power Boat Company set about designing a specific MGB. The first of these came into service in 1942; they were 71½ feet overall, 47 tons, powered by three Packard engines of 4,050 bhp giving a top speed of 40 knots, armed with one 2-pounder, one twin 20mm and two twin .303 machine-guns, and carried two depth charges. The crew consisted of two officers and ten men. Seventy-eight of these craft were built in 1942. A further forty-one Elco and Higgins boats of 70-80 feet built in America were transferred to the Royal Navy under lend/lease between 1940 and 1942, and used as MGBs.

For the first three years of the war, Coastal Forces were composed mainly of short MTBs and MGBs built of hard chine, double-skin mahogany hulls. But there were also several other types of craft, primarily the ML (motor launch) and HDML (harbour defence motor launch).

The round-bilge HDML was an Admiralty designed craft of 72 feet overall, displacing 54 tons, built of double-skin diagonal mahogany, powered by twin diesel engines of 150 hp each that gave a speed of 11½ knots, and armed with one 2-pounder and two twin .303 machine-guns. They were used for patrol work in harbours, estuaries and coastal waters. The simple construction enabled them to be built easily in yards abroad and they saw service in many different ways in every theatre of operations. Six hundred boats of this type were built between 1940 and 1944, including a number for India, Australia, New Zealand and South Africa; twenty-six were transferred to the French Navy in 1944.

The MLs were even more versatile. The first was the Fairmile 'A', a 110-foot craft designed by Norman Hart. Twelve of them were built in 1940 by ten different firms, including the Fairmile Marine Company. Displacing 57 tons and powered by three Hall Scott 600 hp petrol engines that gave 25 knots, they were armed with one 3-pounder and two single .303 machine-guns, and carried a crew of sixteen. Of prefabricated, hard chine construction, they were used for many purposes, including patrol and escort duties. In 1942, these 'A' type boats were converted to minelayers.

Meanwhile, working in cooperation with Fairmile, the Admiralty had in 1940 prepared a round bilge design which resulted in the ubiquitous 'B' type Fairmile. These craft had even more uses and were variously employed on Commando raids as troop carriers, for patrol and escort duties, air/sea rescue, minesweeping and minelaying, ambulance launches and as navigation leaders for the Normandy invasion. Over 650 were built between 1940 and 1944, again many of them for use by Commonwealth navies overseas. They were 112 feet overall, displaced 65 or 73 tons, powered by two Hall Scott Defender petrol engines of 600 hp each which gave up to 20 knots, and carried similar armament and crew to the 'A' boats.

The proved seaworthiness of these boats led to a modified version of the Fairmile 'A' being developed for use as motor gunboats in 1941. Known as the Fairmile 'C' Type, they were 110 feet overall, displaced 72 tons, were powered by three Hall Scott petrol engines of 2,700 bhp, supercharged to give a greater speed of up to 27 knots, were armed with two 2-pounders, two twin .5 and two twin .303 machine-guns, and carried a crew of sixteen. Twenty-four were built in 1941 and they were the first of the long MGBs (over 100 feet).

By the following year, it was felt there was also a demand for a long MTB which could operate further afield in heavier weather and which could also carry more powerful armament. At the same time, operations with the small type of craft had shown that MGBs often missed opportunities by not carrying torpedoes; there was a requirement in fact for a combined MGB/MTB. Accordingly, the Fairmile 'D' was developed and began to come into service in 1942. Although short boats continued to be built it was these craft, the 'Dog-boats' as they were called, which bore the brunt of operations during the latter stages of the war. Over 220 were built between 1942 and 1944. Of a similar hard chine, prefabricated, double-skin, diagonal, mahogany construction, they were 115 feet overall and powered by four Packard supercharged engines of 1,250 hp each. As combined MGB/MTBs, they displaced 105 tons and had a top speed of 29 knots; as MGBs they were 90 tons and as MTBs 95 tons, with speeds of up to 31 knots. They paid a great penalty in size and speed over the shorter boats for their greater sea-keeping qualities and heavier armament, making it very hard for them to close an enemy unseen. The different displacements resulted from differing forms of armament, which varied considerably, and the crews required to man the boats also varied from fourteen for the single-purpose craft to thirty for those of dual purpose. As MGBs they first carried one 2-pounder, one twin Oerlikon 20mm, two twin .5 and two twin .303 machine-guns, two depth charges and one Holman illuminant projector; the MTBs carried the same armament plus two 21-inch torpedoes. Eventually, the combined MGB/MTBs carried a formidable armament of two 6-pounders, one twin 20mm, two twin

.5 and two twin .303 machine-guns, and four 18-inch torpedoes. They were the most heavily armed boats of their kind in the world.

There were four further developments in long boats of the combined MGB/MTB type before the end of the war. In mid-1942 the first of the Denny-type steam gunboats (SGBs) came into service. They were the largest of the Coastal Force craft at 145½ feet overall, displacing 165 tons, powered by two geared turbines of 8,000 hp which gave up to 35 knots, were armed with one twin 2-pounder, two twin .5 machine-guns and two 21-inch torpedoes, and carried a crew of twenty-seven. Early operations showed their steam machinery to be highly vulnerable to machine-gun fire. Extensive modifications had to be carried out to fit heavier armour plate, and at the same time their armament was increased to one 3-inch gun, two 6-pounders, and three twin 20mm, as well as the two 21-inch torpedoes. This in turn meant a larger complement of thirty-four and displacement went up to 260 tons. With the resulting drop in speed to 30 knots and the fact that their size made them an easier target for the enemy to hit, they were not a great success. Of the sixty originally envisaged, only seven were actually built.

Also in 1942, eight Camper & Nicholson craft were built, originally intended for the Turkish Navy but taken over by the Royal Navy, the first three being completed as MGBs and the remainder as mercantile blockade runners, named *Hopewell, Nonsuch, Gay Viking, Gay Corsair* and *Master Standfast*. They were 117 feet overall, displacing 95 tons, powered by three Davey Paxman diesel engines of 3,000 bhp which gave up to 30 knots, and were armed with one 2-pounder, two twin .5 and two twin .303 machine-guns, and two 21-inch torpedoes. A second series of eight craft was built in 1944.

Finally, in 1943, there were two experimental boats which came too late, however, to be developed before the end of the war. Vosper's built a 100-foot craft of 75 tons, powered by four Packard engines giving 35 knots and armed with one 6-pounder, one twin 20mm and two twin .303 machine-guns, and two 18-inch torpedoes; this was completed as an MGB. And Fairmile produced one 'F' Type craft which had four Bristol petrol engines totalling 7,000 hp giving a speed of 36 knots; it was one of the most powerful petrol-engined boats ever built.

From a modest beginning of only eighteen MTBs and six MA/SBs at the start of the war, Coastal Forces grew into a 'private navy' of over 1,700 craft, including 641 MTBs and MGBs, with a peak manpower of 3,000 officers (98 per cent of them RNVR) and 22,000 men. In nearly 800 separate actions fought in all theatres of operations, but primarily in home waters and the Mediterranean, they sank more than 500 enemy vessels at a cost of 178 craft to themselves. Many of the actions were fought against enemy motor torpedo boats, and in thus defending Allied coastal convoys they were responsible for saving hundreds of merchant ships. Coastal Force craft also carried out more than twice as many minelaying operations as all other naval minelayers put together.

German Boats

After the First World War, the Reichsmarine was left with only thirty-two destroyers and torpedo boats out of the large fleet it had built up; of the remainder, eighty had been destroyed in action, 143 were given up to the Allied powers and 117 were broken up. The Versailles Treaty restricted not only the number but also the size of the destroyers that Germany could build. When in the mid-1920s the Germans began to reconstruct their fleet, they were limited to torpedo boats of not more than 900 tons. Soon after, partly as a result of having seen the British and Italian boats in action during the First World War, and also because the Treaty restrictions limited the building of other craft, they turned their attention for the first time to the possibilities of motor torpedo boats.

In 1928, the Reichsmarine obtained from the Lürssen shipyard in Vegesack the plans of a luxury motor cruiser that was being built for an American customer. Powered by three Maybach engines, it had a speed of 30 knots. From this basic design, the *Schnellboot* (fast motor torpedo boat) was born. Because of the Versailles Treaty, it was falsely called a submarine chaser and it was so constructed that the torpedo tubes on the forecastle could be rapidly set up or removed, and the grooves in the hull which made it possible for the torpedoes to clear the boat when fired were made to look like part of the streamlining, in order to deceive any curious visitors to the yard.

Germany had a great advantage over all the other powers in having developed the first-class Daimler-Benz diesel engine for use in small boats. Diesels were used in S-boats soon after they first began to be built and proved far less hazardous during war operations than the highly inflammable petrol engines of the British, American and Italian craft. S1 was completed in 1930, a hard-chine boat, 81 feet overall, 39 tons, powered by three 1,000 bhp engines giving a top speed of 37 knots, and armed with two 21-inch torpedoes and a light machine-gun. Five more of these craft were built up to mid-1932 and formed into the beginning of the 1st Flotilla under Kapitänleutnant Bey. But trials showed them to have only limited seaworthiness, and as the newly developed 1,320 bhp diesel engines needed more space, their size was increased to 106 feet overall, 80 tons, with a round bilge design built of two or three skins of teak on light metal frames. The wheelhouse was enclosed, a 20mm anti-aircraft gun replaced the light machine-gun and the crew now numbered twenty-one. Eight of these boats were built in 1934. Then their size was increased again to 114 feet overall, 85 tons, in order to take the three even more powerful diesels totalling 6,150 bhp that gave a top speed of 38 knots in 1938 and finally, in 1939, succeeded in achieving 40 knots. With only slight modifications, twelve of these craft were delivered between 1938 and 1939. They were armed with the two 21-inch torpedoes and two 20mm anti-aircraft guns. Range was 700 miles at 30 knots and they carried a crew of twenty-one.

These twenty-four craft, S2 to S25 (S1 had been scrapped) were the only motor torpedo boats in service with the German Navy when war began, and the first five were by then obsolete. But plans had been drawn up by the Lürssen yard for a new design which was to be the basis for all S-boats built during the war. The most notable alteration was that the two forward 20-inch torpedo tubes were enclosed by a partially raised forecastle, with flanges that opened when the torpedoes were to be released. This gave the S-boats their distinctive low and lean shape, and contributed greatly to their seaworthiness and speed.

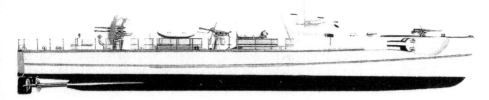

The Schnellboot S.170 series which entered service in 1944 was powered by three 2,500hp Daimler Benz diesel engines which gave a speed of 42 knots and a range of 700 miles at 30 knots. The bridge was armour plated. Four torpedoes were carried in the two torpedo tubes. The 20mm Flakvierling mounted on a quadruple rapid-fire turret to the rear was very effective against low-flying aircraft, and there was also a 37mm anti-aircraft cannon on the bow.

S.80 series

Displacement: 82 tons
Dimensions: 108 ft x 16 ft x 6 ft
Engines: 3 Daimler Benz diesels of 1,600 bhp each
Maximum speed: 36 knots
Endurance: 800 miles at 30 knots
Armament: 2 x 1 21inch torpedoes, 2 x 1 20mm AA guns
Crew: 16

S.100 series

Displacement: 100 tons
Dimensions: 115 ft x 16½ ft x 6½ ft
Engines: 3 Daimler Benz diesels of 2,000 bhp each
Maximum speed: 42 knots
Endurance: 700 miles at 30 knots
Armament: 2 x 1 21inch torpedoes, 2 x 1 20mm AA guns; later development included 4 x 1 21inch torpedoes and either 1 x 1 40mm AA and 3 x 1 20mm or 1 x 1 37mm AA and 5 x 1 20mm or 3 x 2 30mm AA
Crew: 23

GERMAN S.80 SERIES

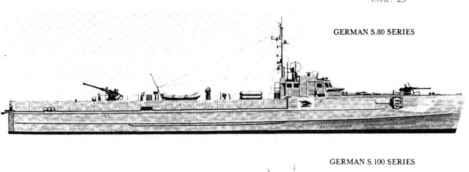

GERMAN S.100 SERIES

The first of these boats, *S26*, came into service early in 1940. It had a similar performance to the earlier craft and carried the same armament and crew, the only difference being that it now displaced 100 tons. A further ninety-three were built over the next three years, with only slight modifications, mostly by Lürssen, but a number by the Schlichting yard at Travemünde. Sixteen boats of a smaller 108-foot version were built in 1941, in which the top speed was reduced slightly to 36 knots and five fewer crew were carried, but the operating range was increased to 800 miles. An even smaller craft of 92 feet was built in 1943 and eight were completed by the Werf Gusto yard in Schiedam.

Also in 1943, a 40mm cannon was added to the larger version in place of one of the 20mm AA guns, its crew increased to twenty-three, and three new diesel engines were installed that gave 7,500 bhp and pushed the top speed up to 42 knots. The size of the craft was increased slightly to 115 feet overall, displacing 105 tons, and in this form seventy-five were brought into service in 1943 and 1944. The later boats carried two 30mm guns in place of the former armament and speed was increased even further to 45 knots with the introduction of 3,000 bhp engines. They also carried either two spare torpedoes or six to eight mines. From 1944 onwards, the gun armament of the larger boats was either one 40mm and three 20mm, or one 37mm and five 20mm guns.

Twenty-six boats were completed in 1945, including nine which carried four 20-inch torpedo tubes and which were armed with three twin 30mm guns. A large number of others were in various stages of completion, but were scrapped when the war ended. In all, 244 S-boats were brought into service during the war. They took part in operations in the North Sea, the English Channel, the Baltic and Mediterranean, and were responsible for sinking over 100 Allied warships and 500,000 tons of merchant shipping for a loss to themselves of 170 craft.

The Germans also developed another type of coastal craft known as the R-boat (*Raümboot*), which was similar to the British ML and used for coastal convoy protection, minelaying, minesweeping and air/sea rescue. The first of these craft were built in 1934 by Lürssen. Those used during the war were between 116 and 134½ feet overall, displacing from 110 to 175 tons, with two- or three-shaft diesels giving speeds of 20 to 24 knots, and armed variously with 37mm and 20mm AA guns; 325 were brought into service with crews of between thirty-four and thirty-eight.

American Boats

The lack of interest shown in motor torpedo boats by the US Navy during the First World War continued in the post-war period, and the only development which took place was in 1920 when the Navy bought two of the British Thornycroft CMBs for experimental purposes. It was not until 1937 that President Roosevelt, who as Assistant Secretary of the Navy in the First World War had been amongst the few to appreciate the value of motor torpedo boats, sponsored an appropriation of $15 million for the development of suitable boats.

This was partly due to the interest in MTBs being shown by other countries. At the same time, the Americans were already familiar with the possibilities that these craft offered, for a number of Thornycroft ex-CMBs had entered the

United States privately, their chief use being to smuggle liquor from Canada along the east coast during the Prohibition era. This 'rum trade' led to the smugglers carrying out extensive experiments to improve the performance of these and other craft, including the adaptation of the Liberty engine for marine use; experiments which were to prove of considerable value during the war.

In 1938, as a result of President Roosevelt's appropriation, the Navy offered prizes to private designers for a number of small-boat designs, including 54-foot and 70-foot MTBs. This competition resulted in Higgins Industries of New Orleans being given a contract in May 1939 to build two PT (patrol torpedo) boats, numbers 5 and 6, based on the 70-foot winning design of Sparkman and Stephens, the naval architects, but scaled up to 81 feet. The Navy also began to build several experimental craft. But all these designs became obsolete when later in 1939 Scott-Paine, the English designer who had failed to get the Royal Navy's contract for MTBs against competition from Vosper, took his British Power Boat Company's 70-foot craft across the Atlantic and sold it to the US Navy. This boat was the ancestor of the American motor torpedo boats. (A second of these private-venture craft was shipped to Canada and became the Royal Canadian Navy *CMTB 1.*) After trials, supervised by Scott-Paine himself, it was arranged for the Electric Boat Company (Elco) to build the craft under licence. In December, Elco was given an order for eleven, *PTs 10-20*, as well as twelve motorboat submarine chasers based on the same design. The only major modification was the substitution of 1,200 hp Packard engines for the original Rolls Royce engines. Scott-Paine's craft had to be used for taking measurements and it was not until 17 June 1940 that it was finally delivered to the US Navy for operational use as *PT 9* – the first American PT boat.

The experimental *PTs 1-8* were still building and were intended to form MTB Squadron 1, commissioned in July 1940 under Lieutenant Earl S. Caldwell, while *PT 9* and the Elco boats were to make up Squadron 2. None of the experimental boats proved to be very satisfactory, however. Then Higgins carried out modifications to the original 81-foot design and their new 78-foot craft, which was delivered in February 1941, was received with enthusiasm; many in fact thought it superior to the Scott-Paine boat. In the meantime, the Navy had called for modifications to the Elco boats to make them bigger in order to carry four 21-inch torpedo tubes. *PT 20* and the twenty-nine boats that followed were 77-foot craft. Most of the earlier boats, including *PT 9*, were transferred to the Royal Navy in April 1941, under lend/lease, and used in operations in the Mediterranean.

By now, other American boatbuilders wanted to compete for contracts, and in the summer of 1941 the US Navy held what was called the 'Plywood Derby' to test all the various types of craft against each other in a 190-mile race off the New England coast. Elco were the winners, with Higgins second, and from this time on those two companies were responsible for building most of the American PTs. (Third in the race was a 72-foot boat designed and built by the Huckins Yacht Company; ten were later built but they were not used in combat.) Further modifications were made to the Elco design, and eventually the US Navy settled on two standard types of boat, the Elco 80-footer (38 tons) and the Higgins 78-footer (35 tons). Both were powered by three 12-cylinder Packard

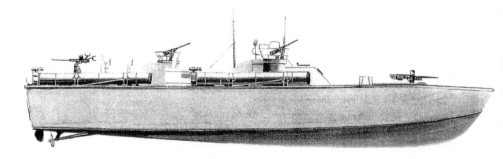

The 80-foot Elco PT boats came into service in 1942. Later boats in the series were powered by three 1,350hp Packard liquid cooled engines which gave speeds in excess of 40 knots. Armament consisted of four torpedo tubes, two twin .50-inch machine guns, one 20mm cannon at the stern and, on some boats, a 37mm cannon at the bow which was found to be an excellent weapon for "barge busting" – attacking Japanese landing craft.

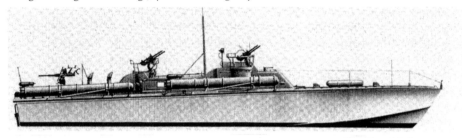

US Elco 80 ft PT boat

Displacement: 38 tons

Dimensions: 80 ft x 20¾ ft x 5 ft

Engines: 3 12-cylinder Packard, originally rated at 1,200 bhp each but progressively increased to 1,350 and finally 1,500

Maximum speed: 40 knots

Endurance: 500 miles at 20 knots

Armament: 4 x 1 18inch torpedoes, 2 x 2 .5inch machine-guns; later developments included 4 x 1 21inch torpedoes, 2 x 1 20mm, 1 x 1 37mm or 2 x 1 40mm, and finally experiments with 75mm, 4.5inch barrage rocket projectors, and 5inch spin-stabilized rockets

Crew: 14

marine engines, burning 100-octane gasoline, originally rated at 1,200 hp but as the boats increased in weight with heavier armament, modified to 1,350 hp and finally to 1,500 hp. Many changes had been made, but both boats owed much to the original Scott-Paine design, maintaining the hard-chine, stepless bottom hull and the outward flare of the sides. Elco eventually built 320 and Higgins 205 of these boats, including some for lend/lease.

Both boats were designed for top speeds of at least 40 knots with a full load and a cruising range of 500 miles. While following a similar basic design, each had its own distinctive below-deck arrangement of engine room, fuel tanks to carry 3,000 gallons of gasoline, fresh water tanks, chart room and living quarters. The Elco boat was slightly faster, but the Higgins was more manoeuvrable, so that each had its proponents depending on the conditions under which they were used. In terms of armament, the first boats carried four torpedo tubes – 18-inch to begin with, then 21-inch – and two twin .5-inch machine-guns. Then a 20mm cannon was added, useful both against aircraft and surface craft. Automatic 37mm guns, mounted in the bow, became standard in 1943, but were replaced by two 40mm cannons. Towards the end of the war, experiments were made with 75mm cannons, 4.5-inch barrage rocket projectors and 5-inch spin-stabilized rockets.

The increase in weight of gun armament was made possible by a reduction in the weight of torpedoes. The original four Mark VIIIs fitted in the first boats were manufactured to a 1920s design; intended for use by destroyers, they were heavy and slow, given to erratic runs, especially at shallow depth settings, and had to be launched through tubes to avoid tumbling the gyro which added to the weight. The Mark XIII torpedo when it was introduced avoided many of these drawbacks. It was not only faster (45 knots), more powerful and more reliable, but its non-tumbling gyro made it possible for it to be launched from simple racks on each side of the boat, instead of through heavy torpedo tubes.

Japanese Boats

The Japanese did less than any of the major powers in the development of motor torpedo boats, concentrating their efforts in the years preceding the war on building bigger warships, the construction of which had been denied to them in the 1920s and early 1930s by the naval treaties of that period. Most of the small boats built or converted from merchant vessels were landing craft, primarily intended for use during the invasion of China in 1937.

In 1938, however, the Japanese captured a Thornycroft CMB at Canton and from this the Tsurumi yard developed an experimental motor torpedo boat. This led to the *T1* type, seven of which were built in 1941. They were 59 feet in length, powered by two petrol engines of 1,800 bhp which gave 38½ knots, and armed with two 7.7mm guns and two 18-inch torpedoes or six depth charges.

Later types of this boat built of wood or steel in 1942 and 1943 were simplified so they could be constructed quickly by small boatyards, but the result was that speeds were reduced to between 17 and 27 knots. They were generally armed with either one 13mm or one 25mm AA gun and two 18-inch torpedoes. During this period, a much bigger craft was also built, the *T51* type: 104 feet, 75 tons, powered by four type-6 or two Vulcan petrol engines which gave 29 or 30 knots, and armed with two or three 25mm AA guns, two or four 18-inch torpedoes and eight depth charges.

In 1944, a new *T14* type was designed, smaller than the others but with a better performance: 49¼ feet, powered by one type-91 petrol engine which gave 35 knots, and armed with one 13mm or one 25mm AA gun and two 18-inch torpedoes.

Throughout the war, the Japanese suffered seriously from a shortage of engines, consequently many hulls were never completed and were still on the stocks at the end of the war when they were surrendered to the Allies. Of the more than 250 motor torpedo boats that were completed, a number developed engine trouble and were only used for harbour duties. Forty-nine were lost during the war, the remainder being surrendered and scrapped after 1946.

As a result of acquiring a former Italian MAS boat in 1940, the Japanese developed from this several types of motor gunboat, powered by aircraft engines giving between 17½ and 34 knots, of which more than a hundred were built at Navy and small private yards during the war. Most were 59 feet overall and armed with two 20mm AA and two 7.7mm guns, or three 25mm AA guns; all carried two or four depth charges. They were originally intended to escort MTBs on their missions. But the Japanese left the development of their coastal craft too late for them to make much of a contribution during the war.

As a last resort during the closing months of the war, the Japanese introduced the one-man *Shinyo*-type suicide motorboat. They were 16 to 18 feet long, powered by one or two automobile engines giving speeds of up to 30 knots and loaded with a charge of over 4,000 lb of TNT in their bows, which was armed by the pilot when on a collision course with an enemy vessel. Over 600 were built, most of them in 1944 for use during the Okinawa campaign, where they were hidden in coves and inlets until they could be launched from their trolleys on a one-way journey for both man and boat. Fortunately, the American PTs succeeded in locating most of their hiding places before they could be used. There is no record of any Allied ship being seriously damaged by one of these craft.

These then were the main types of motor torpedo boats used in the Second World War. They were built up into formidable fleets of small craft that saw some of the most fiercely fought battles later in the war, after they had proved their value to the sceptics who existed in all the major navies. At the beginning of the war there was just a handful of boats – untried in combat, some of them already obsolete, and with no one being sure just how they could be used.

CHAPTER 3

Into Battle

At the end of April 1940, seven boats of Kapitänleutnant Rudolph Petersen's 2nd Schnellboot Flotilla were patrolling the waters off the Norwegian coast. A few days earlier, German troops had invaded Norway and Denmark and were now preparing to sweep through Holland, Belgium and France. This would give the S-boats their much-needed bases in the North Sea and English Channel, but for the moment they were based at Wilhelmshaven, where they came under the general command of Konteradmiral Bütow, as 'Führer der Torpedoboote'.

On 30 April, Petersen's flotilla was ordered back to Wilhelmshaven. Here the boats were overhauled and then sent on the first S-boat mission into the English Channel, a round-trip voyage of some 400 miles. No one knew quite what to expect as none of the boats had operated so far from base before, but the general orders were to attack British shipping in the area.

At 22.00 on the night of 9 May, four of the boats were on patrol north-east of the Dover Strait when the commander of lead boat *S32*, Leutnant Kosky, signalled to Petersen on *S30* that he had sighted shadows on the horizon to the east. He was ordered to keep them in sight while the other boats closed up behind him. Peering into the gloom, Kosky studied the outlines of the ships. Thick bridges, long low sterns, pointed bows…There was no doubt about it. They were British destroyers. The group had in fact run into a force of cruisers and destroyers of the Home Fleet that had been out searching for enemy minelayers.

Quietly, on single engines, the S-boats circled eastwards so they could attack from the dark horizon. They hoped they had not been seen, but suddenly a light signalled from one of the destroyers. Petersen was unable to reply with the correct identification code and seconds later the destroyers began firing. Flashes lit the night sky and the sea near the S-boats boiled with falling shells.

Petersen ordered his force, which also included *S31* and *S33*, to start all engines and turn hard to port. The boats heeled over and with bows lifting out of the water at 40 knots, they sped out of range of the destroyers' guns. At this point, because fuel was running low, Petersen and Kosky were compelled to set off on the long haul home. Meanwhile *S31*, under the command of Kapitänleutnant Opdenhoff, had lost contact with the other boats and suddenly found one of the destroyers dead ahead. In the darkness the boat had obviously not been seen for the destroyer was not firing. Opdenhoff approached closer, then at a range of 800 yards gave the order to fire two torpedoes. The splash as they leaped from the bows and hit the water was seen from the destroyer and her guns began to open rapid fire. Even as *S31* turned away there were two deafening explosions as the torpedoes struck. Because of gunfire from other ships in the area, Opdenhoff could not wait to see their effect, but he signalled 'Destroyer torpedoed, two hits'.

The crew of the fourth boat, *S33*, saw the explosions and, in order to get away, the commander headed into a fog bank, later reporting: 'Suddenly, right in the middle of the fog, there was a grey shadow in front of us.' It was another of the British destroyers. Unable to turn in time, the boat crashed straight into her. 'Our bow slipped along the side of the destroyer and eventually came free, but before we had got over the shock there was another bump and this time we were colliding with the stern. By now the destroyer was firing, not at us, but simply in any direction. They must have been nervous.'

The destroyer steamed away and *S33* was left alone in the fog. Not knowing whether his boat was still seaworthy or not, the commander ordered a smokescreen to be made and set course for home. An inspection showed that not only were the forward compartments full of water, but about 18 feet of the bows had simply disappeared, leaving a large jagged hole. There was much other damage as well. It was in this condition, with pumps working at full pressure to keep the boat afloat, that *S33* made the 200-mile journey back to base. The shipyard was so impressed with her stability in such a condition that they requested to keep the boat for experimental purposes. This was refused by Naval Command and after a new bow had been fixed the boat was ready for active service again.

The German radio announced the next day that in the first motor torpedo boat action of the war, a British destroyer had been torpedoed and sunk in the North Sea. This was not true, although it might well have been. The destroyer concerned, the *Kelly* (1,695 tons) was very badly damaged and it was only by the skill of her crew and a tow lasting ninety-one hours that she was brought safely back to the Tyne for extensive repairs. Nevertheless, this example of what a small boat could do against such a ship came as a shock to the Admiralty. And when later that day the Germans invaded Holland and Belgium, and it seemed only a matter of time before France fell, it was realized that the war of the small boats was being brought right to Britain's doorstep. At one stroke the Germans had access to bases all along the coast of Western Europe from which they could attack British coastal shipping. Commanders like Petersen would no longer have to make the long haul across the North Sea from the German Bight.

It was at this point that the Admiralty became really concerned about the threat from German motor torpedo boats and gave orders for the construction of motor gunboats for the specific purpose of combating this menace.

At the beginning of the war, the opposing motor torpedo boat forces were roughly similar in number: the Germans had twenty-five boats, the British twenty-two, although the German craft were larger and better armed, carrying 20mm guns as against .303 machine-guns. Both forces were some distance from what was to become their main areas of operations, in the English Channel, Dover Strait and North Sea. The Germans were based at Wilhelmshaven, whereas the only fully operational British MTB flotilla was at Malta. During the so-called Phoney War of the winter of 1939, there was nothing peaceful about the fight at sea. Warships, submarines and merchant vessels were in action from the very beginning. But the motor torpedo boats did not come into the picture until later. The German S-boats spent the first months on uneventful patrols in the North Sea, close to their base. Meanwhile, the 60-foot British Power Boat Company boats of the 1st MTB Flotilla were ordered home from the Mediterranean and left Malta on 11 November, accompanied by their depot ship *Vulcan*, an ex-trawler. It was an eventful voyage. During a gale off Sardinia on 30 November, en route for Marseilles, *MTB 6* broke down and sank while being towed by a merchant vessel – the first MTB casualty of the war. The remaining boats made their way up the Rhône, were then towed through the French canals to the Seine, and under their own power again passed through Paris and across to the Channel, arriving in Portsmouth on 8 December. After refitting, most of the boats made their way to Felixstowe on the east coast where, with the depot ship *Vulcan*, a base was operational by January 1940. Although Portsmouth was the first MTB base, where the new 70-foot Vosper boats were forming up into the 4th Flotilla, the first operations were carried out from Felixstowe.

As the German boats had found, there was little opportunity for action in the early months of 1940, which were spent on uneventful coastal patrols and air/sea rescue missions. At this time the main role which the Royal Navy saw for MTBs was to escort coastal convoys, and possibly to act as submarine hunters as well. This was primarily because while Britain had many merchant ships, there were far fewer escort vessels available to protect them in convoy. The Germans faced a different problem: they had many more escort vessels than merchant ships, including destroyers, torpedo boats, armed trawlers and minelayers, as well as S-boats and R-boats. And so from the start they could use their S-boats aggressively to attack British convoys without depleting the forces available to protect their own. As operations were to prove, this was also the most effective use for MTBs, designed as they were as weapons of attack rather than defence.

By early May, three more flotillas were operating from Felixstowe – the 3rd, 4th and 10th – comprising an assortment of Vosper, BPB, Thornycroft and old experimental craft. Following the German invasion of Holland on 10 May, three boats of the 3rd Flotilla, commanded by Lieutenant Commander Anthony Cole, were sent across to operate against the enemy in the Zuiderzee. They arrived at Ijmuiden on 12 May and in a confused situation, which included constant air raids, they journeyed via the canals to Amsterdam and then down to the Zuiderzee. There was little they could do, in fact, except evacuate a number of refugees and servicemen, including the crews of ships being used to block Ijmuiden harbour. The three craft, *MTB 22, 24* and *25*, set off on the afternoon of 14 May to return to Felixstowe. At 22.00 they were attacked by two seaplanes, a Dornier and a Heinkel. It was at this point that the MTBs scored their first success of the war, ironically against an aircraft. Able Seaman Stanley Aldridge, the gunner on *MTB 24* (Lieutenant R. Parkinson), shot down the Heinkel while

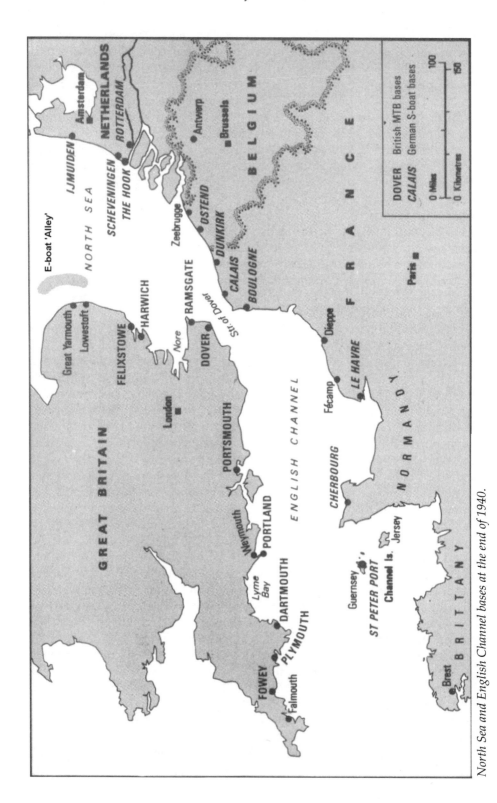

North Sea and English Channel bases at the end of 1940.

the gunners on the other two craft hit and possibly downed the Dornier. The boats were undamaged and arrived back at base the next morning.

Two weeks later, together with every other available craft in Britain, the MTBs left to take part in the evacuation from Dunkirk. Stewart Gould, at that time commanding *MTB 16* before he transferred to MGBs, reported:

We left Dover at 06.35 on 28 May and it was not long before we came under fire from the guns in Calais and Gravelines. The MTBs scattered and eventually reached Dunkirk at 08.30. I took *MTB 68* under orders and reported to the Senior Naval Officer. Destroyers were embarking British troops from the East Pier. The town was being bombed and there was a great deal of shelling.

MTB 68 was sent back to Dover with a hand message from the Senior Naval Officer. We anchored close inshore and began embarking troops under fire. They were exhausted and still carrying full equipment. Few were able to climb on board and had to be hauled in through the torpedo stern doors. [The early BPB craft launched their torpedoes tail first from the stern.] Able Seaman Schofield swam voluntarily several hundred yards to save the lives of exhausted men.

We made several trips to and from the beach and transferred over 300 troops to the destroyers. Enemy aircraft attacked and *MTB 16*'s Lewis guns, manned by Able Seaman F. Clark and Telegraphist H.F. McCutcheon, brought down a twin-engined bomber.

During one trip inshore we ran aground, damaging the propeller. The centre engine was out of action and the tide was falling. We returned to Commander Maund, who was controlling the evacuation of the beach, and took up duties towing destroyers' whalers. At 21.00 the wind began to freshen and the evacuation continued from Dunkirk itself, to where Maund marched the troops. We left there at 05.50 on 29 May and returned to Dover and then to Felixstowe for repairs.

Such was Gould's report on the evacuation from Dunkirk, which took place from 26 May to 4 June. Many accounts have been written describing the desolation of the scene, the charred wrecks in the harbour and the men who had to be left behind while the town of Dunkirk went up in flames. But there is something in the factual terms of Gould's report, part of the record of one boat which was on continuous duty for more than twenty-four hours, under heavy gunfire, and which then only returned home when damaged, that sums up as much as anything the spirit that was Dunkirk. Every available boat in Britain had been called upon to take part in the evacuation, known by the code name of Operation Dynamo, including seven MTBs, three MA/SBs, one ML and one old CMB. Other commanders were present whose names were also to become legend in the battles of Coastal Forces: Christopher Dreyer, Bill Everitt, Hillary Gamble and 'Harpy' Lloyd. One of them, John Cameron, was the last to leave Dunkirk, in a 40-foot MTB that was one of the smallest craft to take part in the operation. Lieutenant W.G. Everitt, commanding *MA/SB 6*, was responsible for bringing home Lord Gort and General Leese. Also evacuated in MTBs were members of the Belgian Cabinet, Admiral Keyes and General Alexander. Perhaps their most noteworthy contribution to the evacuation was in patrolling the eastern flank of the area to hold off marauding S-boats. But even so, these craft achieved a notable success by sinking the British destroyers *Wakeful* and *Grafton*. One of them was sunk by a boat (*S25*) commanded by Kapitänlieutnant Siegfried Wuppermann, who was to become one of the best-known German 'ace' commanders in the Mediterranean.

It was as a result of the MTBs' exploits that the commanding officer of the MTB base at Dover, Lieutenant Commander S.H. Dennis, who was himself at Dunkirk each day and night with the boats of his flotilla, submitted a report to the Admiralty that made the following main points.

1. The MTBs have proved themselves invaluable for such operations.
2. Aircraft are quite unable to destroy them. Many attacks were made, by dive bombing and machine gunning, but no boats were lost or seriously damaged. Four ratings only were wounded.
3. Spare crews are essential, as the strain is very great, especially for engine-room staff.
4. Auxiliary engines are of great advantage. Craft entering Dunkirk at night on such engines were not observed by either British or enemy ships and batteries.

Together with the praise that the MTB crews earned from senior naval officers present for their skill and courage, this report helped to dispel some of the doubts which the Admiralty had towards small craft. Lieutenant Commander Dennis had himself served on CMBs during 1917, and was in a position to compare the very different performances of the old and new types of craft.

Dunkirk marked the opening of the first phase of Coastal Force operations. The Germans now occupied the entire coastline on the opposite side of the North Sea, the Straits of Dover and the English Channel, and had ample bases from which their motor torpedo boats could make sorties against British convoys.

In July, the 1st and 2nd S-boat Flotillas were ordered to Boulogne, which became for a while their main base. From the start, however, considerable damage was caused by raiding British aircraft, and so it was here that the idea originated of constructing bomb-proof concrete bunkers in which the S-boats could shelter and carry out maintenance and repairs. Similar bunkers were built at other bases established later in the year at Cherbourg, Le Havre, Ijmuiden, Ostend and Rotterdam.

In Britain, also, there was feverish activity to establish MTB bases along the southern and eastern coasts to receive the new flotillas that were being formed. In addition to Portsmouth (HMS *Hornet*) and Felixstowe (HMS *Beehive*), the 4th MTB Flotilla at Harwich (HMS *Badger*) and the 11th MTB Flotilla at Dover (HMS *Wasp*) were established in June 1940. Before the end of the year there were further bases at Fort William, Portland and Fowey.

In the early days of 1940, Coastal Forces as a separate entity did not exist. Flotillas came under the authority of individual commanders-in-chief who used them as they saw fit. But rapid expansion made it necessary to form a separate organization to coordinate the training of crews, and the construction and manning of all the craft. The base at Fort William, commissioned as HMS *Christopher*, was reorganized in October for this purpose, under the command of Lieutenant Commander A.E.P. Welman. A nucleus training flotilla was allotted to it, and shortly afterwards a school for motor launches was established at Ardrishaig (HMS *Seahawk*). Then, in November, Rear Admiral Piers K. Kekewich, formerly on the staff of the Vice Admiral Northern Patrol, was appointed Rear Admiral Coastal Forces (RACF), and the term Coastal Forces came into official being for the first time. Flag officers continued to remain responsible for the operations of flotillas under their command, but every other detail of technical development and personnel was directed by Kekewich and his staff. It was not, in fact, an ideal arrangement and during the three years that Kekewich held the post – until 1943, when it was decided that responsibility for Coastal Forces should come under a separate department within the Admiralty – Kekewich worked under continual frustration in dealing with commanders-in-chief who were reluctant to give up any of the autonomy of their commands, and from Admiralty departments which hesitated to encroach on the established preserves of these commanders. Kekewich first established his headquarters at Fort William but almost immediately, because of more pressing commitments in the south, moved to Portland (HMS *Attack*). In September 1941, he transferred his office and staff, which later included Lord Reith, serving as a Lieutenant Commander in the RNVR, to a secret headquarters in London, in a converted block of flats at Wendover Court, Finchley Road.

During the first twelve months of the war, the number of Coastal Force craft in commission increased more than threefold to a total of 93, of which there were 40 MTBs, 31 MA/SBs (which were converted to MGBs) and 22 MLs. Amongst the craft on order were thirty-three MGBs from the British Power Boat Company (types 60-foot and 70-foot) and 124 larger boats of 110 feet and 115 feet from the Fairmile Company. It was now time for Coastal Forces to strike back at the enemy.

CHAPTER 4

Fight for the Narrow Seas

The first successful torpedo attack by MTBs of Coastal Forces was made on the afternoon of 8 September 1940. Three boats from Felixstowe, *14* (Lieutenant E. Hamilton-Hill RNR), *15* (Lieutenant J.A. Eardley-Wilmot) and *17* (Lieutenant R.I.T. Falkner), set out to attack an enemy convoy of thirty merchant vessels that had been sighted by aerial reconnaissance approaching Ostend. *MTB 14* broke down on the way across the North Sea and when the other two boats arrived off Ostend, they found the RAF heavily engaged in a bombing raid on the anchored vessels. The MTBs made several attacks and released their torpedoes, hitting and sinking at least one ammunition ship and probably a further supply ship. Because of the resulting explosions, together with the bombing and flak that was going on all around, it was not possible to see what further targets were hit by the boats.

Further attacks during the following months revealed only too clearly a lack of training and understanding in the kind of tactics required. An example of this was the abortive attack on a German destroyer on 27 July 1941 by five MTBs of the 11th Flotilla from Dover: two of the boats narrowly escaped collision when crossing each other's bows at top speed, less than 10 feet apart; the torpedoes were fired at too great a distance from the destroyer to have any chance of scoring a hit, one torpedo narrowly missing hitting another MTB; and one of the craft fired at British aircraft flying overhead at that moment. It was a chapter of classic mistakes, with only luck preventing serious casualties. It was no wonder that Coastal Force operations were often summed up officially as amateur and second-rate, with their attacks not pressed home hard enough.

But the crews were gradually learning from such mistakes. They found, for instance, that while approaching a target from behind had the advantage that the enemy usually kept a poorer lookout in that direction, it required high speed and considerable judgement on the part of the Senior Officer to be successful. The ideal firing position was, in fact, from an angle on the enemy's bow from where the torpedo could hit at 90 degrees to his track. With the whole length of the target exposed, there was the maximum margin for error and the enemy had the greatest distance to turn if he wished to take evasive action – to 'comb the tracks'. The actual angle of firing had of course to take account of a number of factors, including the speeds of the torpedo and the target, and the distance the torpedo had to travel, so that invariably from this position it would be aimed some distance ahead of the target.

Firing from the quarter was the worst position of all as the target was narrow and the 'deflection' angle made it narrower still. The time of flight was long and allowed the enemy time to take avoiding action, which could be done by only a small alteration to course. And even if the torpedo did hit, the angle was so fine that it could cannon off without exploding – which did happen on occasion. Only slighter better was firing from the bow, since the deflection increased the hitting angle and the time of flight was shorter. But it was still a chancy method of attack. All torpedo tactics had to be devised to place the boats as near as possible to the ideal 'angle on the bow'.

While cruising, the boats usually maintained a V formation. Station could be kept in line ahead, but this meant that the boats had to keep some distance between each other in order to avoid the wake of the boat ahead, which was often turbulent enough to make a craft uncontrollable. This induced a concertina effect with the boats surging forward and then falling back in an effort to maintain the correct distance, and the longer the line, the worse the effect. It was much easier for two following boats to be on either side of the boat in front, just ahead of the wake in undisturbed water. The distance apart could then be greatly reduced and there was no danger of overriding. However, the V formation was not practical in action – a sudden alteration in course meant that a boat would have to cut across the bows of the next astern, and boats were liable to be screened from the enemy by others in the same unit, an important factor in gunboat fighting when it was desirable to bring as many guns as possible to bear on a target. When an action was imminent, therefore, the boats usually formed up astern, or on a single line of bearing, or were split up to operate individually, depending on the tactics decided upon by the Senior Officer.

As more was learned about fighting in small boats, the need to cover the widest possible area in search of the enemy became apparent. If the original search on silent auxiliary engines failed, then the main engines would be opened up in the hope that the enemy would hear them, open fire and thus give away his own position. The MTBs would then revert to a silent approach.

In the early days, cautious commanders fired their torpedoes at ranges of up to 4,000 yards, with virtually no chance of success. It was found that by using the silent approach, a well-handled boat could creep up unseen to within a few hundred yards of the enemy, even under conditions of nearly full moonlight and good visibility. In fact, to be successful, it became a prime necessity to get up close to the enemy, whether to fire torpedoes or engage in a gun duel. Other points learned the hard way included discretion in the use of smoke, so as not to provide more screen for the enemy than oneself and hamper other craft that might be coming in to attack, and the vital need to report enemy sightings quickly in order that other boats could be sent to the area.

But the biggest handicaps during this period were the boats themselves. Although a large-scale building programme had been got under way, especially of the larger Fairmiles, these did not become available until towards the end of 1941. For the time being, the only boats in operation were those built to pre-war designs, which were never intended for continuous use in rough seas.

The Germans were not slow in exploiting their early success, although it was not until late summer of 1941 that they began attacking the British east coast convoys in earnest. During 1940 they sank twenty-three British merchant ships, totalling 47,985 tons. Even more dangerous were the mines which they frequently laid off the east coast and in the swept channels off the south coast, and which were responsible for sinking at least another 50,000 tons of British shipping.

At this time, because of the daytime sorties by British and German aircraft and the long-range shore batteries which had been installed on either coast of the Dover Strait, both sides were compelled to limit their coastal shipping activities to the hours of darkness. The motor torpedo boats of both sides became night hunters, taking over from the aircraft which were the most effective weapons by day.

In this kind of operation, the S-boats were gaining the upper hand. The MTBs did what they could, but lightly armed as they were they were of little use in combating the enemy boats. It was for this reason that the MGBs were developed, with heavier armament in place of torpedoes. They began to come into service early in 1941 – the first flotilla was based at Felixstowe, followed by bases at Fowey, Weymouth and Immingham. But these were the converted MA/SB craft, unsuited to such operations, and the faster S-boats, acting under specific orders to engage only merchant ships, invariably managed to avoid any action with them. Later in the year the larger Fairmile 'C' Type MGBs began to operate after a crash building programme, but these were too slow, with a top speed of only 27 knots, to be very effective. A number of Elco and Higgins craft, transferred from the US Navy under lend/lease, were more effective when brought into service as MGBs. But it was not until 1942 that the first MGBs designed as such became available.

Meanwhile, the S-boats were continuing their attacks against British shipping, still employed on minelaying for most of the time, but also using their torpedoes when the occasion presented itself. They sank thirteen ships totalling 31,215 tons in this way during 1941, for most of the year having free rein at night over the narrow seas. And then, on the night of 19 November, two months after Pumphrey's action described in Chapter 1, which marked a turning point for the MTBs and established a new pattern of operations against German shipping, came the first decisive victory by MGBs against the S-boats and the first step towards regaining control of British coastal waters. It also brought to public notice for the first time the name of a man who was to become perhaps the best known of all those who served in little ships during the war – Robert Peverell Hichens.

'Hitch', as he was known throughout Coastal Forces, epitomized not only those daring commanders who fought so successfully a new kind of warfare at sea in light fighting craft, but also the whole tradition of the Royal Naval Volunteer Reserve. At the beginning of the war, it was men like Pumphrey and Gould, regular serving officers, who provided the nucleus of this new force and who showed the way it should go. It was RNVR officers like Hichens who took up the fight, to the point where Coastal Forces were manned almost entirely by volunteers. They proved the adage that to scratch beneath the surface of any Englishman is to find a sailor.

In Hichens's case, there was no need to look beneath the surface. He was born a Cornishman, in 1909, and much of his boyhood was spent in sailing small boats along the rugged coasts of his home county and among the Channel Islands. Educated at Marlborough, he took his MA degree at Magdalen College, Oxford, then returned to Falmouth as a solicitor, and partner, in the firm of Reginald Rogers and Sons. He retained his enthusiasm for sailing and at the same time developed a passion for motor racing, driving in many road races on the Continent. He entered the Navy through the Supplementary Yachting Reserve of the RNVR, was commissioned and was serving in a minesweeper during the evacuation from Dunkirk, where he won his first DSC for his work on the beaches, when he rescued several hundred soldiers by getting a rope fixed from a jetty formed of lorries to an anchored yacht, enabling the soldiers to pull themselves out beyond the swell. He was transferred to Coastal Forces in November 1940, and joined the 6th MGB Flotilla which was then being formed at Fowey, following the first S-boat attack on the east coast convoys in what was becoming known as 'E-boat Alley'.

In March 1941, the flotilla, under the command of Lieutenant Peter Howes, was moved to the Coastal Force base at Felixstowe (HMS *Beehive*). But the armament of the converted MA/SB craft was not powerful enough to win a decision over the S-boats, and the few inconclusive brushes with the enemy during the summer of 1941 proved that there was still a great deal to be learned about the tactics that should be employed. Experiments were made on various types of patrol. They tried operating the MGBs with destroyers, but this was not successful; unlike the MGBs, which were too small to be attacked by torpedo, the destroyers were too vulnerable a target to take the chance of stopping to lie in wait for German boats. So the MGBs began to operate alone, patrolling a large area of the North Sea from the Humber to the Thames and the Texel to the Hook of Holland, lying in wait for S-boats either on their way across to raid the British convoy routes, or returning from such raids in the early hours of the morning.

In August, Hichens was promoted acting lieutenant commander and took over as Senior Officer of the flotilla – the first RNVR officer to achieve his own flotilla command. But the patrols continued to be uneventful and the feeling of frustration grew, especially when reports of Dover's MTB success came through. The only reason for some hope came when the boats were fitted with more powerful Oerlikon guns, mainly at Hichens's instigation. It was also Hichens who was partly responsible for pressuring the Admiralty to order BPB boats specifically designed as MGBs.

On the evening of 19 November, while three boats of the flotilla were lying in harbour on short notice, reports came through that S-boats had been seen in the vicinity of the east coast convoy route. The MGBs were immediately ordered to sea. Hichens was the leader in *MGB 64* the other boats were *67*, commanded by Lieutenant L.G.R. 'Boffin' Campbell, and *63*, commanded by Lieutenant G.E. 'George' Bailey. These nicknames, as well as 'Hitch's' own, stood for more than merely a spirit of comradeship. They were the code names by which individual craft were known, so that they could be quickly identified while radio messages were being passed between them during an engagement. The Germans employed the same technique, and eventually 'Rudi', 'Bruno' and 'Karl', heard over the radio during an engagement, became names almost as well known to Coastal Forces as those of their own commanders.

It was an ideal night for small boats – a flat calm sea and an early moon. The unit slowly formed into line ahead and headed past the harbour boom, setting course for the Hook of Holland. But no sooner had the two sparks of light from Hichens's boat signalled full speed ahead when Bailey's boat broke down with engine trouble. The fault could not be corrected, so she had to be left behind. Then, some time later, one of the engines in Hichens's own boat broke down and his maximum speed was reduced to 18 knots, which made it impossible to reach the Hook in time to intercept the S-boats on their return journey, as planned. Meanwhile, further radio reports had indicated that the enemy were out in large numbers. In such a situation, there would have been good cause to turn back and not risk going into action against a much larger enemy force with only one engine working. But Hichens decided to go on, making instead for a point 20 miles to seaward of the area in which the S-boats were operating on the convoy route, in a direct line to the Dutch coast.

The two boats reached this position at 02.00 on 20 November, cut engines, and lay in wait for any sound of the returning S-boats. Reports of their activities were still coming in from the convoy route, so it meant a long wait. It was not until 04.45 that the faintest murmur of engines was heard, bearing west. The moon had set by now and with a mist rising over the sea, visibility was no more than 200 yards. The chances of two small boats, one capable of only 18 knots, intercepting a force of 40-knot S-boats seemed very slight.

The sound became steadily louder for about eight minutes and then seemed to bear slightly to the south. Hichens started up, guessing at the enemy's course and headed south-east in the hope of intercepting them. After a short time he stopped again to listen. The sound was much louder now. Altering course slightly, the MGBs set off once more. Suddenly, Hichens caught sight of a tiny blue light winking quite close to port. The faint outline of a hull loomed out of the mist. Although certain that it was an S-boat, he had to identify before attacking. A challenge was flashed. The reply was faint and indecisive. And then, there they were ahead, five S-boats, their hulls low and painted white, clustered together, almost stopped or moving very slowly, having arrived at their rendezvous position.

The two MGBs surged in amongst them, firing at a range of only 50 yards. Before the Germans knew what was happening, one S-boat was engaged to starboard, another to port, and one which was moving slowly across Hichens's bow was given a burst of fire by the forward guns at less than 20 yards. A fourth was attacked on a parallel course. Most of the enemy fire was erratic and passed harmlessly overhead, but a burst from the fourth boat put Hichens's main gun out of action.

By now the S-boats had somewhat recovered from their initial surprise and were scattering in all directions. With the speed of the MGBs insufficient to keep up with them and deciding that the enemy's general disengaging course was likely to be south-east towards the Dutch coast, Hichens headed in that direction, followed by Campbell. Suddenly, a fifth S-boat loomed up to starboard, taking a similar course. It was at this point that Hichens found his starboard guns had either been knocked out or were jammed. He had nothing with which to engage the S-boat except a stripped, hand-controlled .303 Lewis gun. As he wrote: 'The sense of frustration that I experienced at this moment is one of the liveliest and most vivid memories of my life. After a year's search for the elusive E-boat, to have one ranging nearer and nearer alongside at point-blank range, to be unable to fire anything at her except a rifle bullet, was utterly exasperating.' And more than that, at any moment he expected a hail of 20mm shells to come from the enemy boat, which at that distance could hardly fail to hit.

Then Campbell came up in the other MGB with all guns firing. The S-boat swung hard to starboard, firing wildly, and in a minute was out of sight. At 18 knots, the MGBs had no chance to catch her. They kept on the same south-easterly course for a time, when Hichens stopped again to listen. There was no sound of the enemy. The sheer closeness of the range in which the action had been fought had undoubtedly caused considerable damage to the S-boats, but without heavier armament, the MGBs had apparently not been able to make it decisive. On the other hand, a quick examination showed that they themselves had been incredibly lucky. There were no serious casualties and although Hichens's boat was slightly damaged, Campbell's was almost unscathed. They were wondering what to do next when Hichens's coxswain reported hearing a faint sound to the south-west.

Engines were started up again and the two MGBs headed in that direction. Dawn was beginning to show in the eastern sky when suddenly, out of the mist, there appeared ahead of them the long hull of a stationary S-boat, lying low in the water. There was no sign of life on her and after a few moments of suspense and suspicion that it might be a trap, the enemy vessel was found to be abandoned. She had been badly damaged in the action and left in a sinking condition, after her crew had been taken off in another S-boat. It had been the sound of that boat that Hichens's coxswain had heard.

The enemy boat, *S41*, was boarded and every effort made to keep her afloat so that she could be towed back to England. But the seacocks had been opened and the engine room was full of water, making it impossible to get near to close them again. As the water level rose, she began to settle by the stern. Everything possible was removed from the boat – guns and ammunition, W/T equipment, charts, books, logs, compasses, searchlights, revolvers, even pictures of Hitler – and transferred to the gunboats. As she began to wallow in the water, Hichens reluctantly gave the order for her to be abandoned. The MGBs pulled away and stood off at about 50 yards to watch the end. As the stern settled the bow lifted slowly until, for several seconds, the boat hung vertically poised in the air. Then she slid quickly into the water and disappeared from view.

A cheer went up, but it was ragged and feeble. The crews felt something of the sadness of the sight of any ship going down. The MGBs returned home to a triumphant welcome, flying the Nazi flag beneath the White Ensign. They had achieved their first success against the S-boats. Later reports showed that RAF fighters had engaged three which had been found limping home, so it was possible that the MGBs had, in fact, sunk one more. But in any case, two had been very badly damaged at point-blank range and two others roughly handled. Two small MGBs had taken on and beaten five larger and faster S-boats at their own game. It was a turning point in the fight between the little ships.

Lieutenant Commander Hichens went on to serve with distinction in Coastal Forces, not only as a flotilla leader but as the originator of most of the tactical theory that came to be used in motor gunboat warfare. He was awarded the DSO twice and the DSC three times, and was three times mentioned in despatches. He was offered senior posts ashore, but preferred to remain in action with the fast boats he loved so much, and of which he wrote:

> I think one of the most lovely sights I have ever seen is a gunboat unit at speed in moonlight, with the white pluming wakes, the cascading bow waves, the thick black outlines of the guns darkly silhouetted, the figures of the gunners motionless at their positions as though carved out of black rock, all against the beautiful setting of the moon-path on the water.

He was killed in the early hours of 13 April 1943, by a final burst of enemy fire after a minor engagement had been broken off. He had taken part in 148 operations, of which fourteen were actions against the enemy. Peter Scott MBE DSC and Bar, who himself served with distinction in Coastal Forces as a Lieutenant Commander in the RNVR, broadcast at the time on the BBC:

> The chief thing about him was the way he could lead and the confidence he instilled into the officers and men of his flotilla. I remember one of them telling me that his only fear on going into action was that he wouldn't satisfy 'Hitch'. And it wasn't limited to his flotilla, this inspiration. It spread around and developed the spirit which put our Coastal Forces on top whenever they met the enemy, by virtue not of their guns but of their determination.

Hichens's action had shown that if the conditions were right and the attack pressed home with sufficient determination, the S-boat could be defeated. But the battle for Britain's coastal shipping was by no means over. The real fight was to come the following year when, with better MGBs coming into service, Coastal Forces got down in earnest to combating the German boats and fierce fights raged almost nightly in the narrow seas. The summer and autumn of 1942 were to see the peak of Coastal Force operations in this area.

Meanwhile, from mid-1941 until the end of the year, the Germans were getting a substantial number of convoys and warships through the English Channel under cover of air escort and coastal guns. Enemy minesweepers were operating in these waters with considerable freedom, and between April and June alone, no less than twenty-nine merchant ships of over 1,000 tons each, and eleven destroyers, were known to have made the passage. On 3 November, Pumphrey and Lieutenant P.A. Berthon between them sank a 5,000-ton ship and got away without casualties, while Gould's MGBs kept the escort vessels busy and severely damaged a German torpedo boat – a class of craft which was in fact a small destroyer. The tactics developed in this kind of combined attack by MTBs and MGBs were to prove of the greatest value later, for by now further Coastal Force bases were being set up on the east and south coasts to receive the new flotillas being formed. After the winter when weather conditions would severely restrict all small-boat operations, these would be able to launch a major offensive against enemy shipping.

Other methods of attack by MTBs were also devised during this period. On 1 October, the Norwegian destroyer *Draug* left Scapa with *MTB 56* (Lieutenant Per Danielsen RNN) in tow. Thirty miles from the Norwegian coast the MTB slipped away from the destroyer (the MTB would not have been able to make the passage across under her own power) and quietly entered a fjord south of Bergen. Here, Danielsen came upon a fully laden tanker, escorted and northward bound. He sank the tanker by torpedo and also one of the escorts before speeding away to rejoin the parent destroyer and be taken in tow once again for the passage home. Both returned safely without suffering any casualties.

Such operations, unexpected and irritating to the enemy, brought a glimmer of hope towards the end of a year that had seen little but one defeat after another for Britain, both on the home front and in the Mediterranean. The last three months were described by the First Lord of the Admiralty as 'the crisis in our fortunes'. And then, in December, there came a further blow from yet another enemy when the Japanese in a series of lightning strikes brought disaster to the Far East. Once again, a few ill-equipped and outdated little ships were to find themselves in the forefront of the action.

CHAPTER 5

Disaster in the Far East

On the morning of 7 December 1941, the Japanese invaded Siam and Malaya, launched simultaneous attacks on Hong Kong, the Philippines and various Pacific islands, and carried out a devastating air raid on the American fleet at Pearl Harbor. Within hours the whole balance of the war was tilted alarmingly in favour of the Axis powers.

Based in Hong Kong were the six 60-foot MTBs of the British Power Boat Company that had been formed into the 2nd MTB Flotilla after their arrival in 1938, plus two Thornycroft 55-foot boats that had been acquired from the Chinese Navy. The local Chinese graphically described them as 'wind thunder boats' as they took up their duties with the Hong Kong Auxiliary Patrol, a force that included a minesweeping flotilla and two Admiralty tugs.

When war broke out in Europe, the Auxiliary Patrol was transferred to Aden and most of the RN personnel were relieved by the Hong Kong RNVR, commanded by Commander J. Petrie OBE DSC, who had been first lieutenant to Lieutenant Roland Bourke VC DSO and Bar, on *ML 276* during the raid on Ostend in the First World War. Only the 2nd MTB Flotilla remained, commanded by Lieutenant Commander G.H. Gandy RN, but the rest were officered and crewed by the Hong Kong reservists. These eight boats were virtually the only naval defence left when the Japanese launched their attack.

The first task of the MTBs, together with several commandeered ferry-boats, was to evacuate troops retreating along the Kowloon Peninsula. This was done after dark to avoid attack by the Japanese aircraft which commanded the skies. On 15 December, as the result of a bombing raid on Aberdeen harbour, *MTB 08* was set on fire and blew up, *MTBs 10* and *26* were damaged, and the RNVR headquarters ship, HMS *Cornflower*, was sunk at her moorings.

Working in pairs, the MTBs kept up their patrols, frequently engaging enemy minesweepers which were clearing the Bay in preparation for an amphibious landing. At 08.00 on 19 December, *MTBs 07* and *09* were sent into Hong Kong harbour to attack the boats and ferries in which Japanese troops were crossing from Kowloon Bay towards Taikoo. Expecting little resistance, the Japanese were taken completely by surprise. The attack was led by Lieutenant R.R.W. Ashby, on *MTB 07*, whose orders were to 'proceed into the harbour and shoot anything inside'. In spite of heavy fire from both shores and from Japanese craft in the harbour, the two MTBs came speeding in amongst the invasion craft, overturning many of the smaller boats in their wash.

Ashby later reported:

I opened fire on the enemy landing craft with all my guns at 100 yards range, with excellent effect, and passed down the leading strings at a distance of about five yards, firing continuously. I dropped two depth charges, which failed to explode. I then came under machine-gun fire from both shores and from wrecks in the harbour, from howitzers and light artillery fire from both shores, also from cannon and machine-gun fire from aircraft. The boat was hit several times and a cannon-shell exploded in the engine room, putting the starboard engine out of action and killing the leading stoker. I ordered the telegraphist to the engine room to investigate. My speed was reduced to 22 knots. However, I turned and attacked a second bunch of landing craft with machine-gun fire at point-blank range with most satisfactory effect. Another cannon-shell now put my port engine out of action. The boat was making water in the engine room, so I had no alternative but to try to extricate myself and endeavour to reach base. I headed for the Naval Yard under intense machine-gun fire and under attack from three aircraft. I directed fire against the diving aircraft and tracers were observed to enter the fuselage of two of them, one of which made off towards Kowloon low down and did not return.

MTB 09 had followed up the attack and the result was that the landing, for a time at least, was completely dispersed. On rejoining the lead craft, *MTB 09* found her to be lying stopped, with her third and last engine out of action. *MTB 09* took her in tow while her crew plugged the bullet holes below the waterline and by continual pumping managed to keep her afloat. In this way, both craft were able to return to Aberdeen harbour. For this action, Lieutenant Ashby was awarded the DSC and recommended for transfer to the Imperial RNVR. He later served with Coastal Forces in home waters, then in the Mediterranean and finally in Burma.

Later that day, *MTBs 11* and *12* set off to repeat the same kind of attack, but they found the landings abandoned for the time being. The Japanese were now on the alert and the two boats came under heavy fire. *MTB 12* was hit and stopped. She was not seen again and was presumed to have been blown up. The same fate overtook *MTB 26* which made another sortie into Hong Kong harbour a few hours later to shoot up Japanese craft if the landings had been resumed.

On 20 December, the flotilla commander received instructions for what to do in the event of the MTBs being ordered to escape from Hong Kong, the order coming in the early hours of 25 December, the day Hong Kong fell. The five remaining boats of the flotilla left Aberdeen for Mirs Bay. They travelled by night, lying up by day in creeks and inlets under camouflage. It was during one such stop that an MTB picked up survivors from a launch that had attempted to escape from Hong Kong but had been intercepted and sunk by the enemy. One of the survivors was Admiral Sir Andrew Chen Chak, the President of Southern Kuomintang. He only had one leg, but when the launch was attacked he had thrown his wooden leg over the side, jumped into the water after it and managed to swim to shore. He was not only an incredible character but he was later to be of the utmost help to the MTB crews.

The nearest friendly territory was far beyond the range of the MTBs. As it was, they had to go out to sea and then return to the coast of the Chinese mainland in order to avoid Japanese patrols, but by luck, they happened to land on a part of the coast controlled by Chinese guerrilla forces. The MTB crews had been ordered to scuttle their boats to prevent them falling into Japanese hands and then try to cross China to reach Rangoon – a journey of 3,000 miles. It would have been an impossible undertaking but for two unforeseen events: having Chen Chak in their party, with his knowledge of the country and ability to communicate on the right terms with the guerrillas; and coming across the guerrillas themselves.

Just before dawn on Boxing Day the boats were scuttled and, accompanied by the guerrillas who were to lead them through the Japanese-occupied coastal territory, the party set off inland. It took them three days to cover the 80-mile trek into Free China. Arriving at Wei-Chow they marched through the main street carrying the Chinese flag and the White Ensign side by side. The travel-weary remnants of the 2nd MTB Flotilla were the first the local Chinese had ever seen from the Royal Navy and the party was given a royal reception, complete with firecrackers.

From here on the going was easier, but it was still a tortuous journey as it was impossible to head directly westwards. On 31 December, they left on the second stage of the trek by sailing 200 miles inland in a river junk, which took four days. Then came another 200 miles by road to Kee Kong, the wartime capital of Kwantung Province, which before the war had been Canton. Here followed another great reception by the Governor of the Province, helped by the discovery that one of the RNVR officers had been at Cambridge with the Governor's ADC. It was only slightly marred when at the special banquet laid on for them, the hungry mariners wolfed all the rice served at the end of the meal which etiquette demanded should only be toyed with to show that the host had provided more than could be eaten.

After a short rest the party set off again, this time by rail through a section of the country that was not held by the Japanese, until they reached the Burma Road. They then travelled by truck for two weeks, covering over a thousand miles. After the discomfort of this ride, the last stage of the journey was a pleasant two-day trip southward by train through Mandalay to Rangoon, which they reached on 14 February 1942 – only to find that their arrival coincided with that of the Japanese. Singapore surrendered the following day and Rangoon itself fell three weeks later, on 8 March. Although most of the party managed to get away safely – one of them who later served in an aircraft carrier in the Pacific had the satisfaction of returning to Hong Kong to witness the official surrender of the Japanese – it was a bitter end to such a momentous and hazardous trek.

There were no MTBs stationed in Singapore or Rangoon – those originally intended for Singapore had been reassigned to Malta in 1939 and the urgent demand for coastal craft in home waters had prevented them from being replaced – and the brunt of the Japanese attacks was borne by a few slow and outdated MLs, manned by officers and men of the Dominion and Colonial RNVR. They fought against overwhelming odds for as long as they could, but when the Japanese entered the harbours, they undertook the evacuation of refugees and Service personnel, operating all the time under heavy fire and bombing attacks. They were compelled to move in the hours of darkness, hiding by day in creeks under makeshift camouflage. It is estimated that from 19 February, when the evacuation of civilians from Rangoon began, over 100,000 escaped by sea to Calcutta in MLs and other auxiliary craft of the Burma RNVR, a force which had only come into existence in June 1940.

Most of these craft were destroyed when Rangoon fell, marking the end for the time being of any Coastal Forces activity in South-East Asia. At the end of the year, twenty-two lend/lease MTBs from America, the 16th and 17th Flotillas, were shipped to Madras and Trincomalee from where they carried out patrol duties with the Royal Indian Navy as part of the defence of India. They saw no action and, because inadequate maintenance facilities resulted in their rapid deterioration, they were scrapped in 1944.

It was not until towards the end of 1944 that British Coastal Forces in the Far East saw action again, during the Arakan campaign in Burma, when fittingly the Senior Officer Arakan Coastal Forces was Commander Ashby, one of the Hong Kong reservists who had made the great trek across China. But by then large numbers of American motor torpedo boats – PT (patrol torpedo) boats – were already being used with great effect in the Pacific campaigns.

CHAPTER 6

The PTs in Action

When Japanese aircraft attacked Pearl Harbor on the morning of 7 December 1941, precipitating America's entry into the war, there were no more than twenty-nine PT boats in service with the United States Navy, namely Elco 77-foot craft which were formed into the 1st, 2nd, and 3rd MTB Squadrons. The twelve boats of Squadron 1, under the command of Lieutenant Commander William C. Specht, were based at Pearl Harbor. Squadron 2, under Lieutenant Commander Earl S. Caldwell and comprising eleven boats at that time, were fitting out in the New York Navy Yard for shipment ten days later to Panama to augment the defences of the Canal. And the first six boats of Squadron 3, commanded by Lieutenant John D. Bulkeley, were at Manila Bay, having arrived in the Philippines on 28 September.

These boats of Squadron 3 were to be the first US motor torpedo boats to see combat during the hopeless four-month struggle to defend the Philippines from the invading Japanese hordes. After that, PTs were not used to any extent in further action until America began to take the offensive in the Pacific War on 7 August 1942, with the Marine landings on Guadalcanal. From that point onwards, in numbers that were continually increasing as more and more squadrons were formed, PTs were in the van of the American drive across the Pacific to the Solomon Islands, New Guinea and on to the liberation of the Philippines. And they played an important part, with British Coastal Forces, in the Mediterranean War and in the English Channel during and after the Normandy landings.

At the time of the Japanese attack on Pearl Harbor, six of the boats of Squadron 1 were moored in the submarine basin, with their crews either on board or having breakfast on a nearby tender. As the bombs began to fall, the PT crews rushed to man their guns. The craft were armed with nothing heavier than .5-inch machine-guns in those days; nevertheless the gunners on *PT 23*, J. Van Zyll de Jong and George B. Huffman, managed to shoot down two of the Japanese torpedo planes, and the other boats also scored hits. None of the craft were damaged, unlike the bigger ships which were the main target of the attack and which suffered disastrously. After the raid the boats helped to clear up the resulting chaos, ferrying wounded to the hospital and undertaking many other duties. They remained in Pearl Harbor until six months later, when they took a minor part in the great Battle of Midway.

Bulkeley's boats in Manila were in similar action three days later when the Japanese launched their first heavy air attack on Manila Bay. Having been given warning of the raid, unlike the boats in Pearl Harbor, they managed to put out into the bay and, by manoeuvring to avoid the diving bombers, they escaped damage while at the same time bringing down three enemy planes. But the Navy Yard had been virtually destroyed, including thousands of barrels of gasoline and much of the PT equipment and spares. The boats moved to a new base in Sisiman Bay, at the tip of the Bataan Peninsula. During the rest of December, while the Japanese were free because of their air superiority to bomb Manila at will, and while the US Asiatic Fleet withdrew to the south, the PTs carried out constant night patrols. These were mostly uneventful for the Japanese were concentrating on overrunning the islands to the north. But on 17 December, three of the boats were sent out to rescue some 300 survivors from a Filipino ship, the SS *Corregidor*, which had sunk after hitting a mine while trying to take refugees to Australia. One of the boats, *PT 32*, a 77-foot craft designed to carry two officers and nine men, took on board no less than 196 passengers from the sunken ship.

Towards the end of December, General Douglas MacArthur and Rear Admiral Rockwell, the naval commander, established their headquarters on the island of Corregidor. Manila was declared an open city and the US Army withdrew onto the Bataan Peninsula. The situation was becoming grimmer every day. The PTs, which by the end of the month were virtually the only US fighting craft left, were rapidly deteriorating. Not only did they suffer from a lack of spare parts and a shortage of gasoline, but much of the gasoline and oil that remained was found to be sabotaged. Wax deposits that had been put into the fuel dumps caused the carburettors to become clogged, so that they had to be cleared almost hourly, and it was never known when an engine would suddenly stop. And sand was often found in the lubricating oil. The first casualty came on Christmas Day when *PT 33* ran aground on a coral reef after engine failure while on patrol south of Manila Bay. All attempts to move her failed, so she was set on fire to prevent her falling into the hands of the enemy. The Japanese Army entered Manila a week later, on 2 January 1942.

On 18 January, Bulkeley received orders to make a night attack on four enemy ships, possibly including a destroyer, that had been sighted in Binanga Bay. He selected two boats which seemed to be in the best condition, *PT 34* for himself, and *PT 31*, commanded by Lieutenant Edward G. DeLong. They set off that night and separated at the mouth of Subic Bay with the intention of making rendezvous at Binanga.

PT 34 entered Subic Bay shortly before midnight. Avoiding a challenging light from the shore, she managed to creep in at 10 knots and arrived at the rendezvous point. *PT 31* was not there, however, and when she still had not arrived after half an hour, Bulkeley decided to go in alone. Just inside Binanga Bay he was challenged by a two-masted freighter and replied by firing two torpedoes. One hit the ship and exploded – Army observers later reported seeing her sink and believed her to be a 5,000-ton merchant ship armed with 5.5-inch guns – but the other torpedo stuck in the tube while running at top speed. Without water resistance to slow it down, the metal was becoming white-hot and the torpedo was in danger of disintegrating. At the same time, the boat was now under fire from the shore batteries and having to make a run for it out of the bay at top speed. The chief torpedoman, John Martino, managed to stop the turbines of the torpedo by closing the valve in the air line, in itself a dangerous task involving contact with the roaring torpedo that threatened at any moment to shatter into fragments as deadly as an exploding grenade. But now a new danger became apparent. The torpedo was hanging halfway out of the tube, and as the boat raced through the choppy sea each wave that washed over the torpedo's warhead turned the blades of its impeller. After a certain number of turns the warhead would be armed, at which point it would take no more than a slight blow for it to explode and destroy both the boat and its crew. Faced with this threat, Martino clambered out along the torpedo and stuffed a wad of toilet paper into the impeller blades to stop them turning. A few hours later, the torpedo shook loose and fell harmlessly into the sea. *PT 34* returned to base without further mishap, but there was still no sign of the other craft, *PT 31*.

What had happened was that shortly after separating at the entrance to Subic Bay, *PT 31* had broken down because of the now familiar problem of waxy petrol clogging the carburettors. After drifting helplessly, the craft ran aground on a reef. For some hours the crew tried to get her off but it was hopeless and eventually, Lieutenant DeLong gave orders to abandon ship. The second officer and the nine men of the crew departed on a raft while DeLong remained behind to destroy the boat by chopping holes in the petrol tanks and then setting it on fire. On taking to the water after the boat had started to burn, DeLong was unable to locate the raft and it was over an hour before he managed to clamber onto the beach. Finding tracks on the sand shortly after dawn, he followed them to a clump of bushes where seven of his men were hiding. The second officer and two men were missing; they were never seen again. The Japanese were already attacking to the south and Japanese planes were active overhead. DeLong and his men remained in hiding all day, within earshot of Japanese soldiers who had come down to the beach. Then, when darkness fell, they made their way cautiously to where they had previously spotted two native canoes and paddled clear of the beach – within 200 yards of where hundreds of Japanese soldiers were now camped. After an exhausting few hours, during which time they capsized once, they landed further along the coast and soon after dawn the following day were rescued by Philippine Army Forces.

This now left four PT boats. They were barely in an operational condition, but the patrols continued and they were even able to score some further successes against the invading Japanese.

In view of the relentless advance of the Japanese forces, General MacArthur was instructed early in March to leave Corregidor. It was intended that he and other Senior Officers, including Admiral Rockwell, should make the first leg of the journey by submarine, with the PTs being used as escort. But it soon became apparent from a sharp increase in the activities of enemy warships off Subic Bay that the Japanese were intent on intercepting him, and so it was decided to make the evacuation earlier than planned, on 11 March, and to leave by PT boat. Bulkeley, with *PT 41*, was to carry General and Mrs MacArthur, their son, and Major General Richard K. Sutherland, MacArthur's Chief of Staff. *PT 35*, commanded by Ensign Anthony B. Akers, would carry Admiral

Rockwell and his Chief of Staff, Captain Ray. Other passengers would be taken by *PT 34*, commanded by Lieutenant Robert B. Kelly, and *PT 32*, commanded by Lieutenant (junior grade) Vincent E. Schumacher.

It was an extraordinary operation for such high-ranking officers to evacuate in boats that were almost falling to pieces, commanded by young men of no higher rank than lieutenant, and itself pointed to the extreme gravity of the situation. The boats made rendezvous at 20.00 on 11 March at the entrance to Manila Bay and proceeded in column ahead, *41* leading, towards Taganayan Island, in the Cuyo Group, where they were to hide up during the hours of daylight on 12 March. Then they were to get under way again for Cagayan on Mindanao, arriving there, if everything went according to plan, at 07.00 on 13 March. It meant a 560-mile voyage through Japanese-patrolled waters. Should any boat break down, she was to transfer her passengers to another boat and continue independently; if necessary all personnel would be transferred and the boat scuttled. Boats were to take every means of avoiding the enemy. If they were discovered and attacked, *41*, with General MacArthur on board, was to turn away and try to escape while the others engaged the enemy. Other precautions, such as alternative routes and hideouts, were also laid down.

The possibility of attack seemed more than likely when, just as the boats were leaving Manila Bay with their passengers on board, air reconnaissance reported that an enemy cruiser and destroyer had been sighted west of Mindoro. It was already known that a Japanese destroyer division was heading for the area at top speed.

There were difficulties from the very beginning. A strong easterly wind made the going very rough, putting the boats to an even greater strain; because of the enemy ships, a wide detour had to be made west of Mindoro Strait, thus losing time; and the boats found it impossible to keep together, according to plan. All of them were suffering from mechanical defects and, apart from these, they had to stop every hour or so to clean the carburettors of waxy gasoline. By morning, in spite of the efforts of the crews, all the boats were separated. *PT 32* was limping on two engines and *PT 34* could only keep up speed by tying down the throttles in the engine room. This, in fact, led *34* to arrive first at Taganayan, albeit two hours late. Kelly and his passengers passed an anxious day waiting for the others until, late in the afternoon, *41* and *32* came creeping into the cove. Unable to make the rendezvous point in time, they had been hiding amongst the other islands to avoid air attack. *PT 35* remained missing. After a hurried conference and examination of the boats, it became obvious that *PT 32* could not continue on the mission. She had lost most of her fuel, only one engine was working and there were leaks in the hull. Her passengers were therefore transferred to the other two boats and Schumacher was ordered to wait for *35*, to pass on directions and then independently try to make for Cagayan.

It was 18.00 when the two remaining boats, *PT 34* in the lead with *41* following, set off again on the last leg of the voyage to Cagayan. After less than an hour, a Japanese cruiser was suddenly sighted to the north but luckily the PTs were hidden in the glare of the setting sun and the enemy warship turned away without seeing them. With only a sketchy idea of the navigation of these waters,

Bulkeley cautiously led the boats from one island to another, keeping as close inshore as he dared. Soon after midnight a storm blew up, and the heavy seas and frequent rain squalls which drenched passengers and crews alike lasted until daylight. But they also helped the boats to slip undetected through the most heavily patrolled area, in which every Japanese ship was keeping a sharp lookout for them. And so they arrived safely at Cagayan on the morning of 13 March, exactly on time, after thirty-seven hours of constant danger from the enemy, the weather and the boats themselves. Later that day the missing boat, *PT 35*, also made it to Cagayan. After a further four days of anxious waiting, two B-17s flew in to take General MacArthur and his party to Australia, from where he set about building the force which was ultimately to return to liberate the Philippines.

Bulkeley was ordered to continue his attacks on enemy shipping for as long as his boats lasted. His first thought was for *PT 32*, which had been left behind at Taganayan. An air search for her proved fruitless. It was only much later that he heard the boat had been scuttled when Schumacher found her to be no longer seaworthy.

During the following weeks the three battered boats fought with grim determination while the Japanese completed their occupation of the Philippines. At various times all of them were out of action because of breakdowns and could only be put to sea in a patched-up condition. Nevertheless, they continued their attacks on enemy shipping. On the evening of 8 April, Bulkeley and Cox in *41* and Kelly in *34* made for the eastern side of Cebu to lie in wait for two enemy destroyers that had been reported heading through the Tanon Strait. To their astonishment, what emerged round the southern tip of the island was not a destroyer but a light cruiser, complete with 5.5-inch and 3-inch guns.

Both PT boats crept forward to within 500 yards of the cruiser and fired torpedoes. Bulkeley and Cox saw their first two miss; the next two ran true and hit beneath bow and bridge but failed to explode. Kelly's first two torpedoes also missed astern by which time the cruiser's searchlight was sweeping over the water. The beam caught *41* for a moment, then settled on *34*. The cruiser's guns opened fire while at the same time the vessel rapidly increased speed. Kelly's boat was riddled with holes and the mast shot away, in spite of Bulkeley's attempts to strafe the decks of the cruiser and draw her fire from *34*. Kelly moved closer to within 300 yards of the cruiser, to a point where the searchlight was beamed almost vertical to keep the PT boat illuminated, and fired his last two torpedoes. Then he turned away at maximum speed, only to find himself simultaneously under fire from a destroyer which suddenly loomed up some 2,000 yards away. It looked as if the boat was trapped. The cruiser turned to prevent her escaping, while the destroyer closed to port. Then Kelly and another member of his crew saw two spouts of water shoot up amidships at the cruiser's waterline. The searchlight faded as if from a power failure aboard and her guns stopped firing. This gave Kelly a chance to escape and it was the last he saw of the cruiser. After being chased and engaged by three more destroyers, the PTs managed to escape in shallow water south of Mindanao, where the destroyers could not follow.

Kelly's first thought on seeing the spouts of water was that the cruiser had been hit by the destroyer which was firing on the PT from the opposite direction. But his chief torpedoman reported them as torpedo hits and several observers who saw the action from the shore confirmed this, stating that the cruiser later sank. Japanese reports, however, indicate merely that the 5,100-ton *Kuma* class cruiser had been hit only once – and by a torpedo that failed to explode. Whatever the damage actually caused, the *Kuma* remained afloat until 11 January 1944, when she was sunk by a British submarine off Penang.

That was the last action fought by Squadron 3. Later the same night, while Kelly was trying to reach Cebu City to obtain medical aid for the wounded, *PT 34* was bombed and strafed by Japanese aircraft. One of the planes was brought down, but the boat was finally set on fire and exploded after beaching. Two of the crew were killed but Kelly managed to get the rest ashore, including three wounded.

The next boat to go was *PT 35*, burned in the slipway at Cebu as the Japanese were entering the city on 12 April. *PT 41*, her career as a torpedo boat ended because there were no torpedoes available, was also destroyed later when the Japanese closed in for their final onslaught in the Philippines. Bulkeley, later to be awarded the Medal of Honour and the Navy Cross for his exploits during those desperate four months before the final fall of the Philippines – Kelly and Cox also received the Navy Cross – was flown to Australia on 13 April under orders from General MacArthur. Returning later to the United States, he brought with him a message from MacArthur stressing the effectiveness of motor torpedo boats, especially in the coastal waters of the Pacific islands, and the need for them to be formed into a separate branch of the Service. MacArthur wanted 200 boats made available to him within eight months. Although his request was not fulfilled in that time, it was the start of the build-up of a motor torpedo boat force that before the end of the war totalled 212 PTs, operating from bases strung out through the whole of the South-West Pacific.

CHAPTER 7

Battle of the Mediterranean

Together with the prevention of a German invasion of the British Isles by the Battle of Britain, and the keeping open of American supply routes in the Battle of the Atlantic, the Battle of the Mediterranean was one of three key factors which made a German victory in Europe impossible and gave the Allied forces time to prepare and launch the Second Front. It was a battle in which the outcome depended largely on sea power as the Allied and Axis nations strove to keep open supply routes to their land forces, at the same time denying the use of such routes to the opposing side. And it was a battle in which small craft of all types, employed in large numbers by the major powers concerned, played a vital part in contesting for supremacy of coastal waters where larger warships and submarines were seldom able to penetrate because of the shallow depths, minefields and shore batteries.

The role motor torpedo boats had to play did not begin in earnest until 1942, and it was not until 1943 that they came into direct conflict with each other. By that time the fight for the narrow seas off Britain had passed its peak, with the MGBs gradually gaining ascendancy over the German S-boats. Increasing numbers of craft were sent to the Mediterranean, together with many of the commanders and crews of both sides, who had learned the techniques of small-boat fighting in the North Sea and English Channel.

But the scope for small-boat warfare in the Mediterranean was much greater. In a complicated and constantly changing situation, they could be used in many more ways; as many in fact as their individual commanders could devise, for they were operating without precedent and naval chiefs tended just to let them get on with it. The Germans and Italians used motor torpedo boats to attack Malta and other British bases, and to attack not only merchant shipping, as in the North Sea, but warships as well, up to the size of cruiser. British, Commonwealth and American boats took part in Combined Operations raids and assisted partisans operating behind enemy lines. Some of the patrols they carried out sometimes kept them away from their main bases for weeks at a time, hiding by day in the coves and inlets of the numerous islands in the region and fuelling from small forward bases. It was only in the Mediterranean that motor torpedo boats of both sides were able to claim the sinking of submarines.

The main areas of operation were along the North African coast, off Sicily and the west coast of Italy, amongst the islands of the Adriatic and Aegean Seas, and off southern France, following in fact the broad pattern of the war on land. The Battle of the Mediterranean began with Italy's entry into the war in June 1940. Her aims were basically to seize the Suez Canal with land forces

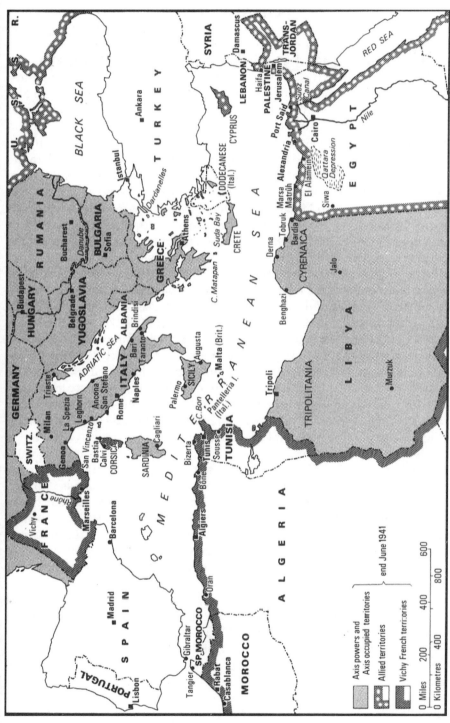

The Mediterranean theatre; summer 1941.

based in Libya, strike north-east through Palestine, Syria and Iran to capture the Middle East oilfields, and then south to create Mussolini's dream of an East African empire. Looking even further ahead, the Axis forces could sweep north to outflank the Russians; India would be open to them together with a direct sea route to their Japanese ally. With the fall of France, only Egypt, Palestine and Gibraltar, and the two islands of Malta and Cyprus, were in British hands; it was not long before those countries that had remained neutral were held by the Axis, so that they controlled the entire northern coastline from France to the Balkans, including Greece and Crete, and the southern coastline from Algeria to the Egyptian border.

The Italian Fleet greatly outnumbered Admiral Cunningham's Mediterranean Fleet, composed as it then was of outdated battleships and a few cruisers and destroyers – all that the Admiralty could spare from Home and Atlantic waters – with the immense task of covering both the western and eastern Mediterranean from a limited number of naval bases at Gibraltar, Malta and Alexandria. Even in terms of coastal craft, the Italians predominated. Against over 100 Italian MAS boats based at Taranto, Naples, Sicily (Messina, Augusta and Palermo), Tripoli, Sardinia, the Dodecanese (Leros), the Adriatic, Spezia and the Red Sea, reflecting the attention the Italians had devoted to coastal defence, all that Britain could muster were nine of the old type 55-foot Thornycroft MTBs that they had been building for the Finnish and Philippine navies, and which were hastily formed into the 10th MTB Flotilla before being shipped to Alexandria. (The only other MTBs that might have been available – the twelve BPB boats of the 1st Flotilla – had returned from Malta to Home waters at the end of 1939.) Shortly after the arrival of the Thornycroft boats, five of them under the command of Lieutenant Commander E.C. Peake were sent to help in the defence of Crete. But they suffered continually from engine breakdowns and a lack of petrol supplies, and were finally destroyed during a German air attack on Suda Bay on 23 May 1941.

That left just four MTBs, which were used mainly for patrol work in the harbours of Alexandria and Haifa. But the value of such craft was by then well appreciated and larger numbers were urgently requested for use in the Mediterranean. At that time, the Admiralty had none to spare from Home waters, where they were desperately trying to cope with the German S-boat menace. It was at this point that the Canadian Government offered to supply twelve of the 70-foot BPB craft they were building, and arrangements were made under lend/lease for two flotillas of ten boats each of the American Elco type to be transferred to the Royal Navy in the Mediterranean. None of these boats would be available until early 1942, by which time the rapid building programme in Britain was also making it possible for MTBs, MGBs and MLs to be allocated to this theatre, together with trained British, Dominion and Commonwealth crews. It was from this time that the build-up of Coastal Forces in the Mediterranean began.

Meanwhile, the overall war situation in Mediterranean waters had undergone violent fluctuations. The entry of Italy into the conflict, with her impressive fleet and especially her large submarine force, had been taken so seriously that for a time the Admiralty even considered abandoning the eastern Mediterranean. Two factors made such a drastic step unnecessary. Firstly, the Italian fleet showed itself unwilling to engage in battle, which meant that the British could retain the initiative, even with outnumbered forces. And secondly, the Italians failed to realize the overriding importance of air power in the struggle to keep control of the Mediterranean routes. They did not take the necessary steps to eliminate Malta, which became even more vital as an air base than as a naval base. And so, although Britain was denied an open sea route through the Mediterranean, except for occasional fast military convoys from Alexandria to Malta or from Gibraltar to Egypt under cover of all available naval strength, and most of her supplies for Egypt had to go the long way round the Cape, the strategic situation at the end of 1940 was by no means unfavourable. British forces had occupied Crete, following Italy's invasion of Greece in October 1940, which gave greater control over eastern Mediterranean waters. Malta had not only withstood Italian air attacks but had received reinforcements so that Italy's supply lines to Libya remained under constant attack. And the build-up of British forces in Egypt and East Africa had been proceeding steadily, so that there was good reason to hope that the Italians would be pushed out of Libya and East Africa the following year.

All this changed abruptly with the intervention of German forces into the Mediterranean theatre early in 1941 to strengthen their Italian ally. The Luftwaffe, based in Sicily, began a devastating onslaught on Malta and British shipping. German troops arriving in Greece forced the eventual evacuation of British forces at the end of April, thus gaining control of the Aegean and the approaches to the Dardanelles for the Axis powers. Meanwhile, the arrival of General Rommel's Afrika Korps in Libya not only prevented a probable defeat of the Italians but resulted in British forces falling back to a besieged position in Tobruk.

The only bright spot in the picture was the advance of British Empire troops from Sudan and Kenya into Eritrea, Abyssinia and Somaliland, which by early summer finally shattered Mussolini's dream of an East African empire, and gave the Allies complete control of the sea routes in the Red Sea and along the East African coast. But this did little to compensate for the defeats elsewhere. The fall of Crete at the end of May not only resulted in the loss or capture of thousands of troops and large quantities of supplies, but in the 'little Dunkirk' evacuation of those who could be got away to Alexandria, many ships were lost. And the German occupation of Crete gave the Luftwaffe bases from which they could carry out bombing raids over a wider area.

In spite of this, the Royal Navy still managed to keep Tobruk supplied and Malta continued to hold out against the mounting fury of air attacks. Planes and submarines based on the island kept hammering the enemy convoys bringing supplies from Italy to Tripoli – to such effect that over 100 German and Italian ships totalling more than 270,000 tons were lost between June and September. This in turn helped the British Army offensive in Libya, which by the end of the year was to lead to the reoccupation of Benghazi. But it was a success that could not be exploited, for the Royal Navy could no longer guard the Army's flank or guarantee its supply. German countermeasures to the British offensive had included the diversion of U boats from the Atlantic and a stepping-up of Luftwaffe attacks from Sicily against the Libyan supply routes. Combined with daring attacks in coastal waters by Italian one-man torpedo boats and the laying of large numbers of mines, these operations resulted in the complete elimination of the Mediterranean Fleet's battle squadron during the last three months of the year. Amongst those lost were the aircraft carrier *Ark Royal* and *Barham*, the first British battleship to be sunk at sea; those cruisers and destroyers that were not sunk outright were badly damaged and in need of extensive repairs. The end of 1941 brought the Allied situation in the Mediterranean to its lowest ebb. It was one of the worst crises of the war.

Up to this point, the only successful motor torpedo boat operations in the Mediterranean had been carried out by the Italians, as might have been expected with their considerable force of small but very fast craft. The stress on individual effort, rather than teamwork, which the handling of these boats required was something particularly suited to the Italian temperament. While the larger ships of the Italian Fleet may have been unwilling to fight, this certainly did not apply to their small-boat forces. And in what was to be the very smallest craft used in this type of operation – the 'human torpedo', in which one man or possibly two sat astride a torpedo and used this to guide them to a target, where they detached the warhead and secured it to the hull, then turned away in the hope of escaping the resulting explosion or being detected by lookouts – the Italians performed these dangerous tasks with ingenuity and extreme bravery. Their attacks on ships in British bases or in coastal waters caused serious losses right up to the time of Italy's surrender from the war. One attack by three 'human torpedoes' on Alexandria harbour caused the battleships *Queen Elizabeth* and *Valiant* to be put out of action for many months.

And the more orthodox motor torpedo boats were far from inactive. MAS boats based on the island of Pantellaria made regular attacks on Malta-bound convoys and succeeded in torpedoing a number of merchant ships. On 12 March, the cruiser *York* was sunk off Crete, as was the submarine *Union* of the Malta flotilla, on 20 June; and on 26 July, together with aircraft, MAS boats took part in a heavy attack on Malta itself. It was only through the alertness of the defences that they were beaten off, with considerable losses.

During this time, boats from Coastal Forces in Britain were already on their way to take up the challenge against these craft and also to operate in the same way against Italian ships. But just as the Germans had sent reinforcements to help their Italian ally in so many other ways, now they decided to extend this to small-boat warfare as well. In July, the 3rd S-boat flotilla that had been operating in the English Channel was transferred to the Mediterranean, under the command of Korvettenkapitän F. Kemnade and including Kapitänleutnant Siegfried Wuppermann as a group commander. Their specific purpose was to support the attack from the sea that was to be Operation Hercules – the invasion and conquest of Malta, the island that for so long had been a thorn in the side of the Axis powers.

The only route the boats could take to reach the Mediterranean was via the German and French canals to the Ligurian Sea, but the undertaking required the utmost secrecy, and the sight of motor torpedo boats bristling with guns in such normally peaceful inland waterways would be certain to attract considerable attention. So they were disguised to look like tugs: their white hulls were painted black and brown, dummy wheelhouses of wood were built round their bridges, false funnels erected, painted in the colours of an imaginary shipping company, and all signs of armament removed. It was in this manner that they made the journey through the Rhine-Rhône Canal and down past Lyon and Avignon – ironically taking part of the same route travelled by the British MTBs when they returned from Malta to the English Channel in the early days of the war.

At La Spezia, the boats were converted back to their normal shape and colours before sailing for Sicily, where they were based at Augusta, arriving in time for the concerted drive on Malta in the early months of 1942.

While the Luftwaffe increased the intensity of its attacks on the beleaguered island and U-boats had a field day with the British convoys that were desperately trying to keep the garrison supplied, the first main task of the S-boats was to lay mines. It was only 60 miles from the southern tip of Sicily to La Valletta, a distance that the boats could easily cover in two hours. Operations were always carried out at night, for once again, as they had found in the English Channel, the S-boats were vulnerable by day to attack from aircraft – in this case from Malta-based Spitfires. And these planes, though few in number, were taking a heavy toll of German forces. Increasingly, the S-boat crews found themselves having to be ready by day to pick up Luftwaffe pilots whose planes had been brought down in the narrow waters.

April saw the peak of the offensive against Malta. From the time of the arrival of the last convoy at the end of March, there were savage air raids almost every day. Two British submarines were sunk and others damaged. The dockyard was put virtually out of action, and with the sinking not only of the destroyers *Lance* and *Kingston* but most of the available minesweepers as well, the harbour entrances were closed by mines, many of which were laid by the S-boats. With the loss of 126 aircraft on the ground and twenty more in aerial combat, the Malta-based RAF strength faced extinction.

But still Malta held on. With supplies rapidly dwindling, desperate attempts were made to get convoys through to the island. Of the first, Operation Harpoon from the west, only two out of six merchant ships managed to arrive on 16 June, for the loss of two destroyers sunk and a cruiser, three more destroyers and a minesweeper seriously damaged. A convoy coming from Alexandria at about the same time, Operation Vigorous, fared even worse. Not only were a cruiser, three destroyers and two merchant ships sunk, as well as others damaged, but the sheer weight of the enemy's attack with aircraft, submarines and surface warships made it impossible to get through to Malta. The convoy was recalled to Alexandria.

It was during an attack on this convoy that the 3rd S-boat Flotilla achieved its first resounding success in the Mediterranean. In May, the flotilla had been moved to a new base at Derna, 35 miles west of the British garrison at Tobruk, to patrol the waters off the North African coast through which supplies were arriving in preparation for Rommel's big offensive. On 14 June, the British convoy coming from Alexandria, including eleven merchant ships, eight cruisers and twenty-six destroyers, was spotted by German aircraft. Wuppermann, as senior commander of the flotilla, was ordered to attack the convoy with five boats. They set sail at 17.00, intending by evening to be on station between Derna and Crete to make an interception; and at 22.00, they succeeded. They were picked up by radar on the British ships but mistakenly identified as U-boats. Wuppermann let the ships sail past, then ordered S59 (Leutnant Muller) to lead S55 into an attack from the south while he on S56 led S35 and S34 to attack from the north. Both groups were to come up astern of the convoy where there was less chance of them being seen. It took more than an hour to get into position. Then, just as they were creeping towards the escort screen to get in close to the supply ships, they were spotted by destroyers and driven off by heavy gunfire. By the time they had safely dispersed, shortly before midnight, they had lost contact with the convoy.

That might have been the end of the operation, but earlier in the evening Rear Admiral Vian, commanding the convoy, had received word that the superior Italian battle fleet had left Taranto with the intention of attacking the convoy and would make contact the following morning. Vian was ordered by the new Commander-in-Chief, Admiral Sir Henry Harwood, who had recently taken over from Admiral Cunningham, to continue on course until 02.00 the next morning, then reverse course in the hope of throwing the Italian fleet off the scent. With some fifty ships involved it was a difficult manoeuvre, causing a certain amount of confusion, but it was completed successfully. As luck would have it, however, the new course brought the convoy right back to S56, which at some time after 03.00, after searching unsuccessfully to regain contact with the convoy, suddenly found herself amongst a group of destroyers and a cruiser. One of the destroyers signalled a challenge. While the crew of Wuppermann's boat waited, scarcely daring to breathe, his signalman replied with the same group of letters. The ruse seemed to succeed for the destroyer remained silent. S56 was now right alongside her, close enough to see the men on the bridge clearly, and only 400 yards away from the cruiser. Wuppermann gave the whispered command for the torpedoes to be made ready.

Suddenly, the beam of a searchlight from the destroyer cut through the darkness, wavered over the boat and held her. Alarm bells rang in the cruiser. Wuppermann ordered the rudder hard to port and fired two torpedoes at the cruiser before making off at top speed for the gap between two destroyers that were following her. By now all guns were firing at the little boat. They had to cease for a moment as she passed between the destroyers for fear of hitting their own ships before opening up again as S56 sped away. It seemed impossible that she would not be hit, but at that moment there was a violent explosion as the torpedoes struck home, throwing the gunners off their aim. It was only for a minute or so, but it gave Wuppermann time to get away unscathed. In jubilation he reported to base that he had torpedoed a cruiser of the Dido class. In fact, it was the larger Southampton class cruiser *Newcastle* (9,100 tons), which was damaged by the hits and operated for the next four months with a hole in her bow.

The escort destroyers chased *S56* for ninety minutes before being shaken off. It was during that time that the destroyer *Hasty* was also hit by torpedoes, possibly fired by *S55*, although she claimed no hits. The damage was so serious that the destroyer eventually had to be sunk by a consort. And so, as in the English Channel, the S-boats were the first to strike a major blow.

By this time the build-up of British Coastal Forces was well under way. A main base had been established in an old yacht basin at Alexandria (HMS *Mosquito*). Under such experienced Coastal Force officers as Lieutenant Commander C.S.D. Noakes, Lieutenant Dennis Jermain and Lieutenant Robert Allan, all of whom had seen action against S-boats in the English Channel, the American Elco boats were formed into the new 10th and 15th Flotillas, and by early May the first half dozen craft had moved up to a skeleton base at Tobruk, under Jermain's command. Here they helped to keep the garrison supplied from Egypt, patrolled the offshore waters and took part in a number of clandestine operations ('false-nose jobs' as they were called) such as landing agents on German-held Crete. Four of them were meant to play a part in Operation Vigorous by being towed behind merchant ships and slipped should the convoy be attacked by surface ships. As such, they might have had their first meeting with Wuppermann's S-boats. But that would have to wait until later, for shortly after leaving Alexandria the convoy ran into rough seas and the alternately tautening and slackening tow ropes soon caused damage to the lightly built MTBs. It was intended that on arrival in Malta, the MTBs would remain there as an operational unit under Lieutenant Allan as Senior Officer. But it was not long before Allan's own boat *MTB 259* was sinking under the strain of the tow. The other boats fared little better; they were forced to leave the convoy and put in to Tobruk, after picking up Allan and his crew when *259* finally sank.

It was not an auspicious start for the MTBs, but worse was to come. In June, Rommel launched his big offensive and British troops began withdrawing from the Gazala Line. The last time this had happened in 1941 it had been possible to retain Tobruk as a garrison behind enemy lines, kept supplied by the Navy from Alexandria. But Rommel was determined this should not be so again. On the morning of 20 June, Jermain and several of his boats returned from a night patrol to find the town under a heavy bombing attack while German tanks were battering their way through the perimeter defences. In the desperate hours that followed the MTBs fought gallantly to rescue troops, lay smokescreens so that some of the harbour craft could escape, and in the last stages were actually involved in sea-to-shore duels with German tanks, infantry and artillery. Then Tobruk fell. The MTBs returned to Alexandria which itself, by the end of the month, was in danger with Rommel's forces just two days' march away.

But Rommel was stopped by the Eighth Army at the El Alamein line, within one last throw of taking the Suez Canal and trapping the Mediterranean Fleet between Alexandria and the Sicilian Narrows to the west, where the Luftwaffe held virtually undisputed control. Again it was on lines of supply that the outcome was finally decided, for as long as the Royal Navy could continue running vital supplies to Malta, so the attacks could be maintained on the enemy supply lines to Africa, thereby keeping Rommel starved of the petrol he needed for his last armoured thrust into Egypt.

The MTBs played little direct part during the momentous events of the months that followed the fall of Tobruk, up to Rommel's defeat in the last battle of El Alamein at the end of October, followed by the British and American landings in North Africa on 8 November, and the grim struggle to keep Malta supplied. Many had been lost at Tobruk. Those of the Elco boats that remained were reformed into one flotilla, the 10th, commanded by Lieutenant Jermain. The first of the Vosper 70-foot and 72½-foot boats had arrived and were being formed into the 7th and 8th Flotillas for initial use mainly on anti-submarine patrols off Beirut and Cyprus. And in September, Coastal Forces in Alexandria were reorganized under Captain G.V. Hubback. The most significant operation during this period was the part the 10th Flotilla played in the Battle of Alamein on the night of 23/24 October by making a feint seaborne landing at Ras-el-Kanais, 60 miles west of Alamein, to mislead the Germans into thinking they were being attacked in force behind their lines and thus cause a diversion of their troops. The MTBs closed the beaches and simulated a landing by sending up showers of tracer, dropping lights and smoke-floats in the water, and broadcasting a variety of noises over loudspeaker systems to sound like anchors dropping and large bodies of troops going ashore. The plan was a complete success; the MTBs were later attacked from the air but suffered only minor damage.

But it still brought no direct confrontation with the enemy, even though for the rest of the year the MTBs hunted along the North African coast from operational bases set up at Benghazi and Ras-el-Hilal. In the meantime, the S-boats had augmented their earlier successes by sinking another Southampton class cruiser, the *Manchester*, off Cape Bon on the Tunisian coast in the early hours of 13 August, operating now with Italian MAS boats based at Porto Empedocle on the west coast of Sicily from where they could cover the Sicilian Narrows. The cruiser was part of the Operation Pedestal convoy bringing much-needed reinforcements and supplies to Malta. In the confusion of the engagement it could not be ascertained who fired the torpedoes which hit, and the cruiser's sinking was credited equally to both S-boats and MAS boats. In addition, the motor torpedo boats sank four of the convoy's merchant ships and damaged one other. The following day, German bombers took up the attack and out of a heavily escorted convoy of fourteen merchant ships, only five, including the crippled US tanker *Ohio*, managed to get through to Malta. In addition to the *Manchester* and the nine merchantmen lost were added the aircraft carrier *Eagle*, the anti-aircraft cruiser *Cairo* and the destroyer *Foresight*, while the carrier *Indomitable* and the cruisers *Nigeria* and *Kenya* were all damaged. It was a heavy price to pay but the arrival of even five of the merchant ships, and especially of the *Ohio*, enabled air strikes to be restarted from Malta just as Rommel was preparing his offensive to drive the Allies out of Egypt.

Nevertheless, the S-boats had achieved considerable successes during their first year of operations in the Mediterranean, especially in their major task of helping to tighten the blockade round Malta. And in spite of the fact that flotillas were heavily engaged in fighting in the English Channel, the North Sea, the Baltic and the Black Sea, more boats were on their way, ordered to what seemed a very fruitful hunting ground by Fregattenkapitän Rudolph Petersen, who now commanded all S-boat flotillas as *'Führer der Schnellboote'*.

But although slow in starting, from the beginning of 1943, British Coastal Forces, later joined by an American PT squadron, began to hit back.

CHAPTER 8

In the Balance

If 1942 had been a quiet year for British coastal craft in the Mediterranean, with most of the effort directed at building up bases and flotillas, this was far from so in home waters. In fact, apart from the fierce fighting that took place in the narrow seas during the Allied landings in Normandy in 1944, the summer and autumn of 1942 was the busiest period of all for Coastal Forces.

As the British and German boats increased the pressure of their attacks on each other's merchant shipping, success went first one way then the other. For most of 1942, the balance was about even and only towards the end of the year did it begin to swing in favour of the British. One reason for the greater activity was the rapid build-up in the number of boats coming into service. At the beginning of the year, Coastal Forces in home waters consisted of seven MTB flotillas, plus a training flotilla; nine MGB flotillas, of which two were 'C' Type Fairmiles, with the others made up of an assortment of converted MA/SBs, small BPB craft and the early 77-foot lend-lease Elcos; and eighteen ML flotillas. These operated from twenty Coastal Force bases that had been established along the east and south coasts. By the end of the year, the MTB flotillas had been increased to fourteen, the MGBs to thirteen (including forty of the large 'D' type Fairmiles), the MLs to twenty-two; five HDML flotillas and one SGB flotilla had also been commissioned. The Germans had eight flotillas of twelve S-boats, each operating in home waters, together with a similar number of R-boats. Until April 1942, the S-boats operated under the overall control of the torpedo boat flotillas and it was only after then that they were established as a separate command, with Petersen as their first Commander-in-Chief.

The successful MTB and MGB attacks at the end of 1941 had shown the way – now there were the boats with which to carry these out on a large scale. There were two distinct areas of operation: the North Sea (Nore Command) and the English Channel (Dover, Portsmouth and Plymouth Commands). Following the tactics that had proved so successful in U-boat warfare, the Germans shifted the emphasis of their attack abruptly from one area to another. Thus, for the first six months of 1942, the S-boats were most active in the North Sea. Then came a sudden shift to the Dover Straits and English Channel, followed by a brief spell of activity in the Western Channel (by an S-boat flotilla operating from Cherbourg and the Channel Islands), then back to the North Sea again.

In the meantime, the MTBs carried on the Dover tradition by concentrating their efforts in the Channel for the first half of the year. But with longer ranges being made possible with bigger boats, they began to operate further afield, crossing the North Sea from east coast bases to attack enemy shipping off the

Dutch coast, and even operating from the Shetlands across to the Norwegian coast.

Finding that the direct use of aircraft by day and S-boats by night had not been sufficient to prevent Allied east coast convoys getting through, the Germans began 1942 with a concerted drive to lay mines in the British shipping routes. Mines had always been an important factor in German policy. Apart from those laid from the air, a number of different types of surface vessel were fitted for minelaying, including destroyers, torpedo boats and S-boats, as well as submarines. In many ways the S-boats were the most dangerous, for not only could they more easily escape detection, but they were the only craft small enough to lay mines close inshore. In the first six months of 1942, they alone laid 260 mines off the east coast, both magnetic and acoustic, which were responsible for the loss of more than thirty Allied merchant ships totalling some 100,000 tons, as well as the escort destroyer *Vimiera.* Also taking into account their torpedo attacks on Allied shipping, which sank several more merchant ships and another destroyer, the *Vortigern* (on 15 March), the S-boats had become an alarming menace. Their main area of attack was that part of the coastal convoy route which lay off Yarmouth which became known as 'E-Boat Alley'. The S-boats reached this area from their main bases at Ijmuiden and The Hook by crossing the North Sea past the Brown Ridge shallows, and so confident had they become towards the end of 1941, and so few were the forces ranged against them, that they were often still at sea in the hours of daylight.

The task of defending coastal convoys was shouldered primarily by the destroyer escorts, with some help from the MLs. But these smaller boats, because of their slow speed, were seldom able to cope with an S-boat attack by themselves, and they sometimes had the unfortunate experience of being mistaken for the enemy and shot at by their own forces. It was for this same reason that the MGBs were not used as convoy escorts. They would have been far more effective in this way, for the historic reason why convoys are both the best means of defence and attack – they allow forces to be concentrated where the enemy ships must come in order to attack. It was using these tactics that the Atlantic convoy escorts were eventually able to get the upper hand of the U-boats. But in the case of the MGBs, as there was an even greater danger of them being mistaken for enemy motor torpedo boats, they were sent out instead to patrol the lines of defence some miles to seaward of the convoy routes.

When they could be spared, which was not often, planes of Fighter Command defended the coastal convoys from air attack by day, and also attacked S-boats when they happened to see them, which was usually when returning from other missions. But it was on a haphazard and generally unplanned basis. From the beginning of 1942, however, Fighter Command began to take part with other naval and air forces in a coordinated offensive directed specifically against S-boats, their part being to attack the boats as they returned to base by day. These sorties eventually compelled the S-boats to operate only at night, which reduced the number of hours they had available for minelaying and convoy hunting. But it then put the burden of coping with them onto the MGBs, especially when from April onwards the S-boats began to operate from Ostend as well, thereby halving the distance they had to travel to the English coast.

There were pitifully few MGBs at this time to take such countermeasures. Night after night all those that were available set out from their bases at Felixstowe, Great Yarmouth and Lowestoft to stand guard off the convoy routes, but the S-boats usually managed to slip past them. Hichens had shown, however, that when they could make contact with them, the MGBs could take on and beat the bigger German craft. And on the night of 14/15 March, three of the fast Elco boats of the 7th MGB Flotilla from Lowestoft scored another major success.

The Senior Officer of the flotilla, Lieutenant J.B.R. Home, on *MGB 88*, was accompanied by *MGB 87* (Lieutenant S.B. Bennett) and *MGB 91* (Sub Lieutenant P.A.R. Thompson, a Canadian from the RCNVR), and had left harbour late in the afternoon to take up station on an all-night patrol off the Dutch coast. No sooner had they crossed the North Sea when reports came through that a large force of S-boats was active on the east coast convoy route – it was one of these boats that sank the destroyer *Vortigern* in the early hours of 15 March. The MGBs were ordered to approach Ijmuiden to wait for the S-boats on their return. For hours they patrolled close to shore without sighting the enemy, then just before sunrise they intercepted an S-boat heading for home and obviously thinking she was safe in her own waters. The MGBs came roaring towards her, firing with everything they had, and in spite of the S-boat's 40 knots, the Elco craft found they could easily keep up with her. Such was the force of their attack that some of the enemy crew jumped overboard while the others scrambled on deck with their hands up. The MGBs had received the first surrender of a German S-boat – number *S111*.

Although badly damaged, the S-boat was still afloat and Lieutenant Home believed she could be brought home. The survivors from the water were picked up while the rest of the German crew were herded on board *MGB 87*. A boarding party led by Lieutenant Bennett's first officer, Sub Lieutenant A. Phillips, tried to get the boat working again, but in the middle of this, four more S-boats were sighted to the eastward, converging on the MGBs at full speed. With reluctance, the prize had to be left, her bow well down by now but still flying the White Ensign that had been exchanged for the Nazi flag. Then followed a running fight with the other S-boats in which both sides suffered casualties and some damage. Nevertheless, all the MGBs managed to get home.

It was in actions such as these that the MGBs began to come to terms with the German boats, and, if they did not always result in decisive successes, they kept up a harassment of the enemy that often forced them to turn back from an intended raid. Meanwhile, in the Channel, the initiative was also beginning to pass into British hands, largely due to the effectiveness of shore radar that led the Germans to complain that the British could actually see what was happening, while all they could do was to listen to the British wireless traffic as the only way of deducing the situation. Pumphrey's earlier success in the Straits was quickly followed by others, and the names of such MTB commanders as Hillary Gamble, H.L. 'Harpy' Lloyd, Mark Arnold Foster and the New Zealander G.J. Macdonald were appearing with increasing frequency in the press, creating, whether they liked it or not – and most did not – a new kind of war hero. There was something in the exploits of small boats setting out into the night to attack vastly bigger ships than themselves that captured the imagination and gave to Coastal Forces the kind of aura and prestige that Fighter Command possessed, particularly in the days of the Battle of Britain. And their exploits struck a note of good cheer at a time when the news from the main fronts was mostly depressing.

One of the most dramatic operations early in 1942 was the attack by MTBs on the battlecruisers *Scharnhorst* and *Gneisenau,* and the heavy cruiser *Prinz Eugen,* during their escape up-Channel from Brest. Although warned by the German Naval Command of the risks involved in such a move, Hitler was adamant that these important warships should not remain at Brest but were to be brought back into German waters to be ready in case Britain invaded Norway, which Hitler, wrongly, thought to be imminent. It was this same consideration that had led to the transfer of the new battleship *Tirpitz* from the Baltic to Trondheim in January.

Plans for the breakout from Brest were carefully laid with the utmost secrecy. Channels were swept through the British minefields, strong fighter protection was arranged for the midday passage of the Dover Strait, and in addition, the ships were to be escorted by six destroyers to Cap Gris Nez, where ten torpedo boats and a large number of small escort craft, including S-boats and R-boats, would also join the force. All these activities were observed by the pilots of Coastal Command on their patrols, so that by the time the ships left Brest on the evening of 11 February, four days before the new moon to gain the longest period of darkness possible, the Admiralty had guessed the enemy's intention. They should have been ready to take countermeasures but the forces available were very few and the measures taken, both by the Royal Navy and the RAF, were hopelessly inadequate.

The first attack was made soon after midday on 12 February by all the serviceable MTBs from Dover – a total of just five boats, led by Lieutenant Commander Pumphrey (*MTB 221*), with *219* (Sub Lieutenant Mark Arnold Foster), *45* (Lieutenant L.J.H. Gamble), *44* (Sub Lieutenant Richard F. Saunders, RANVR) and *48* (Sub Lieutenant Anthony Law, RCNVR). They left harbour at 11.55 and sighted the enemy ships half an hour later, proceeding through the Dover Straits between Calais and Gravelines. But all the MTBs were suffering from engine trouble – *44* in particular, having lost one engine completely, was straggling some way astern – and a swarm of escorting torpedo boats and S-boats barred them from getting closer than 4,000 yards, while squadrons of Messerschmidts flew guard overhead. As Pumphrey later reported, the situation was impossible. Whenever the MTBs increased their speed to try to slip through the screen, the S-boats easily increased theirs to maintain the barrier. They did not attempt to turn on the MTBs, as they could have done, with what would have been disastrous results; neither did the German planes make any move to attack. They were obviously conserving their ammunition for the expected onslaught by British bombers, and all the German escorting forces were carrying out their orders to concentrate solely on defence to guard the big battlecruisers.

Pumphrey had two courses open to him. He could either try to battle through the S-boats, or fire torpedoes at long range. He had just decided on the first, almost suicidal course, when fate took a hand and one of the engines of his boat broke down. His speed was reduced to 16 knots, which put an end to any last chance of a direct attack. And so the MTBs fired their torpedoes from long range and turned away. There was only a forlorn hope of hitting any of the targets, and even this was dashed when three minutes later the battlecruisers changed course and continued on their way unharmed.

The MTBs were glumly gathering together for the journey home when suddenly a German destroyer came looming at speed through the smokescreen that had been laid by the S-boats. The MTBs scattered, making more smoke, but with all their torpedoes fired they were helpless against the destroyer, which by now was fast overtaking them and firing its heavy guns. The situation was becoming desperate when, at the last minute, two of the fast 63-foot MGBs (43 and 41) from Dover arrived on the scene, led by Stewart Gould. They had left Dover after the departure of the MTBs and on the way over had shot down two Messerschmidts. Now they made straight for the destroyer with guns blazing, at which point the German ship made a fast turn and retired to rejoin the main force.

So ended the MTBs' abortive attempt against the German convoy. Shortly afterwards, six Swordfish of the Fleet Air Arm, led by Lieutenant Commander E. Esmonde, came over to make a gallant but hopeless attack against overwhelming odds. All the planes were shot down. Only five survivors were picked up – two of them by *MTB 45* on the way back to Dover. Esmonde was posthumously awarded the Victoria Cross. Further aircraft attacks were made later in the day but all were beaten off without causing any damage to the enemy; a torpedo attack by destroyers from Harwich, made in the early afternoon, had the same disappointing result. By evening the German ships were off the Dutch coast and it was here that both the *Scharnhorst* and *Gneisenau* hit mines that had been laid earlier by the RAF. The *Scharnhorst* in particular was seriously damaged and the *Gneisenau* was never effective again, but all the ships had arrived safely in German waters by the morning of the 13th. The gamble had paid off. With skill and determination, the Germans had successfully run the gauntlet through English home waters, a fact which caused a public outcry in Britain at the time and which led to the setting up of a Board of Inquiry to investigate the escape of the enemy squadron.

Not all such passages through the narrows were so successful, however. During an action on 12 May against an armed merchant raider making the passage with an escort that included four Möwe class torpedo boats, eight minesweepers and many smaller craft, two of the torpedo boats, *Iltis* and *Seadler*, were sunk, for the loss of one MTB (*220*, in which the Senior Officer, Lieutenant E.A.E. Cornish, and most of his crew were killed). In fact, the summer of 1942 proved so hazardous for German convoys in the Dover Straits that the enemy were forced to make a major effort to lay defensive minefields in mid-Channel to protect their shipping lanes. As usual the work was mostly carried out by S-boats and

R-boats, which meant that craft that had been engaged in offensive action in the North Sea against British convoys had to be transferred to the English Channel for this purpose.

With MGBs from Dover, Folkestone and Ramsgate nightly patrolling the area, minelaying proved to be a dangerous operation. There were a number of encounters between British and German craft in which the S-boats tended to come off worse against the new MGBs, faster as they now were and more heavily armed. And so the Germans decided to try a new ruse, by setting out before dark in the hope of completing the task before the British night patrols were in position and at the same time choosing evenings of poor visibility to reduce the chance of being spotted by aircraft.

The first that Coastal Forces knew about this was on 16 August, when shortly after 20.30, radar stations at Dover detected a large force of enemy craft leaving Calais on a north-westerly course at 15 knots. This was unusually early for such a sortie. Although visibility was less than a mile because of the overcast weather, the sun was still up and it would not be dark for more than another hour. But a number of R-boats were known to be based at Calais and it was suspected that these had set out to lay mines in the southern approaches to the Channel. This proved to be the case and the force was found to number between twenty and thirty R-boats. Two of the smaller-type MGBs, numbers 6 and 10 under the command of Lieutenant G.D.K. Richards DSC, had already sailed from Ramsgate on anti-E-boat patrol, and three larger 'C' Type MGBs, 330, 331 and 609, under Lieutenant D.C. Sidebottom, were just preparing to leave Dover. Both groups were immediately ordered to converge on the enemy force in mid-Channel, in spite of the odds of five to one that they might be up against. Their action was to become a classic in Coastal Force operations.

Half an hour after leaving harbour the steering of Richards's craft, *MGB 10*, broke down when the rudder connections parted. Leading Motor Mechanic John Wibrin crawled into the after compartment, and in the heat and noise of the cramped space under the exhaust pipes held the connections in place throughout the following seventy minutes of the engagement. In the words of the citation awarding him the DSM: 'His outstanding stoicism was essential to the success achieved and was a feat requiring almost incredible endurance and devotion to duty.'

The three MGBs from Dover were speeding in line ahead at 23 knots, led by Sidebottom in 330, when at 21.25 they sighted six enemy vessels steaming in line across their bows on a south-westerly course. These had in fact parted from the main enemy force. They were closed and challenged by Sidebottom, but made no reply. So the MGBs altered course to the south-west and took station just ahead of the last boat in the enemy line at a distance of 200 to 300 yards.

At this point two more boats were seen approaching from the north-west on the starboard beam. They too were challenged and proved to be *MGBs 6* and *10*. In order not to engage Sidebottom's force by mistake, which was moving in to attack the rear of the enemy line, Richards took his two MGBs forward at 35 knots to engage the leading enemy vessels.

The enemy had not increased speed to escape, thereby helping Sidebottom to identify them as R-boats which were not capable of more than 20 knots. His three MGBs were now on a parallel course and gradually overhauling the enemy line to port. The R-boats had not made any attempt to open fire and may have mistaken the MGBs for their own craft. Whatever the reason, they had a rude shock when at 21.27, two minutes after the first sighting, Sidebottom pressed the button which sounded the open-fire signal at every gun position, and a broadside swept from the three boats towards the last two enemy vessels. This fire was returned almost immediately from four of the enemy boats, whose gunners must have been waiting with fingers on the trigger to see what would happen.

At such a short range, with the distance continually closing, neither side could miss. The wireless in Sidebottom's boat was hit immediately, so that no enemy report could be made to base. Then the pom-pom gun and crew were knocked out after firing only thirty rounds, and the same thing happened to the Rolls Royce gun. The following boats, *609* and *331*, were also heavily hit. But the two enemy craft had fared even worse with 2-pounder shells bursting all over their hulls.

With nearly all his guns out of action, Sidebottom faced a difficult decision. If he turned away to disengage, the other MGBs would probably take this as a signal to follow, for the action was too fierce for any signals to be passed between them, and they would lose the chance of finishing off the two enemy craft. If he stayed where he was, on the other hand, a sitting target with no guns, he would almost certainly be sunk.

He took the only other course, turned sharply to port and tried to ram the last enemy boat, thus enabling the other two MGBs to move forward and engage the enemy more closely. Just before the impact, the enemy's after gun scored hits on the bridge, wounding everyone including Sidebottom. As the coxswain collapsed, the wheel spun free and the boat lurched further to port, passing just under the enemy's stern, with Sidebottom the only one still on his feet. He grabbed the wheel and turned it hard to starboard, the boat swung round again, aided by the force of the enemy's wash, and her bows ripped into the R-boat's port quarter. The impact was so great that Sidebottom's first lieutenant was thrown across the bridge and knocked partly unconscious. The enemy boat heeled sharply over to starboard and her guns stopped firing. Locked together, both boats turned out of line, leaving the other craft to speed away from them. The MGB's starboard .5-inch gunner continued to keep up his fire on the next ahead in the enemy line, which was also coming under increased fire from the other two boats moving up to take *330*'s place.

With the MGB's engines still running at high speed, keeping her bows forced into the side of the enemy, it was apparent that the number of casualties made boarding impossible. As the telegraphs had been shot away, Sidebottom's order to stop engines had to be passed to the engine room by messenger.

As they slowed down, the enemy boat pulled clear and drew slowly away into the gathering darkness, making a great deal of smoke and with water pouring into the gaping hole in her side.

With the engines now stopped, Sidebottom had a chance to take stock of the situation. It was found that all the guns except the starboard .5-inch pair were so damaged that they were useless; the steering and port engine were out of action; the telegraphs were cut and fires had broken out in six places. Two members of the crew were dead, eight wounded by gunfire and two were suffering from carbon dioxide poisoning in the engine room. But in spite of the fumes, they managed to put out a fire that had started when the petrol tanks were punctured by a shell, restarted the engines, and remained at the controls until the boat had been brought safely back to harbour, when they were taken to hospital. Able Seaman Trevor Strachey-Hawdon, the gunner who had kept up fire from the .5-inch guns after the ramming, although under heavy fire himself in an unprotected position, rigged up the hand tiller and from then on took charge of steering the craft. He was helped by Able Seaman Richard Jane. Another gunner, Able Seaman Victor Willingdale, a member of the pom-pom crew who had been wounded along with the others when the gun was knocked out of action, attended to those who were wounded more severely than himself and then helped to put out the fires. One of the worst was under the bridge – its glow showing through a shell hole was attracting renewed firing from the enemy. So Willingdale lay down in front of the hole and screened the glow until the flames could be put out.

Meanwhile, *MGBs 609* and *331* had continued on their original course, engaging the remaining R-boats at close range. The boat that was now last in the enemy line was very badly damaged, but the other craft ahead of her kept up intense fire on the gunboats and *609* suffered heavily. Two of the crew were killed, another two mortally wounded, and her commanding officer, Lieutenant Alan McIlwraith, and first lieutenant, Sub Lieutenant L.B. McIlhagga, RCNVR, along with most members of the crew were wounded. Still she kept going, with only the twin Oerlikon gun working, until a shell hit the engine room and she had to disengage. As she did so, she struck some underwater wreckage which damaged the rudders and the propeller of the one engine that was still working.

The third MGB carried on alone until her guns were also put out of action and her commanding officer, Lieutenant N.R. Weekes, and two other members of the crew, were wounded.

While this short and fierce battle was taking place at the end of the enemy line, Richards had taken his two smaller boats up to the front to attack the leader. They were much faster than the R-boats and were able to engage first to port, then circle and attack to starboard. After two such circuits at a range of no more than 150 yards, the enemy's speed was reduced and a fire broke out amidships. Two more circuits and the R-boat was brought to a standstill, firing a six-star distress signal, three red and three green. At 21.45, the MGBs ceased fire, having in eighteen minutes expended 900 rounds of Oerlikon and all ready-use .5-inch and .303-inch ammunition. By now, the whole area was enveloped in smoke. Further six-star signals were being fired into the air. At one point, Richards had a glimpse of Sidebottom's boat, but all the other craft had disappeared except for the R-boat.

During the engagement, *MGB 10* had been hit on the water line and one engine was out of action, but there were no casualties. Some of the most accurate and damaging fire against the R-boat had come from the Oerlikon gun, manned by Able Seaman Tom Macreath. At one point, when a stoppage occurred, he stripped the gun whilst under fire and got it working again. *MGB*

6, commanded by Sub Lieutenant R.M. Barge, had also been hit on her side and superstructure, and the port Lewis gunner, Able Seaman Edwin Cunningham, was mortally wounded while at his post. An incendiary round had entered the engine room and set fire to one of the engine covers; this might have had serious consequences had it not been promptly extinguished by Acting Chief Motor Mechanic Leonard James. But generally most of the enemy fire had passed over the gunboats; being smaller and faster, they were more difficult targets than Sidebottom's craft.

Ordering *MGB 6* to stand by, Richards came up alongside the R-boat. Smoke was still coming from her, although the fire appeared to be out. Sub Lieutenant Philip Lee and Leading Stoker Robert Mackenzie jumped on board with the intention of overpowering the crew and making fast the towing ropes. They found six or seven dead bodies strewn across the deck, but the rest of the crew had abandoned the boat. Suddenly there was a loud explosion amidships as ammunition that the R-boat was carrying blew up and flames swept the craft from stem to stern. The MGB alongside was showered with glass and burning debris, and Lee and Mackenzie were only just able to jump clear in time. They had already secured the tow ropes and these had to be cut immediately to allow the gunboat to pull away from the burning wreck.

MGB 6 in the meantime had picked up eight survivors of the R-boat's crew from the water, six of them badly wounded. Later, *MGB 10* found another seven, two of whom were wounded. The two MGBs stood by the wreck until 22.45, then returned to Dover with their prisoners. As they left, the German shore batteries at Cap Gris Nez began firing at the remains of their own vessel.

Sidebottom's three craft managed to limp home in a battered condition. But the whole engagement had been highly successful. Further German survivors who were picked up the following night confirmed that the R-boat rammed by Sidebottom had sunk. And in addition to the boat sunk by the small MGBs, three more were badly damaged, two of them to the extent that they might well not have been able to return to base. A long list of awards resulted from this 'brilliant and successful action, in which there were many acts of individual bravery', as the official report read. The DSC was awarded to Sidebottom, Lee and Barge; the DSM to Wibrin, Mackenzie, Ordinary Seaman Harold Weeks (the Oerlikon gunner on *MGB 6*) and Acting Petty Officer Richard Yarnall (who carried on at the wheel of *MGB 330* although wounded); and Mentioned in Despatches were Richards, McIlwraith, McIlhagga, Robinson, Seymour, James, Cunningham (posthumously), Macreath, Jane, Strachey-Hawdon and Willingdale.

By the summer of 1942, three new types of Coastal Force craft had made their appearance – the more heavily armed 71½-foot MGBs of the British Power Boat Company, the large 115-foot 'D' Type Fairmiles that were intended as combined MTB/MGBs but which were in fact first used primarily as MGBs, and the even bigger steam gunboats.

The SGBs answered the seeming need for a craft that was large enough to put to sea in rough weather and which could operate both as a super-gunboat and a torpedo carrier, combining the functions of the MGB and the MTB, as did the

German S-boats. Displacing 165 tons, 145¼ feet overall, and powered by two 4,000 hp steam turbines using special flash boilers, they were the largest of the small boats, resembling, in fact, a miniature destroyer. Their hulls were built of steel whereas all the other Coastal Force craft were of wood. They were perhaps the most graceful of all the craft produced during the war, and with formidable armament of one 3-inch gun, two 6-pounders, several 20mm and two .5-inch twins, plus two 21-inch torpedo tubes with reloads, they should have been a devastating adversary. But they suffered from two drawbacks: they were too slow, capable of a maximum speed of only 35 knots, with a limited endurance of 350 miles at 12½ knots; and, more importantly, their boilers proved to be particularly vulnerable to attack. Once they had broken down, they required a major effort to repair. There could be no ingenious improvisation at sea as with the other types of engine, which could be kept going at least long enough to get the boat back to base. In an effort to overcome this weak spot additional armour was fitted, increasing the displacement to 260 tons, which had the effect of even further reducing the speed to under 30 knots. With their comparatively large silhouette and without the necessary speed to manoeuvre quickly, they made too easy a target for the much faster German craft. Only seven of these experimental craft were built. And one of these was lost during their very first torpedo action.

The 1st SGB Flotilla had been formed at Portsmouth by mid-June. On the evening of the 18th, three of these, *SGBs 6, 7* and *8*, under the command of Lieutenant J.D. Ritchie, acting Senior Officer of the flotilla, set out in company with the Hunt class destroyer *Albrighton* to intercept two German merchant vessels which were known to have left Le Havre with an escort of S-boats. The plan was to make for the enemy shipping route east of Cape Barfleur by 01.00 the following morning, and then sweep eastwards to intercept the west-bound convoy.

Passage to the Baie de Seine was made without incident. Shortly after 01.00, *SGB 6* had an engine breakdown, lost contact with the others and had to return independently to Portsmouth. An hour and a half later, while on a course parallel and slightly north of the enemy route and cruising at 12 knots, *Albrighton* made RDF contact with the enemy force, some 2½ miles ahead. A warning signal was flashed to the SGBs. A minute later, a German merchant vessel of about 1,000 tons was sighted, accompanied by several S-boats. *Albrighton* led the attack, firing starshell to illuminate the target and engaging with her 4-inch guns. The commanding officer, Lieutenant Commander R.J. Hanson, ordered the after torpedo fired, but the firing crew were momentarily blinded by gunfire and the torpedo missed. By now the SGBs were closing the target, so *Albrighton* withdrew to allow them greater freedom of movement, continuing to fire starshell, which revealed a second and much larger merchant ship of 3,000 tons coming up behind the first.

SGB 8, commanded by Lieutenant J.R. Griffiths, with Lieutenant Ritchie on board, and *SGB 7*, commanded by Lieutenant R.L. Barnet, both turned to port and passed astern of the enemy column, engaging the S-boats with gunfire, one of which was considerably damaged by pom-pom fire from *SGB 8*. Then the gunboats reduced speed and turned to fire their torpedoes at the larger merchant vessel. *SGB 8* fired first and one torpedo was seen to hit. *SGB 7* attacked next and as her torpedoes hit there was a loud explosion, a large column of water spouted into the air, and a dull orange glow spread along the ship. By this time *SGB 8* was involved in a fierce battle with S-boats. When Ritchie next had a chance to look round, both the target and *SGB 7* had disappeared.

After the engagement had been broken off, *Albrighton* remained to search for the missing gunboat, but there was no sign of her and at 04.15, as it was growing light, the destroyer withdrew and followed the other gunboat home. It was later discovered that *SGB 7* had been sunk, with most of her crew being rescued and taken prisoner, including Lieutenant Barnet.

The tactical idea of using a destroyer and Coastal Force craft together on an operation, so that the larger ship could give covering fire and illuminate the target, had been proved successful by the sinking of the German merchant vessel; the loss of the gunboat was due primarily to its lack of speed and there was little that the destroyer could have done to prevent this. This kind of combined attack had, in fact, been suggested at the beginning of the war when the Admiralty was considering how coastal craft could best be employed. But most available destroyers were required more urgently elsewhere, as convoy escorts in the Atlantic and to combat the U-boat menace. Now, the kind of operation in which the SGBs had been involved was employed increasingly in the Channel, and later in highly successful operations carried out from the Shetlands.

After this first action by the steam gunboats, no further craft of this type were ordered, although as many as sixty originally had been envisaged. As an Admiralty report at the time stated, the loss of *SGB 7* revealed only too clearly their vulnerability. Nevertheless, the remaining six continued to give strenuous service until the end of the war. While they were being refitted and provided with additional armour, it was discovered that they came within the specified length which entitled them to be known by names instead of numbers. And so they became *Grey Goose*, *Grey Wolf*, *Grey Seal*, *Grey Fox*, *Grey Shark*, and *Grey Owl*, the only Coastal Force craft to achieve such a distinction. They fought many spirited actions and were credited with the sinking of six enemy ships and damaging many more.

Command of the SGB Flotilla was taken over by one of the best-known RNVR officers to join Coastal Forces, Lieutenant Commander Peter Scott MBE DSC & Bar, son of Captain Scott of the Antarctic, and later to achieve distinction as an artist and ornithologist. It was he who was responsible for creating the most successful ship camouflage used in the war, blending duck-egg blue, off-white and green to such effect that on one occasion two ships disguised in this way collided in mid-ocean before they saw one another. This camouflage was designed primarily for invisibility at night and broke away from the entirely false idea which had previously been accepted that because night is dark, dark colours should therefore be used. The opposite was found to be true – if a ship was seen at night, it was in the form of a dark shape, so the purpose of camouflage should be to lighten her.

Meanwhile, the 71½-foot MGBs had also been in action. The building of these craft had been largely due to the persuasion of Robert Hichens, and it was he who took command of the first boats to come into service, formed into a renumbered 8th MGB Flotilla. At about this time, because their S-boat attacks on east-coast convoys had become increasingly unprofitable, the Germans made a sudden and unexpected switch to a new area of operations. At the end of June, two S-boat flotillas were transferred to Cherbourg with the object of attacking convoys in the Western Channel.

Plymouth Command was far less prepared than Nore Command had been to meet such a threat – there had been much less S-boat activity in this area generally and defensive measures against them had not seemed to be very necessary. Nore Command had already appointed a Coastal Forces operational executive (Commander J.L. Younghusband DSC) whose job it was to study the tactics and methods to be employed by the small boats in coastal defence. So successful had this proved that it was suggested his area of operation should be extended to other commands as well, to advise them on Coastal Force work in general. But this idea was rejected as it would mean treading on the toes of local commanders-in-chief who were touchy about retaining sole authority in their own areas. When a force of S-boats attacked an Allied convoy in Lyme Bay on 7 July they scored a substantial success by sinking six ships of 12,356 tons with no loss to themselves. Now the danger was apparent and, as the activity in the North Sea had lessened somewhat, Hichens and his new 8th Flotilla were immediately transferred to the West Country, based at Dartmouth.

He achieved his first success on 14 July, the night after his arrival – not, ironically, against the S-boats but by sinking a tanker off Alderney in a depth-charge attack, coming across the German convoy by accident after waiting fruitlessly all night for the targets they had expected. It was not until just over two weeks later, on 1 August, that he met the S-boats in this area, operating as they now were from St Peter Port in Guernsey as well as from Cherbourg. The encounter was decisive. Four MGBs, commanded by Lieutenant R.A. 'Bussy' Carr, Lieutenant L.G.R. 'Boffin' Campbell, Lieutenant G.F. 'George' Duncan RCNVR, and Lieutenant T.R. Ladner RCNVR, with Hichens on board Carr's boat, took on an equal force of S-boats just off Cherbourg, and in a twelve-minute action succeeded in destroying two of them at virtually no cost to themselves, leaving the scene as the German shore batteries began to fire on their own boats.

It was not long after this that the Germans transferred their main activities back to the North Sea, and Hichens and his flotilla themselves returned to Felixstowe in September. But his operations, not only against the S-boats but against the enemy's own convoys as well, had shown the Western Channel to be a fruitful hunting ground for MTBs. As there was less danger from mines in the deeper waters of the Channel, destroyers could operate in combination with the smaller boats, as had originally been planned. A strong force of MTBs, MGBs and Hunt class destroyers was formed at Dartmouth, Plymouth and Portsmouth, and from this point onwards, until the Channel was cleared of enemy ships after the Normandy landings, they carried out many successful sorties amongst the Channel Islands and between Cherbourg and Ushant. One such operation took place on the night of 13 October, when the Germans tried to bring the armed merchant raider *Komet* through the Channel to Cherbourg, from where she could set out to attack the Atlantic convoys.

The *Komet* (4,000 tons) was an important ship – new, fast and heavily armed – and a powerful escort of minesweepers and torpedo boats was provided for her. Five destroyers from Portsmouth, under Lieutenant Commander J.C.A. Ingram on *Cottesmore*, four more from Plymouth and eight MTBs from Dartmouth were sent out against the convoy. The destroyers made contact in the early hours of the 14th off Cap de la Hague and succeeded in setting the raider and two of her escorts on fire. Then *MTB 236*, commanded by Sub Lieutenant R.Q. Drayson, arrived. While the destroyers were forced to turn their attention to the remaining escorts, damaging every one of them in the resulting action, *MTB 236* slipped unseen between the shore and the enemy ships. Although damaged, *Komet* was still making 15 knots and in danger of getting away in the confusion of the battle. The MTB crept ahead of the raider on silent engines and at a range of 500 yards delivered the *coup de grâce* with two torpedoes. The *Komet* blew up

E-BOAT RUNNING ATTITUDES

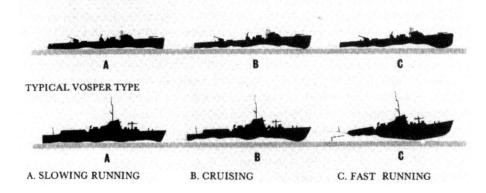

TYPICAL VOSPER TYPE

A. SLOWING RUNNING   B. CRUISING   C. FAST RUNNING

These illustrations show one of the major differences in design between the hard-chine planing hull of the British and American boats, and the round-bilge displacement hull of the German E-boats. The planing hull was more or less mandatory in order to achieve high speed with a short boat, but although it gave inherent lateral stability it did restrict speed in rough weather because of slamming of the flat bottom as the bows lifted out of the water.

Another disadvantage was the high plume of water created in the wake which could be seen from miles away at night. The German boats on the other hand remained nearly horizontal even at a top speed which certainly matched and sometimes was higher than the Allied craft. This was partly due to the sheer power of the DaimlerBenz diesel engines, but another factor was the special Lürssen-designed rudder arrangement. Each

boat had one main and two side rudders. By steering with the main and turning the side ones outwards to an angle of 30 degrees, an air-filled hollow space (cavitation effect) was created behind the three propellers. This not only improved speed and efficiency, but also reduced the high stern wave and kept the boat almost horizontal at high speed.

with an explosion that was seen from the English coast, some 60 miles away. Drayson was awarded the DSC.

The first 'D' boat to see action was *MGB 601* (Lieutenant A. Gotelee) in the Dover Straits on 20 July, during an attack on a heavily escorted German convoy when, together with two smaller MGBs, one escort vessel was sunk but when also one MGB was lost, including the Senior Officer, Lieutenant H.P. Cobb, and his crew. As a result of this action, modifications were made to all the other 'D' boats that were still building and it was not until towards the end of the year that they began to come widely into service with the opening up of a new theatre of operations off the Norwegian coast.

In the meantime, from August onwards greater activity was resumed in the North Sea when the S-boats returned from their efforts during the spring and summer in the Channel. They found to their cost a greatly changed situation. With more boats available, some of them of the newer and improved types, Coastal Forces had established permanent MGB and ML patrols some 8 miles to seaward of the east coast shipping lanes. The shortwave shore radar and VHF wireless stations that were being built began to play a major part in keeping these patrol craft informed of the enemy's movements. By the end of the year the whole of the coastal area of Nore Command was covered by radar, which could detect and plot enemy boats up to 20 miles offshore, and, to increase the advantage, radar sets were now being fitted in the Coastal Force craft themselves. Many fierce actions were fought in E-boat Alley, often at close range, but it was seldom that the S-boats could achieve any marked success. One such occasion was in mid-December, when a force of S-boats slipped through the patrol line undetected and sank five merchant ships of convoy FN 889. But such success was rare. Of the 63,350 ships that had sailed in east coast convoys during the first three years of the war, only 157 had been lost from all causes; the more serious losses of the early months had mostly been among ships routed independently. In 1942, S-boats in all theatres sank only twenty-three merchant ships of 71,156 tons; mines were responsible for the loss of another fifty-one Allied ships of 104,588 tons in all waters, including twenty-one ships of 43,000 tons off the east coast. During the year, Nore Command minesweepers swept no less than 707 ground and 157 moored mines.

While countermeasures against the S-boats were proving so successful, Coastal Forces now began to take the kind of offensive in the North Sea that was already in progress in the Channel. A new figure emerged as a pioneer of MTB tactics in the North Sea –Lieutenant Peter Gerald Charles Dickens RN (son of Admiral Sir Gerald Dickens, great-grandson of the novelist, later promoted Lieutenant Commander and awarded the DSO, MBE and DSC).

Earlier in the war Dickens had been first lieutenant of a Hunt class destroyer. It was while escorting cargo ships bringing coal from the north to London down the east coast – the most economical and indeed the only practical means of doing so when one ship could carry more than hundreds of wagonloads – that he first realized the importance of coastal convoys and their vulnerability if coastal waters were not sufficiently protected. The lesson was soon to be sharply underlined when on 20 April 1942, as a result of hitting one of several mines laid by S-boats off the east coast the night before, his ship, the *Cotswold*, was severely damaged. At different times that night, another destroyer and two merchant ships also hit mines in the same field. Casualties from the *Cotswold* were picked up and brought back to shore in an MGB, the commander of which was Robert Hichens. Although Dickens was not himself wounded, he and Hichens did meet fleetingly for the first time. They were later to work closely together as Senior Officers respectively of the MGBs and MTBs at HMS *Beehive*.

Dickens accepted with enthusiasm his appointment as Senior Officer of the 21st MTB Flotilla. He started at HMS *Bee* in Weymouth, where the first three boats were working up, and in May, he and the flotilla were sent to Portsmouth. His first action was nothing if not dramatic and could well have been his last. While leading two other MTBs in an attack on a German convoy off Pointe de Barfleur, the rudder of his craft jammed as they were heading directly for an enemy merchant ship. Unable to turn, he had no alternative but to carry on straight ahead at top speed, under constant fire by now. The starboard boat's steering was hit by enemy fire, forcing her to turn away, but the port MTB, commanded by Sub Lieutenant G.J. MacDonald DSC RNZNVR, thinking it was Dickens's tactical intention to maintain a direct course, stayed with him. The two boats shot between two merchant vessels, missing the stern of the first by a few feet. Dickens's craft was badly shot up and on fire, although incredibly there were no casualties. The other MTB had not even been hit at all and MacDonald picked up Dickens and his crew before their boat finally sank.

The 21st MTB Flotilla served at various times from Dartmouth, Felixstowe and Lowestoft, finally settling in Felixstowe. It was here that Dickens began the highly scientific study of MTB tactics that was soon to make his name a byword in Coastal Forces and establish him as one of the great small-boat commanders. He approached the problem as a hunter stalking a quarry, in which the best method of attack was not a blind, headlong rush forwards, but a deliberate and unhurried approach. Details were of vital importance – for instance, he always carried plenty of handkerchiefs to wipe the spray from his night-glasses and so keep them in good condition for viewing. When challenged by one-letter morse light from an enemy vessel, the ruse had already been established of turning quickly and repeating the signal to another of the enemy, then on receiving the correct reply, relaying this to the first vessel, thus being allowed to approach without interference. On several occasions Dickens simplified this by replying to the original challenge with any letter and gaining a momentary respite while the enemy, it was hoped, checked this from the code book before opening fire.

He also believed in the importance of firing anything at the enemy, even small arms, in order to make their return fire inaccurate, although only after his presence had been detected. On one occasion, this saved the lives of himself and his crew. Before going out on patrol, the coxswain of another MTB which was in for repairs asked if he could come along in Dickens's boat. Dickens agreed, as long as he brought a gun with him. During an engagement some while later, Dickens found himself with all guns knocked out, one engine broken down, and surrounded by enemy ships that were closing in for the kill. Suddenly, from forward and under the bridge, a single Lewis gun began firing. It was the coxswain who had come along for the ride. Dickens had forgotten all about him. But as a result of his unexpected burst of fire, the enemy's aim was upset, their boats drew back, the MTB had time to get the engine going again and moved away out of trouble. Dickens recalled:

> Our main aim was to creep in unobserved to get as near as possible for a torpedo shot. We developed a system of splitting up, so that if one boat was seen, he would start firing and speed around, not doing any damage but drawing the enemy's fire and attention while the other boats crept in. If they were seen, they would start making a lot of noise and give the first boat a chance to slow down and make an unobserved attack.

Such tactics were highly successful in the increasing number of operations which the east coast MTBs were conducting against enemy shipping off Belgium and Holland towards the end of 1942.

Dickens scored his first great success on the night of 10/11 September when on *MTB 234*, he led another MTB, *230*, (Lieutenant J.P. Perkins), supported by three MGBs, *91*, *82* and *84* commanded by Lieutenant E.D.W. Leaf DSC, against a convoy off the Texel. It was a classic combined attack by the two types of craft that was later to be developed into a regular Coastal Forces operation. While the MGBs kept the enemy escorts busy, the two MTBs slipped in quietly at slow speed from the other side, torpedoed and sank a merchant ship and possibly a flak trawler as well, and escaped unharmed. As Dickens stated in his report, the officers and crews of the MTBs behaved with great coolness and efficiency, 'but no one was called upon to perform any spectacular feat'.

The boats which Dickens had under his command at this time were the 72½-foot second-series Vospers. As in previous years, with the approach of winter, the worsening weather and rough seas reduced the number of operations on which these and other of the small craft could embark. But this year there was a difference, for the larger 'D' boats were now coming increasingly into service, able to withstand heavier weather and, because of their range, were able to operate further afield. It was this consideration that led to the formation of a flotilla of 'D' Type MTBs in the Shetlands, to carry out raids against enemy shipping in the fjords of the Norwegian coast, thus opening up a new area of operations for Coastal Forces. This flotilla, the 30th, was manned by officers and men of the Royal Norwegian Navy, under the command of Lieutenant Commander R.A. Tamber. Their first success came early in the morning of 27 November. In spite of a brilliant moon which gave extremely good visibility, two of the boats managed to enter the Skjaergaard fjord unseen, and torpedoed and sank two large merchant ships, each of about 7,000 tons, to the complete surprise of the enemy. The MTBs returned home unscathed, although they had to cope with a full gale on the way back.

This success was followed by many others off the Norwegian coast. Not only were torpedo attacks carried out but the MTBs also took part in a number of

Commando raids on enemy coastal installations. Eventually the Norwegian flotilla was reinforced by a British one, under the command of Lieutenant Commander K. Gemmel, and operations from the Shetlands continued until the last days of the war.

Thus 1942 ended with Coastal Forces gaining a measure of mastery over the narrow seas. They had fulfilled their prime task, of finding a means of combating the S-boat, and were now going increasingly on to the offensive against German coastal convoys. But the battle was far from over. The Germans tenaciously maintained their small-boat operations in these waters right up until the end of the war. And as if to teach Coastal Forces a lesson in the need never to relax their guard, the S-boats ended 1942 with another lightning switch to the Western Channel where, on 1 December, they succeeded in getting through to attack a heavily escorted convoy, again in Lyme Bay, and sank an armed trawler. This incident, though possibly minor in itself, was regarded as a typical example of serious weaknesses which existed in the defence of south coast convoys, in spite of shore RDF being available to warn of an impending attack. It was surprising that the enemy did not take more advantage in exploiting these weaknesses and were not more enterprising in their attacks on such vulnerable convoys.

The weaknesses on the British side were caused not so much by a lack of initiative as by the system itself, which encouraged each command to think as an autonomous and separate unit – Nore Command had achieved wonders in coastal warfare during the year, but other less prepared commands resented any suggestion that they should receive help and advice from them. The situation might well have been different had Coastal Forces operated as a separate Command with responsibility over all home waters. But they did not and to the end of the war they continued to be operationally responsible to individual commanders-in-chief, which worked well where these were alive to the value of small boats in coastal waters, but not so well where they continued to regard such craft with the Navy's traditional scepticism.

These drawbacks however were minor compared with the overall situation. By the end of 1942 the tide had turned in Britain's favour and Coastal Forces' main activity could now be switched to the more desperate situation in the Mediterranean.

This was a very different picture from that which had existed in home waters at the beginning of the year, when it was the German craft that had held the upper hand. In those anxious days, when the battle for the narrow seas hung in the balance, one of the few rays of hope to lighten the general gloom had been the daring raid on St Nazaire at the end of March by a combined operations group of Commandos and Coastal Forces. It was not only highly successful from a strategic point of view, and morale-boosting for the public at home, but was the forerunner of many later raids of a similar nature both at home and overseas. The experience gained at St Nazaire, and during the Dieppe raid later in the year, was to prove invaluable in planning and carrying out the biggest raid of them all – the Normandy landings. It showed yet another role for Coastal Forces and proved once again the vital need for craft specially designed to operate in coastal waters.

CHAPTER 9

The Big Raid

One of the twenty Coastal Force bases established in Britain during 1941 was at Falmouth, in the Cornish estuary. By early 1942, it was no longer unusual to see a strange assortment of craft gathered in the harbour and moored in mid-channel – trawlers converted into minesweepers, MTBs and motor launches bristling with guns, various types of destroyers. Not all were the sleek warships of modern design. Amongst those that called into Falmouth at various times were some of the fifty obsolete destroyers that the United States had transferred to the Royal Navy under lend/lease.

The *Campbeltown* was one of these, a ship of 1,090 tons that had been built in 1919. But when she steamed into Falmouth harbour on the sunny morning of 25 March 1942, it was not only her prim, old-fashioned lines that aroused curiosity. Armour plating had been constructed round her bridge, giving it a boxed-in appearance, and the deck had been cleared of the main 4-inch guns, the depth-charge throwers and torpedo tubes, so that she rested higher out of the water than usual; on the foredeck there were signs that some kind of construction work had been carried out.

Her arrival was closely watched by two senior officers. Commander Robert Ryder was a determined-looking man of thirty-four, wearing on his uniform the distinctive pure white ribbon of the Polar Medal; Lieutenant Colonel Charles Newman, the bronzed commanding officer of No. 2 Commando, had a more casual air about him but it disguised an equal determination. Both men showed signs of strain. For the past month they had been planning and preparing for one of the most audacious Combined Operations raids of the war and the biggest to be undertaken by Coastal Forces – the attack on St Nazaire. Now there were two days to go and tension was running high. The sixteen motor launches, one motor gunboat and one motor torpedo boat that were to take the military force of 277 Commandos and Special Service demolition experts on the long journey to St Nazaire were already moored and waiting in the harbour. The troops themselves had been accommodated with as little fuss as possible in the converted cross-Channel steamer, *Princess Josephine Charlotte*, which had brought them down from the Clyde ten days earlier. Complete secrecy was vitally important to the success of the mission, and a cover story had been devised to account for all the activity that had been taking place in Falmouth for the particular benefit of a German agent who was thought to be operating in the area. The Coastal Force craft were reported to be units of a new anti-submarine strike force that was being formed. The presence of the troops was explained by the fact that they were supposed to be taking part in an exercise to test the port defences.

But both men, one the naval commander of the operation and the other the military commander, were aware that if the slightest hint of their real purpose leaked out, the raid would end in utter disaster. Involving, as it did, penetrating several miles into heavily guarded enemy territory in the Loire estuary, the only chance of success depended on achieving complete surprise. The sooner they started, the better. The weather for the past few days had held fine, which was just what they wanted for the crossing by such small craft, but it was not likely to last. And the attack had to be made before the end of March while the spring tides remained high enough for *Campbeltown* to negotiate the Loire estuary; otherwise the whole operation would have to be postponed until the autumn.

The date that had been set for departure was 27 March. But as everything was ready, with the final arrival of the destroyer, the two commanders decided that it should be put forward a day. They returned to Ryder's headquarters, which were in the conservatory of a seafront hotel in Falmouth, and a signal was sent to the Commander-in-Chief Plymouth to suggest this. The reply that came back stated that Combined Operations Headquarters had given approval for the force to leave the following day, 26 March. There was just one evening to complete the last-minute preparations. The troops, who would operate in three groups further divided into small parties to undertake specific assignments, were transferred to the motor launches and kept out of sight. Orders were checked and a caution given to commanding officers not to let charts showing the return route home fall into enemy hands. And the 630 officers and men taking part in the raid, 353 of them naval personnel and primarily from Coastal Forces, tried as best they could to snatch the few last hours of undisturbed sleep they were likely to get for several days. Hardly any of them knew their destination but they were under no illusions about the kind of battle they were heading for.

The following morning, just before the force was due to sail, air reconnaissance photographs brought back from St Nazaire showed that the Germans had chosen this very time to berth four torpedo boats in the dock. There was a moment of concern that the raid would have to be cancelled. The torpedo boats, with a speed of 35 knots, could tip the scales heavily against the raiders. But eventually it was decided that the operation should continue as planned, with the difference that two extra destroyers would be sent to reinforce the escort for the return journey. Ryder and Newman boarded the destroyer *Atherstone*, which with *Tynedale* would provide the escort for the outward journey, and soon after midday the expedition sailed from Falmouth. By early afternoon the force had formed up into its cruising order: *Atherstone* in the lead towing *MGB 314*, *Tynedale* in the rear towing *MTB 74* (both boats were being towed to conserve their fuel which was not sufficient for the two-way journey), the sixteen motor launches lined up in two columns between the destroyers, and right in the centre of them the expendable ship *Campbeltown* which was to provide the main purpose of the raid. Operation Chariot was under way.

The target for the raid was the graving dock at St Nazaire, the only dock on the Atlantic seaboard that was capable of accommodating the new German battleship *Tirpitz*. In concept the raid was similar to those on Zeebrugge and Ostend during the First World War, which themselves followed a long naval tradition of attacks on enemy harbours, going back to Drake's famous raid on Cadiz. But now, for the first time, it was to be primarily a Coastal Forces operation.

In the spring of 1942, the war was still very much in the enemy's favour and nowhere was this more apparent than at sea. The one bright event had been the sinking of the *Bismarck* in August of the previous year.

It was discovered at that time that the giant German battleship was in fact heading for St Nazaire, the large port which lay at the mouth of the River Loire some 5 miles in from the estuary. It was here that the French liner *Normandie* had been built in 1935 in a specially constructed dock, 1,140 feet long and 164 feet wide, which at that time was the largest dock in the world, capable of accommodating a ship of over 85,000 tons. Now, in addition to being the only dock outside Germany large enough to take the German battleships, St Nazaire was also a major U-boat base. With the *Bismarck* sunk, the major German warships *Tirpitz*, *Admiral Scheer* and *Lützow*, together with heavy cruisers of the Hipper class, were on the Norwegian coast, and the battlecruisers *Scharnhorst* and *Gneisenau*, together with the cruiser *Prinz Eugen*, were at Brest. If these forces united and made a sortie into the Atlantic, they would cause havoc amongst the Allied convoys. The main factor against this was the difficulty that the German forces would have in making a safe return to the North Sea. But while the Germans had access to ports in the Bay of Biscay and primarily St Nazaire, where their ships could dock and be repaired if necessary, such a move was a dangerous possibility. And the signs were that this was exactly what the German High Command was contemplating.

Heavy bombing of Brest by the RAF had had the desired effect of forcing the three German warships there to leave. The bombing of St Nazaire, however, was more difficult. It was the most heavily defended port outside Germany and some other kind of attack was necessary. The plan for Operation Chariot was put before the Commander-in-Chief Plymouth on 27 February, and by 3 March it had received the approval of the Chiefs-of-Staff Committee. But it was a Commando raid with a difference, due to the very nature of the primary target – the *Normandie* dock within the harbour.

The harbour of St Nazaire lay on the north bank of the River Loire. There were two main basins, the outer St Nazaire Basin and the inner Penhoët Basin, with a channel leading from one to the other. Two entrances through lock gates gave access to the outer basin, which also contained the U-boat pens. The first to be reached when sailing upriver was the South Entrance, which was the more generally used. Between this and what was known as the Old Entrance was an area that was virtually an island, including houses, sheds, gun emplacements and a jetty called the Old Mole. Direct access to the inner basin, if required, was provided by the *Normandie* Dock itself which was furthest upriver of the entrances. At either end were enormous caissons, operated hydraulically as lock gates. Each was 167 feet long, 54 feet high and 35 feet thick, built of such huge proportions not only to withstand the pressure of water outside when closed, but also as protection against accidental collision by ships. It was the outer of these two gates that was the main target.

But just as it had defied destruction by bombing, so it was also considered impractical to try to destroy it by means of the usual kind of demolition charges used by Commandos. This is why a plan to attack St Nazaire put forward in August 1941 had been rejected. But when Captain J. Hughes-Hallett, acting as chief naval planner at Combined Operations Headquarters, suggested the use of a destroyer loaded with explosives to ram the gates and be timed to explode later, the project began to look possible. It had its opponents, but it was finally pushed through by the newly appointed Chief of Combined Operations, Vice Admiral Lord Louis Mountbatten.

When finally approved at the end of February, the plan was for motor launches to carry over the main body of Commandos and Special Service troops who would land at two main points, the Old Mole jetty and the Old Entrance, while other troops would land from the destroyer itself. These three groups were to attack the pumping houses that operated the lock gates of *Normandie* Dock, the anti-aircraft positions, the U-boat base and fuel dump. But most important of all was the expendable destroyer, fitted with an explosive charge in her bows, which was to ram the outer gate at sufficient speed to cut the torpedo net and then scuttle herself so that the delayed-action fuses would not be discovered by the Germans when they came to investigate after the troops had withdrawn. It was considered also that an explosion underwater would have more effect. The objectives of the troops were important, but they were secondary to the basic aim of getting the destroyer into the harbour and rammed up against the gate. A great deal depended on bluff, as well as secrecy. Originally it was planned that twelve MLs would take part, but this was later increased to sixteen with the addition of four torpedo-carrying MLs from Dartmouth. It was also felt that a spearhead force of MTBs and MGBs was necessary to deal with any German craft met en route, but only one of each available – *MTB 74*, commanded by Sub Lieutenant R.C.M.V. Wynn, and *MGB 314*, commanded by Lieutenant D.M.C. Curtis. These were not sufficient for the purpose intended and it was found, in any event, that they would have to be towed for part of the way because their fuel tanks did not have sufficient range. But they were taken anyway. The MGB, fitted as she was with a radar set and echo-sounder, and carrying a 2-pounder gun, was selected as the headquarters ship to lead the force in to the attack. And it seemed that the MTB, which had already been adapted for firing torpedoes over the net defences surrounding the *Scharnhorst* and *Gneisenau* at Brest, might also come in useful.

Apart from Commander Ryder and Colonel Newman who were to lead the force, the other key figures were Lieutenant Commander S.H. Beattie, in command of the expendable destroyer *Campbeltown*, Lieutenant A.R. Green, navigating officer, Lieutenant R.E.A. Verity, beachmaster, and Sub Lieutenant J.E. O'Rourke RCNVR, communications officer.

During the two-day voyage across from Falmouth the weather was mostly fine, but luck was with the attackers and no enemy reconnaissance planes came near. At 07.00 on the 27th, when about 110 miles south-west of Ushant, the sighting of a U-boat gave rise to alarm. The force commanders were on board *Atherstone* at the time and received the report from *Tynedale*. She approached

Lieutenant Commander Edward N. Pumphrey DSO and two Bars, DSC, RN.

Lieutenant P.F.S. Gould DSC and Bar, RN.

Lieutenant Commander Peter Scott MBE, DSC and Bar, RNVR.

Lieutenant Commander Robert P. Hichens DS[O] and Bar, DSC and two Bars, RNVR.

Lieutenant Commander John D. Bulkeley USN commanded the PT boat which evacuated General MacArthur and his family from the Philippines in 1942. During the war, he was awarded the Navy Cross and the Medal of Honor, one of only two such awards made to PT men.

Lieutenant Commander Robert P. Hichens DS[O] and Bar, DSC and two Bars, RNVR (left) and Lieutenant Peter G.C. Dickens DSO, MBE, DS[C] RN, at the time respectively Senior Officers o[f] MGBs and MTBs at HMS Beehive.

e of the best-known American PT boat commanders: (*above left*) Lieutenant Commander John D.
keley Jr; (*below left*) Lieutenant Commander Robert B. Kelly; (*above right*) Lieutenant John F.
nedy; (*below right*) Lieutenant Commander Alan B. Montgomery.

Night patrol – an MTB flotilla sets out from base in V formation.

...per built a number of 50-foot Coastal Motor Boats during the First World War, with a stepped-... design.

...937, Vosper built a private-venture prototype 68-foot MTB which convinced a sceptical ...miralty that it would give the speed and seaworthiness required.

The first MGBs were conversions of the British Power Boat Company's anti-submarine boats (MA/SBs).

One of sixteen 72½-foot Vosper MTBs built in Maryland, USA in 1943 for use in Britain and Russia under the Lend-Lease programme.

'B 523, the first of the 73-foot Type II Vospers, in which the torpedo tubes were reduced to two ause of the scarcity of worthwhile targets in 1945.

tain's experience of fast fighting boat construction and operation during the war led to the t-war development by the now combined Vosper-Thornycroft Group of the Brave Class of Fast rol Boat.

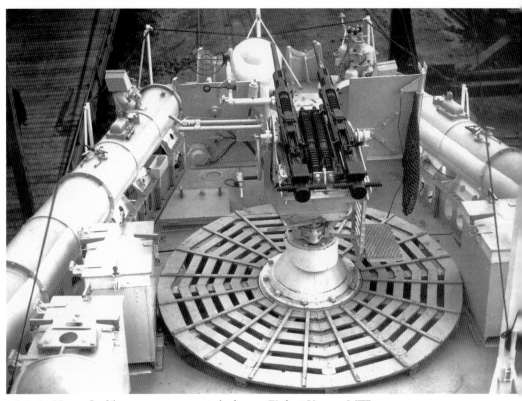

A twin 20mm Oerlikon cannon mounted aft on a 73-foot Vosper MTB.

A 6-pounder gun mounted in a power-operated turret on the forward deck of a 73-foot Vosper M

The wheelhouse of a Vosper MTB showing the lever on the wheel enabling it to be spun for quick manoeuvrability at speed, and two V-shaped torpedo sights on top of the dashboard.

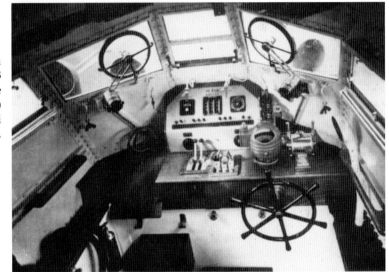

The wheelhouse of a 70-foot Vosper MTB showing the throttle controls (left of the wheel) for the Isotta-Fraschini engines.

By the time Packard engines were fitted in the third-series Vosper boats, there was even less space left in the engine room.

PT-20 – first of the 77-foot American Elco craft, an enlarged version of the British Scott-Paine boat.

A Higgins 78-foot PT boat, which with the Elco 80-foot craft were the two standard types in the U Navy.

experimental zebra stripe camouflage scheme tried out on 80-foot Elco PT boats in the Pacific
d Mediterranean was intended to make it difficult for the gunners on enemy ships to determine
speed and direction of travel of the boat.

any different camouflage schemes were tried out for American PT boats in the Pacific and
editerranean with some interesting local adaptations.

A hole made in the bow of *PT 107* by an enemy aerial torpedo which did not explode (*above*). A Japanese suicide boat shot up by PTs on the beach at Port Saul, Luzon (*below*).

An unusual mottled green and grey camouflage on this 77-foot Elco PT boat was ideal for hiding during the day amongst the islands of the South-West Pacific.

An *S.38* series *Schnellboot* on patrol in the Baltic Sea in 1941. The captain and crew are able to scan the horizon from the bridge above the wheelhouse.

An S-boat of the *S6-S25* series, built shortly before the war, which saw early service in the Baltic, operating from Kiel.

S.26 introduced the new S-boat design with torpedo tubes built into the hull and a cockpit set
ve the wheelhouse roof.

The larger and heavier
S-boats came with the
need for armour-plated
bridges and wheelhouses,
and increased armament,
including flak guns like
the 20mm shown here, for
protection against Allied
aircraft.

Before torpedo tubes
ere built into the hull,
were exposed on the
foredeck of the earlier
S-boats. This shows a
practice shot by the
torpedoman.

The fruits of victory –
surrender of S-boats in t
Mediterranean. Left to
right: Walter Blount, Bo
Ennis, Eric Hewitt and
Tim Bligh.

S-boats in the Baltic wei
camouflaged for daytim
operations against Russ
shipping by a wavy
pattern to match the
waves in northern seas.

the unsuspecting U-boat, opened fire at a range of 2½ miles, and then dropped depth charges. The U-boat quickly submerged and the destroyers spent two hours hunting for her, unsuccessfully. It seemed possible that the submarine had been sunk, but in any case it was doubtful that she had seen the motor launches and given warning of their approach. The presence of the destroyers could easily have been put down by the Germans to the fact that they were on passage to Gibraltar. However, it was one of the risks the attacking force had to take. Later that day a number of French trawlers were sighted. Two of them which lay directly in the path of the expedition had to be sunk, after their crews had been taken off, because of the danger that they might report the expedition's presence. In answer to the apologies of Lieutenant Dunstan Curtis who, commanding *MGB 314*, boarded one of the trawlers, the captain shrugged his shoulders and replied, 'C'est la guerre.'

After darkness had fallen on the evening of the 27th, course was altered for the Loire, and at 20.00 the force stopped to form up into the final approach order. It was now exactly thirty hours since they had originally assembled outside Falmouth. The force commanders, Ryder and Newman, transferred to the MGB which was to lead them in. On either side of this, in V formation, were two of the torpedo-carrying motor launches, on the port side *ML 160* (Lieutenant T.W. Boyd) and on the starboard side *ML 270* (Lieutenant C.S.B. Irwin RNR). Behind these the rest of the motor launches lined up in two columns: on the port side *447* (Lieutenant T.D.L. Platt RNR), *341* (Lieutenant D.L. Briault), *457* (Lieutenant T.A.M. Collier), *307* (Lieutenant N.B. Wallis RANVR), *443* (Lieutenant K. Horlock) and *306* (Lieutenant I.B. Henderson); and on the starboard side, *792* (Lieutenant Commander W. L. Stephens, Senior Officer of the motor launch force), *262* (Lieutenant E.A. Burt), *267* (Lieutenant E.H. Beart), *265* (Lieutenant A.B.K. Tillie), *756* (Lieutenant L. Fenton) and *777* (Lieutenant M.F. Rodier). Behind the MGB and protected on either side by the motor launches was *Campbeltown*. Bringing up the rear, directly in line behind the destroyer, were MLs *446* (Lieutenant H.G.R. Falconer) and *298* (Sub Lieutenant N.R. Nock), and finally the MTB. The two escort destroyers, *Atherstone* (Lieutenant Commander R.F. Jenks) and *Tynedale* (Lieutenant Commander H.E.F. Tweedie) remained a mile behind for part of the way and then patrolled the estuary while the assault took place, ready to take up the escort again when the craft returned.

The force set sail for the mouth of the Loire at a speed of 12 knots. Shortly afterwards, the first casualty occurred, not caused by the enemy but by mechanical failure. The port engine of *ML 341* broke down. When it was found the trouble could not be corrected, the Commandos on board were transferred to other boats, and with bitter regret Lieutenant Briault was forced to turn his boat about and limp home on a previously prepared emergency course. There were thus fifteen motor launches left to make the assault. As a guide during the approach, the submarine *Sturgeon* had been directed to surface at a point 40 miles off St Nazaire and show a screened light to seaward. This was sighted dead ahead at 22.00, showing remarkable navigation on the part of Lieutenant Green, the navigating officer. It was at this point that the destroyers broke off to take up their patrol and the force continued on its way.

Last-minute preparations were being made on board the assault craft. The Commandos were checking their equipment, the crews of the motor launches were emptying the special petrol tanks that had been fitted on deck to lessen the risk of fire if they were hit, and on board *Campbeltown* explosives experts were preparing the delayed-action fuses.

The biggest single problem lay in making an undetected approach up the 5 miles of estuary between the heavily guarded banks. There were two main factors that might result in the force being detected before arriving at St Nazaire – the German radar station on Cap le Croisie, and the noise made by such a large number of MLs. This was assuming, of course, that they had not been sighted previously while making the crossing. A solution to both had seemed to be a diversionary air attack by seventy Wellingtons of Bomber Command just before the assault, with the intention of distracting the radar, drowning the noise of the approaching boats and generally creating confusion among the defenders. And this appeared to be succeeding when, shortly before midnight, while the force was still some 15 miles from the harbour, gun flashes and heavy flak to the north-east indicated that the raid was in progress. Allied to the fact that the weather had now changed and was perfect for the assault – that is, the sky was completely overcast with low cloud and mist while a full moon above the cloud gave just a sufficient degree of light – there seemed to be a good chance of getting close in without being observed. But it was the weather itself that was responsible for the greatest failure of the operation, for when the bombers arrived over the target, they found it to be completely obscured by cloud. Expressly ordered not to make indiscriminate bombing attacks in Occupied France unless targets could be clearly identified, and also aware of the danger of bombing their own forces, the air crews had to make the decision to return home with scarcely a bomb dropped. And so not only were the positive objectives of the air raid unfulfilled, in that no confusion was created, but far worse, the raid had the effect of raising the alarm so that every gun and searchlight was manned, and every lookout system was on the alert by the time the naval force entered the estuary. The attackers were blithely unaware of this, of course, and sailed on towards German defences that were ready and waiting for them.

Land was sighted at forty-five minutes after midnight, dimly at first and then taking shape as hedges and trees as the banks of the estuary gradually drew closer together. And with it came the smell of the countryside, sweet and fresh after the tang of the open sea. All this time the force had remained unobserved, while ahead the diversionary air raid which seemed to be taking place as planned gave heart to the attackers. Tension was mounting and reached a peak when, at a point still about 2 miles from the harbour, a single searchlight from Les Morées Tower suddenly swept across the estuary in an arc towards the ships. It went out before spotlighting them, but it seemed impossible that the force had not been seen. And sure enough, almost immediately afterwards, the searchlights on both banks were switched on and the whole force was floodlit. It was now 01.22. One of the coastal batteries fired a warning shot and a shore signal station flashed a challenge.

In accordance with a pre-arranged plan, Leading Signalman Pike on board the MGB, who could send and receive signals in German, replied to the effect that they were damaged German ships requesting permission to proceed into harbour. The correct callsign could not be given, of course, but it was sufficient to make the German gunners hesitate. The force had now increased speed to 15 knots and was 1½ miles from its objective. Ten minutes more at that speed. How long could the bluff work? The sporadic firing that had broken out ceased and more signals were exchanged with a second shore station. Firing broke out again but it was still intermittent and betrayed the uncertainty of the Germans. There were now six minutes to go and most of the heavy shore batteries had been passed. And then, at 01.27, the firing became really determined. There was no doubt that the attacking force had been identified as hostile. At this point, first *Campbeltown* and then the other ships returned fire and for some minutes there was a violent close-range engagement between the ships and the heavy calibre guns on shore. Both the surprise of the attack and the accurate fire from *Campbeltown* caused the enemy fire to slacken off perceptibly, and it was at just this moment that *Campbeltown*, passing the first entrance to the port, had to aim for the lock gate. The MGB sheered off to starboard, *Campbeltown* increased speed to 19 knots, and, breaking through the torpedo net, hit the lock gate with a loud crash. It was 01.34, only four minutes after the time scheduled in the plan. The bows crumpled back to a distance of 36 feet and the forecastle deck was now projecting over, and a foot beyond, the caisson. This made it easy for the eighty Commandos on board to scramble across to the land, although it prevented the bows of *Campbeltown* from sinking when she was scuttled. But the main object of the raid had been achieved, in spite of the hail of fire which all the time had been concentrated on the bridge of the destroyer.

The fighting now began with a vengeance and continued for the next two hours. It soon became obvious that the bombing raid had failed and that the Germans, in spite of their early surprise, were well prepared to meet the attackers. The motor launches of the starboard column were to land their troops on either side of the Old Entrance. But the lead boat, *ML 192*, was one of the first to be hit. Rapidly catching fire, she staggered across the port column and beached to the south of the Old Mole jetty. In the glare, the following *MLs, 262* and *267*, missed their landing place and went further upriver before realizing their mistake. The next boat, *268*, did turn towards the Old Entrance but was hit and became a mass of flames. *ML 156*, fifth in the column, had been heavily hit earlier, her steering gear was out of action, and most of the military and naval personnel were casualties. She was forced to pull out of line and withdraw on her one remaining engine. Only the sixth boat, *177*, was able to approach and successfully land her troops. She was followed by the MGB, which had been giving covering fire for *Campbeltown*. Newman and his staff were landed, the boat pulled out again and took Ryder to the lock gate so that he could go ashore to make sure that *Campbeltown* was properly scuttled. *ML 177* was ordered to go alongside the destroyer to take off survivors. The two motor launches that had passed the landing place returned and managed to land their troops. But they were repulsed by the Germans who were now rapidly massing and had to re-embark, withdrawing under heavy fire.

The landing on the Old Mole jetty by the port column motor launches fared equally badly. *ML 447* was hit by flak on turning towards the jetty and burst into flames. *ML 457*, now second in line since *341* had turned back because of engine trouble, did manage to land troops on the strongly defended jetty but was hit and caught fire after circling round to return. The third boat, *307*, was beaten off after suffering heavy casualties; she became grounded in shallow water and then withdrew to do what she could against the batteries and searchlights on the east bank. Like other boats which were blinded by the searchlights, *443* missed her way and went too far upriver. By the time she returned, the opposition was too great to be able to get alongside the jetty. The same applied to the last two MLs, *306* and *446*, which were also hampered by the burning wrecks of the two boats that had been hit. They withdrew after most of the troops had been wounded by the heavy gunfire.

The three remaining boats, MLs *270*, *160* and *298*, which were the ones fitted with torpedo tubes, carried no troops and were intended to be used to attack any S-boats or patrol craft that might hinder the approach or come up astern of the force; the same applied to *ML 446* until she had been called upon to take the troops from the broken-down *ML 341*. No such enemy craft were met, and the two lead boats were equally valuable in helping to give covering fire for *Campbeltown*. *ML 270* was hit off the Old Entrance and forced to withdraw with damaged steering. *ML 160* carried out a very effective bombardment in support of the landing parties, fired her torpedoes at a German vessel inside one of the jetties, although the results could not be ascertained, and then went to the rescue of *ML 447* when she was seen to have been hit. At very great risk, Lieutenant Boyd brought *160* alongside the blazing craft and, while under continuous fire from the pill-boxes only yards away on the Old Mole jetty, managed to rescue the survivors, most of whom had been wounded by this time. With only one engine working, *160* pulled away just in time before *447* blew up. *ML 298*, having gone to the Old Entrance to take off troops, but finding none there, circled to the Old Mole jetty, keeping up a constant fire against the German gun emplacements. She was set on fire after passing through petrol burning on the water and eventually blown up by the enemy gunners.

Meanwhile, the last boat in the force, *MTB 74*, had come in and was instructed to wait alongside the MGB near *Campbeltown*; Ryder wanted to keep her torpedoes in reserve in case the destroyer could not be scuttled properly. The charges for this purpose exploded satisfactorily, however, and Ryder returned to the MGB as the destroyer was settling down by the stern. He ordered Lieutenant Wynn to take the MTB to the Old Entrance and fire delayed-action torpedoes at the lock gates leading to the submarine basin. Following Ryder's instructions, Wynn then set off to return downriver, carrying some of the survivors from the crowded deck of the MGB. With a speed of 40 knots, it was thought that the MTB had a good chance of getting home. This certainly seemed so when the boat began to run the gauntlet at top speed with the enemy fire falling well astern. But halfway down, Wynn saw some survivors from one of the motor launches clinging to a raft which had been carried downriver by the current. He stopped to pick them up and was immediately hit by the shore batteries. The boat caught fire and had to be abandoned. Many of those on board who jumped or fell into the water died from exposure, but eventually a few were picked up by a trawler and taken prisoner, including Wynn.

While the Coastal Forces craft were engaged off the harbour, a furious action was taking place on land as those Commandos who had managed to disembark fought their way towards the targets assigned to them. The constant machine-gun and small-arms fire was broken only by an occasional louder explosion as grenades were thrown at the German pillboxes, gun emplacements and fuel storage tanks. The main demolition party reached the two-storied pumping house that controlled the hydraulically operated caissons of the *Normandie* Dock and destroyed it completely. Other key buildings in the port system suffered a similar fate. In spite of the fact that so few of the troops had managed to land, and many of those who did so were wounded, the major objectives were achieved within about an hour. But when it came to withdrawal, it was another story. The sheer weight of the attack had enabled those troops landing from *Campbeltown* and on either side of the Old Entrance to press forward to their targets. But the landing at the Old Mole jetty had failed – and it was from here that the troops were to board the motor launches to return home. German resistance on the jetty stiffened, both driving off the craft that tried to approach from offshore and the troops fighting their way there from land. When Ryder, on board the MGB, left the Old Entrance to see what was happening, he found that the German defenders had mounted machine-guns on the top of nearby buildings and were keeping up a heavy fire from a pillbox on the jetty. While he watched, two motor launches trying to approach were hit and set on fire.

The MGB commander, Lieutenant Curtis, brought his boat to a position 200 yards off the jetty and opened fire on the pillbox that was causing so much of the damage. The pom-pom gunner was Able Seaman W.A. Savage, who sat in his exposed gun position on the MGB's foredeck and kept up a steady bombardment, ignoring the tracer and shells that were bursting all around him. Twice he silenced the German gun but others came forward to replace it. All this time the boat was held in the beam of a searchlight, making it an excellent target for the German machine-gunners and an anti-aircraft gun that had opened fire from the opposite bank. When the pillbox came to life again, the boat was under fire from three directions, being hit many times and very shortly only the pom-pom remained in action, although this too was silenced when Savage was caught by machine-gun fire and killed. For his disregard of danger in the midst of such an inferno, he was awarded the Victoria Cross, in a citation that also expressed 'recognition of the valour shown by many others unnamed in MLs, the MGB and the MTB, who gallantly carried out their duty in extremely exposed positions against enemy fire at close range'.

Ryder ordered the boat back to the Old Entrance, but here again a furious action was in progress. The situation was now desperate. It was 02.50 and there were still forty minutes to go before the two hours which had been allotted to the Commando action were up. But already most of the boats had been destroyed.

As Ryder looked across the river, all he could see of the motor launches were eight blazing wrecks. There were more than forty survivors already on board the MGB, many of whom were badly wounded. There was no chance of any boat being able to moor alongside the Old Mole jetty to take off the troops as planned, even if they could manage to reach the jetty themselves, which was very doubtful. He had to make the bitter decision to leave, and even then it was touch and go whether they would be able to get downriver without being hit by the shore batteries.

It was this same sight, of nothing but blazing wrecks in the river and the Old Mole jetty still in enemy hands, that greeted Newman when he came across St Nazaire Island from the Old Entrance. It was obvious that his force could not be taken off by boat and so he decided they should try to break out inland and make for Spain. The survivors were split up into parties of twenty and fought their way into the town. But by the time dawn began to break, many were wounded and in need of treatment, and ammunition was running short. One by one the parties were forced to surrender. Only five men managed to elude capture and eventually arrived back in England after being sheltered by the French underground.

The MGB with Ryder on board was the last boat to leave the harbour. Earlier, at various intervals, those motor launches that were still afloat had attempted to make the run downriver, all of them in a damaged condition and with many wounded on board. Of these *ML 267* was hit almost immediately and abandoned after being set on fire. *ML 298* suffered the same fate after going only a mile. *ML 177*, carrying some of the crew of *Campbeltown*, including Lieutenant Commander Beattie, managed to keep going for ten minutes but just when it seemed that escape might be possible she was hit and set on fire. The survivors took to the rafts and were eventually rescued by a German trawler, but many did not recover from the ordeal.

In addition to the German shore batteries, there was another danger now to be faced from the four German torpedo boats which had been reported berthed in the dock just before the force left England. They were sighted by the two destroyers, *Atherstone* and *Tynedale*, just as day began to break, heading towards the river in the hope of bottling up and destroying the remains of the British force. The destroyers attacked and tried to drive the torpedo boats westward, towards where the destroyers *Cleveland* and *Brocklesby*, sent as extra escorts, were expected to appear. But after a short battle, the torpedo boats broke off and turned upriver. Here, at 05.30, they trapped *ML 306*. This was the craft that had made repeated attempts to land her troops on the Old Mole jetty. When it became obvious that this could not be done, she left St Nazaire at about 02.00, laying a smoke screen and, going at 18 knots, succeeded in making the passage. But when about 45 miles out, she was caught by the torpedo boats, which circled before opening fire. The ML replied with the only weapons serviceable, one Oerlikon and two Bren guns manned by the Commandos. It was an impossibly one-sided action, but the commander, Lieutenant Henderson, refused to surrender. Only after he and most of the crew had been killed and the guns put out of action did the survivors give in. They were very well treated and the captain of the torpedo boat that took the battered craft in tow commented on their gallantry against such odds.

But apart from this one boat, the German torpedo boats were too late to catch the remainder. It was daylight as they came limping out of the estuary to join the destroyers, first the MGB and *ML 270*, which the gunboat had accompanied downriver as the ML's steering gear had been shot away and she was steering by hand, and then *756* and *446*. Three more MLs – *160*, *307* and *443* – also succeeded in getting away but missed the rendezvous point with the destroyers. Under the command of Lieutenant Platt they set off on the long passage home without escort. They were attacked several times by enemy bombers but managed to beat these off, bringing down one plane into the sea.

These seven boats were the only ones remaining of the seventeen that had entered the river the night before, and soon their number was reduced to six when *ML 156*, which had been badly holed, began to sink. Her crew were taken off by *Atherstone*. The MGB was also seriously damaged and had a large number of wounded on board. The decks were awash with blood, which made them almost too slippery to walk on. The wounded were transferred to *Atherstone*, while *Tynedale* took those from MLs *270* and *446*. Luckily, while this lengthy operation was in progress, the German torpedo boats that had earlier been in action with *Tyndale* held off. As the remnants of the force was forming up at about 08.00 – the two destroyers, one MGB and two motor launches – a German bomber flew over, but appeared to be more interested in the boat that had been abandoned, *756* and sank her by bombing, thus conveniently preventing her from falling into enemy hands. An hour later the force was joined by the two escort destroyers, *Cleveland* and *Brocklesby*. The captain of the *Cleveland*, Commander G.B. Sayer, was the Senior Officer present and Ryder placed the force under his command. He was the same officer who had commanded the 1st MTB Flotilla in the Mediterranean before the war, and he soon had to face a difficult and sad decision. The weather was getting worse, causing the damaged Coastal Forces craft to reduce speed, and enemy aircraft were constantly circling overhead (although after one Junkers 88 was shot down by *Brocklesby*, they kept their distance). But it was essential to get the badly wounded men to hospital as soon as possible, so the crews were taken off and the three boats sunk by gunfire from the destroyers. It was a bitter end, especially for the MGB which had led the expedition so effectively. The three MLs under Lieutenant Platt, which eventually arrived back in Falmouth just as their fuel was exhausted, were the only boats out of the attacking force to survive.

The destroyers returned to Plymouth with 271 survivors of the original force of 630. Of the 277 military personnel who had taken part, 109 were made prisoners of war, including Colonel Newman, 59 were killed, and 109 returned to England. Of the 353 naval personnel, 106 were captured, 85 killed, and 162 returned to England. Nearly all those who returned or were taken prisoner were wounded. As the individual accounts of the action were pieced together, something of the true story became apparent. Many awards for gallantry were made, including the Victoria Cross to Commander Ryder, Lieutenant Commander Beattie and later to Colonel Newman when he returned from captivity at the end of the war.

The casualty rate was high, although not substantially more so than for many similar operations during the war. It was the kind of operation in which the expectation of returning home afterwards was slight to begin with. Any success at all depended on surprise and a quick, simultaneous assault by all concerned. There were no reserves who could be brought in to take care of unforeseen circumstances, and the diversionary bombing raid failed, although the pilots themselves could scarcely have been held to blame for carrying out what was then official policy. What caused so much initial criticism at the time, fed by skilful German propaganda, was that in spite of the high casualty rate, the raid itself had seemed to be a complete failure. It was some days before what really happened after the withdrawal became known.

On the morning after the raid the Germans had thrown a cordon round *Campbeltown*, which was firmly lodged against the lock gate, and a party of about forty senior German officers had gone aboard that part of the ship that was still above water to see how best to move her. Although it cannot be proved and their identities remain unknown, it is thought that two of *Campbeltown*'s officers who had been taken prisoner led the Germans on board to dispel any sense of danger they might have felt, knowing that at any moment the ship would blow up. And at midday, after some of the fuses had failed, the ship did blow up with an enormous explosion, taking not only the lock gate with her but killing all those on board, together with about 340 German officers and men who were in the vicinity. In spite of the great efforts made to repair the damage, the dock was put out of commission for the rest of the war and an Atlantic base was lost to the *Tirpitz*.

But more was to follow. The torpedoes fired by the MTB at the lock gates of the Old Entrance had been set with 2½-hour fuses, but failed to explode in that time. They remained unseen at the bottom of the lock while efforts were begun by the Germans to repair the damage that had been done to the dockyard. At 16.30 the following day, one of these torpedoes suddenly went off. People rushed to the lock to see what had happened. Then, one hour later, the second torpedo exploded, severely damaging the lock gate. These sudden and unforeseen explosions at a time when there was such tension anyway after the raid caused chaos to break out in the harbour. French workers, fearing reprisals from the Germans, rushed towards the one remaining bridge that led to the town. This was barred by German sentries who, in a panic and without their officers who had mostly been killed when *Campbeltown* exploded, opened fire on the crowd. Many Frenchmen were killed or wounded. The firing unnerved German troops in other parts of the dock who, believing the Commandos were carrying out another raid, began firing wildly at anything in khaki – and this included a large number of German workmen of the Todt Organization who happened to be dressed in khaki overalls. Within minutes, the Germans were fighting a pitched battle amongst themselves which went on for several hours, until after dark. It is believed that over 300 German troops and workers were killed.

Unfortunately, a number of Frenchmen took this as a signal to attack their oppressors, believing perhaps that the Allies had landed in force, but they were poorly armed and suffered severe casualties. Later in the week, with the whole of the harbour area closed, the Germans rounded up a hundred male hostages with the intention of shooting them. This was a reduction of their original intention of taking hostage 10 per cent of the male population, and subsequently, in any event, none of the hundred were executed. But the alacrity with which the French rose up, although premature and disappointing to those who thought the Second Front had begun, worried the Germans and caused them to maintain more troops in France instead of sending them to the Russian front.

So ended one of the most successful Combined Operation raids of the war and the greatest single undertaking by Coastal Forces. Not all of the objectives were achieved – the U-boat pens, for instance, and the lock gates at the South Entrance which were to have been blown up by demolition charges. But these were subsidiary targets – in the main objective and the unplanned events that followed, the operation was a triumph. It gave new heart to Coastal Forces at a time when they were entering their fiercest period of fighting in the narrow seas.

CHAPTER 10

The South Pacific Campaign

Before General MacArthur could make his promised return to the Philippines, US forces had to fight their way across the other Pacific territories that had been overrun by the Japanese. This resolved itself into two great campaigns: that of the South Pacific Force in the Solomon Islands, which included Guadalcanal, one of the most savage battles of them all; and that of the South-West Pacific Force in New Guinea. PTs played a vital part in both. But it was not until October 1942 that they saw action again, after the American landings on Guadalcanal in August. During the six months prior to that, following the US withdrawal from the Philippines in April when the last remaining PTs of Squadron 3 had been destroyed to prevent them falling into enemy hands, the US Navy had concentrated on developing the type of boats that it saw would be needed, and then building them in large numbers. At that time there were few bases anyway from which the PTs could operate; the closest they came to any action with the enemy was a brief involvement during the Battle of Midway, in June.

There was much to be done during this six months breathing space, not only on actual construction of boats but in training crews, commissioning squadrons together with PT tenders to be used as servicing and communications centres, and establishing bases, in particular mobile bases of a kind that could be rapidly set up and dismantled, with equipment that could be carried by the PT boats themselves. These mobile bases were to be vital in the wide-ranging war across the Pacific. All this was a new element in naval warfare to the United States, just as Coastal Forces were to the Royal Navy. But the US Navy had an advantage in that the officers and men of Squadron 3 had seen action in the Philippines from the very beginning and had a chance, even under such difficult conditions, of testing out various tactics. These veterans, and they included Lieutenant (Junior Grade) Henry J. Brantingham and Ensigns Cox and Akers of Squadron 3, became instructors at the Motor Torpedo Boat Squadrons Training Centre at Melville, Rhode Island. At the same time experience was gained from studies of the kind of coastal force warfare that was then raging off the British Isles.

Following the attack on Pearl Harbor, Squadron 1 had remained there on patrol duty; then, towards the end of May, the boats were ordered to proceed under their own power to Midway. This voyage of 1,385 miles was the longest ever made across open water by PT boats. With only one having to turn back because of mechanical failure, they all arrived safely, only to be greeted shortly afterwards, on the morning of 4 June, by the same kind of Japanese air attack they had experienced at Pearl Harbor. But this time the Americans were prepared. While the PT boats in the lagoon opened fire on the low-flying Zeros and helped to hold them off, far to the north-west US planes from Midway and the aircraft carriers of the Pacific Fleet were blasting the Japanese invasion force. It was the beginning of the Battle of Midway at which, after the dark days following Pearl Harbor, the Americans turned the tables on their aggressors and the Allies were able to seize the initiative in the long fight across the Pacific to Japan. After picking up pilots who had been shot down in the waters off Midway, and ferrying rescue parties and supplies ashore, just before midnight on 4 June the PTs were ordered out to search for damaged Japanese carriers that were thought to have broken away from where the great sea battle was taking place, and had come to within 170 miles of the island. But the weather was bad, with poor visibility, and the boats made no contact with the enemy, although they searched all night. Only floating wreckage was spotted.

The success of Midway led the way to the first US offensive action of the Pacific war two months later with the landing by the Marines on Guadalcanal on 7 August. It had been apparent for some time that PTs would be extremely useful in the Solomons – Squadron 2 had been carrying out training in Panama for just that purpose. Eight of the boats were designated as a new Squadron 3, under the command of Lieutenant Commander Alan R. Montgomery, and shipped to the island of Tulagi during October. The first division of four boats arrived on the 12th and went into action only two days later when the Japanese, determined to regain control of the southern Solomons, sent a heavy task force to shell the US airfield on Guadalcanal in preparation for launching a major landing on the island. Hearing the sound of the bombardment from Tulagi at 02.00 on the 14th, Montgomery instructed the four PTs to put to sea immediately. Japanese ships were sighted midway between the two islands, the flashes of their guns lighting the tropical blackness of the night sky. The PTs moved in to the attack.

Becoming separated from the others, *PT 38* (Lieutenant (Junior Grade) Robert L. Searles) was swept by the beam of a Japanese searchlight, then passed close by a light cruiser. Searles crept up at 10 knots to within a few hundred yards of the enemy ship and fired the first and second pairs of torpedoes. A hit was observed forward of the bridge as *PT 38* turned away at full speed and passed just astern of the cruiser. Montgomery was on board *PT 60*, which was commanded by Searles's brother, Lieutenant (Junior Grade) John M. Searles. Before he could close to the attack, he was himself illuminated by the searchlight of one destroyer to port and attacked by another destroyer to starboard. Firing two torpedoes at the latter, Montgomery retired at high speed, making smoke. Two explosions were observed on the target. Thinking he was no longer pursued, Montgomery slowed down and was immediately attacked by another destroyer. One shell landed so close astern that the boat was nearly lifted out of the water. Montgomery managed to turn away and eventually eluded pursuit by dropping depth charges in the destroyer's path. But then *PT 60* ran aground on a coral reef. The other two boats, *PTs 46* and *48*, found no targets to attack with torpedoes as the bombardment stopped at about that time, but *48* was involved briefly in a gunfight with a destroyer.

Radio Tokyo later admitted the loss of a cruiser during the action, falsely claiming that of nineteen torpedo boats that had made the attack, fourteen had been sunk.

That first engagement by PTs after the lull in operations following the Japanese occupation of the Philippines was typical of many during the following months. In their fierce effort to drive the Americans from the Solomons, the enemy threw in an increasing number of cruisers and destroyers to make small night landings in such numbers that they could not all be countered. The US forces were stretched to the limit against what came to be known as the Tokyo Express, and in the forefront of the fight to prevent the Japanese ships getting through were the PTs. Night after night the boats of Squadron 3, later supported by the arrival of Squadron 2, lay in wait in the shallow coastal waters to harass the enemy and act as scouts for the larger warships. The climax came during the desperate battle for Guadalcanal, following the enemy's all-out attempt to build up his forces on the island during the middle of November.

The Americans were also in the process of shipping 6,000 men and thousands of tons of equipment to Guadalcanal, and it virtually became a race as to who could get there first with a sufficiently large force to hold the island. US forces did in fact land successfully, in spite of heavy air attacks. While the fighting raged on land, US naval forces were involved in a maximum effort to keep the great Japanese amphibious offensive at bay, and to prevent the US bases on the island being shelled from the sea. Again the PTs proved their value; often, the presence offshore of two or three boats alone was enough to make an enemy force of cruisers and destroyers turn back, for at night it was never known how many of the small torpedo boats might be lurking in the vicinity, and how effective they might be. In fact, although many hits were scored by the PTs, the actual number of proved sinkings was lower than claims made at the time. Even so, at least three enemy destroyers were sunk by the PTs, as well as a number of smaller vessels, and much of the equipment that the Japanese were trying to float ashore. Although the Battle of Guadalcanal showed no sign of abating after the beginning of 1943, and indeed increased in intensity, the Japanese had actually taken the decision to evacuate the island. Their withdrawal was completed on the night of 7/8 February, which also saw the fiercest action in which the PTs had been involved. They claimed to have sunk two destroyers (although only one could be confirmed) and damaged two others for the loss of three PTs. Six months after the Marines had first landed, Guadalcanal was in American hands. The way was now open to the rest of the Solomon Islands.

New bases were set up on the islands that had been recaptured while the Japanese withdrew to the upper Solomons and concentrated on building up their defences. The next big offensive came in June 1943 with the American landings on the New Georgia group of islands, 200 miles to the north-west of Guadalcanal. By then the PTs had been reinforced by the arrival of an additional four squadrons, including Squadron 9 commanded by Robert B. Kelly, now a lieutenant commander. And more squadrons were on their way. While

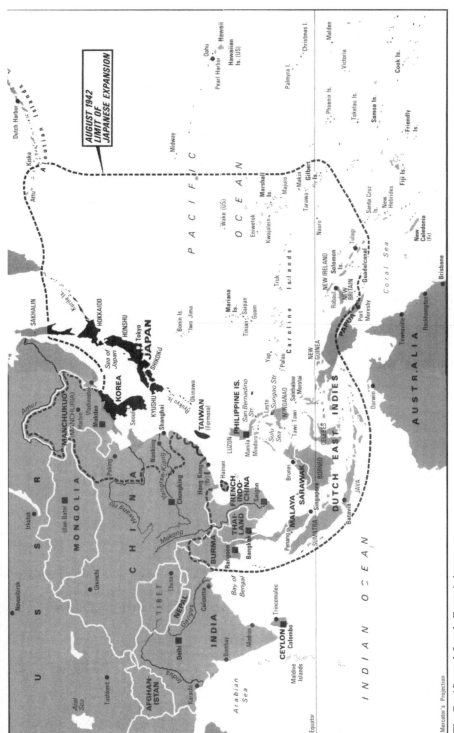

The Pacific and South-East Asia.

operational control of the PTs remained with local naval base commanders, the squadrons were combined into Motor Torpedo Boat Flotilla 1, under the command of Commander Allen P. Calvert, while, for administration and logistic support, Captain M.M. Dupre Jr, was appointed Commander Motor Torpedo Boat Squadrons, South Pacific (Administrative).

A feature of the earlier fighting in the Solomons had been the extent to which the Japanese had used cruisers and destroyers in supporting their Tokyo Express, thus providing the PTs with the biggest and best targets to be found consistently by any motor torpedo boats during the war. In other theatres, such as the coastal waters off Britain and in the Mediterranean, it was only very occasionally that such targets presented themselves; for the rest of the time it was mostly a battle against smaller vessels, such as armed trawlers, coastal merchant ships and opposing torpedo boats. But soon after the New Georgia landings, the Japanese lost so many of their larger warships because of American preponderance of seapower that they turned instead to the use of coastal barges for transporting troops and keeping their island bases supplied. These barges, which could operate in waters too shallow for the larger American ships, and which could hide up close to shore by day to escape attack by aircraft, making their runs mostly at night, became the principal targets for the PTs.

But before this, there was one last major encounter between the PTs and Japanese destroyers of the Tokyo Express, during the night of 1/2 August. Four enemy ships took part, making a run through Blackett Strait to the Japanese base on the southern tip of Kolombangara Island. The only US forces that were in the vicinity to oppose them were PTs based at Rendova Harbour (on Lumbari Island), composed of boats from Squadrons 2, 6, 9 and 10. Knowing this, the Japanese attacked the base from the air in the late afternoon of the 1st. Two boats were destroyed and others damaged. Even so, it was possible to send out fifteen PTs to intercept the four destroyers.

The resulting engagement was a failure for the PTs and, disappointingly, their least effective action since the beginning of the Solomons campaign. The boats attacked independently, without informing the others when they located the enemy, with the result that half of the force found no targets. Uncoordinated attacks by the remainder were easily beaten off and none of the thirty torpedoes fired could be confirmed as hits. The most notable event was the ramming of one of the PTs by the destroyer *Amagiri*, which caused the loss of the boat and damage to the destroyer. In command of the 80-foot Elco, *PT 109*, was Lieutenant John F. Kennedy, later to become President of the United States. His extraordinary exploits as a result of this action have already been the subject of several books. The following extract is quoted from a report prepared on 22 August 1943 by Lieutenant (Junior Grade) Byron R. White and Lieutenant (Junior Grade) J.C. McClure, intelligence officers of Motor Torpedo Boat Flotilla 1:

The time was about 02.30. Ensign Ross was on the bow as lookout; Ensign Thorn was standing beside the cockpit; Lieutenant Kennedy was at the wheel, and with him in the cockpit was Maguire, his radioman; Marney was in the forward turret; Mauer, the quartermaster, was standing beside

Ensign Thorn; Albert was in the after turret; and McMahon was in the engine room. The location of other members of the crew upon the boat is unknown. Suddenly a dark shape loomed up on *PT 109*'s starboard bow 200-300 yards distance. At first this shape was believed to be other PTs. However, it was soon seen to be a destroyer identified as one of the Hibiki group of the Fubuki class bearing down on *PT 109* at high speed. The *109* had started to turn to starboard preparatory to firing torpedoes. However, when *PT 109* had scarcely turned 30°, the destroyer rammed the PT, striking it forward of the forward starboard tube and shearing off the starboard side of the boat aft, including the starboard engine. The destroyer traveling at an estimated speed of 40 knots neither slowed nor fired as she split the PT, leaving part of the PT on one side and part on the other. Scarcely 10 seconds elapsed between time of sighting and the crash.

A fire was immediately ignited, but, fortunately, it was gasoline burning on the water's surface at least 20 yards away from the remains of the PT which were still afloat. This fire burned brightly for 15-20 minutes and then died out. It is believed that the wake of the destroyer carried off the floating gasoline, thereby saving *PT 109* from fire.

Lieutenant Kennedy, Ensigns Thorn and Ross, Mauer, Maguire and Albert still clung to *PT 109*'s hull. Lieutenant Kennedy ordered all hands to abandon ship when it appeared the fire would spread to it. All soon crawled back aboard when this danger passed. It was ascertained by shouting that Harris, McMahon and Starkey were in the water about 100 yards to the southwest while Zinser and Johnson were an equal distance to the southeast. Kennedy swam toward the group of three, and Thorn and Ross struck out for the other two. Kennedy had to tow McMahon, who was helpless because of serious burns, back to the boat. A strong current impeded their progress, and it took about an hour to get McMahon aboard *PT 109*. Kennedy then returned for the other two men, one of whom was suffering from minor burns. He traded his life belt to Harris, who was uninjured, in return for Harris's water-logged kapok life jacket which was impeding the latter's swimming. Together they towed Starkey to the PT.

Meanwhile, Ensigns Thorn and Ross had reached Zinser and Johnson who were both helpless because of gas fumes. Thorn towed Johnson, and Ross took Zinser. Both regained full consciousness by the time the boat was reached.

Within 3 hours after the crash all survivors who could be located were brought aboard *PT 109*. Marney and Kirksey were never seen after the crash. During the 3 hours it took to gather the survivors together, nothing was seen or heard that indicated other boats or ships in the area. *PT 109* did not fire its Very pistols for fear of giving away its position to the enemy.

Meanwhile the IFF * and all codes aboard had been completely destroyed or sunk in the deep waters of Vella Gulf. Despite the fact that all water-tight

---

* IFF is radar interrogation equipment. The letters stand for 'Identification, Friend or Foe'.

doors were dogged down at the time of the crash, *PT 109* was slowly taking on water. When daylight of August 2 arrived, the 11 survivors were still aboard *PT 109*. It was estimated that the boat lay about 4 miles north and slightly east of Gizo Anchorage and about 3 miles away from the reef along northeast Gizo.

It was obvious that the *PT 109* would sink on the 2nd, and decision was made to abandon it in time to arrive before dark on one of the tiny islands east of Gizo. A small island 3½-4 miles to the southeast of Gizo was chosen on which to land, rather than one 2½ miles away which was close to Gizo, but which, it was feared, might be occupied by the Japs.

At 14.00 Lieutenant Kennedy took the badly burned McMahon in tow and set out for land, intending to lead the way and scout the island in advance of the other survivors. Ensigns Ross and Thorn followed with the other men. Johnson and Mauer, who could not swim, were tied to a float rigged from a 2 x 8 which was part of the 37mm gun mount. Harris and Maguire were fair swimmers, but Zinser, Starkey and Albert were not so good. The strong swimmers pushed or towed the float to which the non-swimmers were tied.

Lieutenant Kennedy was dressed only in skivvies, Ensign Thorn, coveralls and shoes, Ensign Ross, trousers, and most of the men were dressed only in trousers and shirts. There were six 45s in the group (two of which were later lost before rescue), one 38, one flashlight, one large knife, one light knife and a pocket knife. The boat's first aid kit had been lost in the collision. All the group with the exception of McMahon, who suffered considerably from burns, were in fairly good condition, although weak and tired from their swim ashore.

That evening Lieutenant Kennedy decided to swim into Ferguson Passage in an attempt to intercept PT boats proceeding to their patrol areas. He left about 18.30, swam to a small island ½ mile to the southeast, proceeded along a reef which stretched out into Ferguson Passage, arriving there about 20.00. No PTs were seen, but aircraft flares were observed which indicated that the PTs that night were operating in Gizo not Blackett Strait and were being harassed as usual by enemy float planes. Kennedy began his return over the same route he had previously used. While swimming the final lap to the island on which the other survivors were, he was caught in a current which swept him in a circle about 2 miles into Blackett Strait and back to the middle of Ferguson Passage, where he had to start his homeward trip all over again. On this trip he stopped on the small island just southeast of 'home' where he slept until dawn before covering the last ½ mile lap to join the rest of his group. He was completely exhausted, slightly feverish, and slept most of the day.

Nothing was observed on August 2 or 3 which gave any hope of rescue. On the night of the 3rd Ensign Ross decided to proceed into Ferguson Passage in another attempt to intercept PT patrols from Rendova. Using the same route as Kennedy had used and leaving about 18.00, Ross 'patrolled' off the reefs on the west side of the Passage with negative results. In returning he wisely stopped on the islet southeast of 'home', slept and thereby avoided the experience with the current which had swept Kennedy out to sea. He made the final lap next morning.

The complete diet of the group on what came to be called Bird Island (because of the great abundance of droppings from the fine feathered friends) consisted of coconut milk and meat. As the coconut supply was running low and in order to get closer to Ferguson Passage, the group left Bird Island at noon, August 4th, and, using the same arrangements as before, headed for a small islet west of Cross Island. Kennedy, with McMahon in tow, arrived first. The rest of the group again experienced difficulty with a strong easterly current, but finally managed to make the eastern tip of the island.

Their new home was slightly larger than their former, offered brush for protection and a few coconuts to eat, and had no Jap tenants. The night of August 4th was wet and cold, and no one ventured into Ferguson Passage that night. The next morning Kennedy and Ross decided to swim to Cross Island in search of food, boats or anything else which might be useful to their party. Prior to their leaving for Cross Island, one of three New Zealand P. 40s made a strafing run on Cross Island. Although this indicated the possibility of Japs, because of the acute food shortage the two set out, swam the channel and arrived on Cross Island about 15.30. Immediately they ducked into the brush. Neither seeing nor hearing anything, the two officers sneaked through the brush to the east side of the island and peered from the brush onto the beach. A small rectangular box with Japanese writing on the side was seen which was quickly and furtively pulled into the bush. Its contents proved to be 30-40 small bags of crackers and candy. A little farther up the beach, alongside a native lean-to, a one-man canoe and a barrel of water were found. About this time a canoe containing two persons was sighted. Light showing between their legs revealed that they did not wear trousers and, therefore, must be natives. Despite all efforts of Kennedy and Ross to attract their attention, they paddled swiftly off to the northwest. Nevertheless, Kennedy and Ross, having obtained a canoe, food and water, considered their visit a success.

That night Kennedy took the canoe and again proceeded into Ferguson Passage, waited there until 21.00, but again no PTs appeared. He returned to his 'home' island via Cross Island where he picked up the food but left Ross who had decided to swim back the following morning. When Kennedy arrived at base at about 23.30, he found that the two natives whom he and Ross had sighted near Cross Island, had circled around and landed on the island where the rest of the group were. Ensign Thorn, after telling the natives in as many ways as possible that he was an American and not a Jap, finally convinced them whereupon they landed and performed every service possible for the survivors.

The next day, August 6, Kennedy and the natives paddled to Cross Island intercepting Ross, who was swimming back to the rest of the group. After Ross and Kennedy had thoroughly searched Cross Island for Japs and had found none, despite the natives' belief to the contrary, they showed the two PT survivors where a two-man native canoe was hidden.

The natives were then sent with messages to the Coastwatcher. One was a pencilled note written the day before by Ensign Thorn; the other was a message written on a green coconut husk by Kennedy, informing the Coastwatcher that he and Ross were on Cross Island.

After the natives left, Ross and Kennedy remained on the island until evening, when they set out in the two-man canoe to again try their luck at intercepting PTs in Ferguson Passage. They paddled far out into Ferguson Passage, saw nothing, and were caught in a sudden rainsquall which eventually capsized the canoe. Swimming to land was difficult and treacherous as the sea swept the two officers against the reef on the south side of Cross Island. Ross received numerous cuts and bruises, but both managed to make land where they remained the rest of the night.

On Saturday, August 7, eight natives arrived, bringing a message from the Coastwatcher instructing the Senior Officer to go with the natives to Wana Wana. Kennedy and Ross had the natives paddle them to the island where the rest of the survivors were. The natives had brought food and other articles (including a cook stove) to make the survivors comfortable. They were extremely kind at all times.

That afternoon, Kennedy, hidden under ferns in the native boat, was taken to the Coastwatcher, arriving about 16.00. There it was arranged that PT boats would rendezvous with him in Ferguson Passage that evening at 22.30. Accordingly he was taken to the rendezvous point and finally managed to make contact with the PTs at 23.15. He climbed aboard the PT and directed it to the rest of the survivors. The rescue was effected without mishap, and the Rendova base was reached at 05.30, August 8, seven days after the ramming of *PT 109* in Blackett Strait.

With the landings on New Georgia, the advance PT bases now moved forward. Apart from that already operational at Rendova Harbour to cover the western area, another was established at Lever Harbour on the north-east coast of New Georgia to cover the eastern area. The main activity of the PTs was now directed at barge hunting, following the first brushes with this type of craft by Rendova-based PTs on 21 July, and Lever boats on 3 August.

The barges were tough opponents – they were so well armoured that gunfire was often ineffective against them. And they were not slow in returning fire, closing the PTs should their attack slacken or stop for reloading. The PT commanders learned the value of having supporting PTs available to cover a retiring boat. At the same time the Japanese also countered these attacks by mounting heavier guns on the barges – up to 40mm – and installing shore batteries along the barge routes. This led to the decision to equip some PTs with 37mm and 40mm guns, and additional armour, making up for the increased weight by the removal of torpedo tubes and depth charges. Their role became that of gunboats, just as in similar circumstances the MA/SBs of British Coastal

Forces in the North Sea had been converted to MGBs, often fighting within range of German shore batteries.

But there the comparison ended. Had the Japanese developed fast motor torpedo boats to the same extent as the other major powers, the Pacific campaigns would have provided ideal opportunities in which to use them, both to combat the PTs and to ferry men and materials amongst the islands, as did the Americans. But they were hampered by a severe shortage of petrol engines, the main reason for their lack of MTB development. Also, the Japanese had to concentrate on other priorities, such as building destroyers, with the result that when these had to be withdrawn because of their vulnerability to attack, barges were the only other alternative, although, considerably armed as they were, they did not have the speed of the PTs with which to avoid attack. The result was that from the beginning, the PTs established a clear ascendancy over them. By the end of August, during ninety-nine engagements against barges, the PTs claimed eleven sunk or destroyed, and twenty-five damaged; by the end of the year, another fifteen were sunk and twenty-one damaged. As it turned out, these claims, unlike some of those made against enemy destroyers, were proved to be conservative. A number of barges were later found by the advancing US ground forces to have been damaged beyond repair as a result of these engagements, and run up on beaches and reefs. And, of equal importance, the presence of the PTs alone was often sufficient to compel the enemy to turn back from attempts to reinforce his island bases.

The PTs had no such problem and were often used for transporting parties of Army and Marine forces to take over the smaller islands, and to carry out reconnaissance for major landings. By now US strategy was not to occupy all the islands entirely but to move forward in a by-passing technique that was to leave tens of thousands of Japanese cut off from their supplies, and even from retreat. And as the advance was made across the Solomons, so the PTs moved on to establish new forward bases. At the end of September, Squadron 11, commanded by Lieutenant Commander Le Roy Taylor, moved to Lambu Lambu Cove on the north-east coast of Vella Lavella, on which US forces had just landed. Soon afterwards the Japanese stopped trying to reinforce Kolombangara, and began evacuating troops from there and Vella Lavella to Choiseul and on to Bougainville, the largest of the Solomon islands. The PTs began a blockade of Bougainville and when the Marines landed at Cape Torokina on 1 November to make an assault on the island, Squadron 11 again moved forward to Puruata Island, just off the Cape. PTs gave covering fire during the beach landings and the bitter fighting that followed, as well as keeping up their attacks on Japanese barges that were trying to evacuate some areas and reinforce others.

It was not surprising in such a widely spread and fast-moving campaign that communications were not only a problem but on occasion broke down altogether. An example of this occurred on a night early in November, during the battle for Cape Torokina. The PTs based on Puruata Island, which were patrolling the eastern coast of Bougainville to prevent the Japanese landing reinforcements, failed to receive a message ordering them to cease patrols for several nights, due to the arrival in the area of two US destroyers which were to carry out their own interception of enemy barges. As the squadron commander did not receive the usual orders to continue the patrol, the boats remained in dock for two nights. The Japanese used this opportunity to land large numbers of troops and supplies on Bougainville and the outraged Marine commander ordered the PTs to put to sea again.

They did so, and early in the morning of the 8th they were picked up on the radar of the destroyers, which had just arrived. Having been told that no friendly boats were patrolling the area, the destroyer commanders assumed them to be enemy craft and opened fire. After some three-quarters of an hour of shelling, they realized their mistake and ceased fire, whereupon the PTs came in to make what seemed a perfectly justified attack on what they thought were enemy destroyers. Only at the last minute was mutual recognition established, just in time to prevent a disaster.

The first 78-foot Higgins craft, Squadrons 19 and 20, arrived in the area in mid-December and were based at Lambu Lambu, from where the main PT operations were now being carried out. As the year ended and 1944 began, the relentless American advance across the Solomons continued, accompanied by bitter and costly fighting. A landing was made on Green Island, to the north of Bougainville, on 15 February. The PTs had led the way for the earlier reconnaissance force and now covered the main assault, after which they immediately set up a new forward base on the island. Meanwhile, heavy fighting was still in progress on Bougainville, with the Torokina-based PTs continuing their attacks on the barges in which the Japanese were desperately trying to bring in reinforcements.

But the end was now in sight. The ultimate objective of the Solomons campaign was the Japanese stronghold at Rabaul, on the north-eastern point of New Britain. US forces from New Guinea, taking part in the South-West Pacific campaign, had already landed at Cape Gloucester at the western end of the island on 26 December. The net was being drawn tighter round the Japanese as US forces of the two great campaigns, the South Pacific and the South-West Pacific, steadily fought their way towards one another. The Japanese knew there was no hope for Rabaul and in mid-February evacuated most of their air strength from New Britain. The 40,000 Japanese troops at Rabaul were less fortunate. They were caught in a trap between the two American armies from which, after the landing of South-West Pacific forces in the Admiralty Islands on 29 February, and the occupation by South Pacific forces of Emirau Island on 20 March, there was no escape.

The first Allied warship to enter Rabaul Harbour since the Japanese occupation was in fact a PT boat, number *319*, one of a force of twelve from Green Island led by Commander Specht, on the night of 29 February/1 March to take part in a joint attack with destroyers. Nothing was found, however, although other boats of the force attacked and damaged several Japanese barges.

From this time on, the PTs in the South Pacific were mainly devoted to preventing the escape of Japanese troops isolated in their areas of occupation, and to strafing coastal installations. These operations lasted until the end of the year, under the overall command of Commander Edward J. Moran, formerly Commander Motor Torpedo Boat Squadrons South Pacific Force, and now commander of the newly formed Task Group 30.3. Many barges were destroyed during this blockade of Japanese-occupied areas. Although from April onwards the Japanese effort in the Solomons declined, it was in some ways the most difficult period of all, involving less danger, perhaps, but much greater monotony in the constant patrol work that was necessary. A number of the PT squadrons were transferred to the South-West Pacific, where heavy fighting was still going on. And then, in October, American forces landed in the Philippines, fulfilling General MacArthur's promise to return, and the remaining squadrons that were not being used for training purposes were shipped to this new area of operations.

CHAPTER 11

The South-West Pacific Campaign

The Japanese occupation of Rabaul had taken place within three weeks of the fall of Manila. With the object of isolating Australia before launching an invasion, the enemy advanced from Rabaul on two fronts, one force extending south-eastward through the Solomon Islands, and the other south-westward into New Guinea. Following the first landings in New Guinea in March 1942, in the Huon Gulf area, they rapidly advanced down the north coast of Papua and across the island towards Port Moresby, the last Allied base north of Australia itself. They were stopped only just in time, within 30 miles of Port Moresby, in a desperate fight by Australian troops in September. With the arrival soon afterwards of US forces, the Allies began the arduous task of driving the Japanese back through the swamps and jungles of eastern New Guinea. Because the interior of the island was almost impenetrable, it was a war fought mainly along the coastline.

The first PTs arrived at Milne Bay, on the eastern tip of Papua, in mid-December. There were only six boats at first, PTs *113*, *114* and *119-122* of Division 17, commanded by Lieutenant Daniel S. Baughman. But as in the Solomons, they were soon to be built up into a large fighting force, playing a vital role in the New Guinea campaign.

As it was, the first actions of these few boats were to be dramatically successful. On the night of Christmas Eve, while on patrol from the PT base that had been set up at Tufi, on the east side of Cape Nelson, Lieutenant Baughman in *PT 122* sighted a surfaced submarine off the Kumusi River. Beyond it was a dark object which could have been another submarine. The boat's commander, Ensign Robert F. Lynch, fired two torpedoes at 1,000 yards and although they seemed to hit, they did not sink the submarine. Coming in closer, the forward torpedoes were fired. This time there were two loud explosions, a sheet of flame, the submarine broke in half and sank. It was later identified as I-22, of 2,180 tons. Minutes afterwards, *PT 122* had to manoeuvre rapidly to avoid torpedoes fired by the other submarine, which had submerged.

That same night, *PTs 114* and *121* were engaged in the first barge action in New Guinea, in which two enemy troop-laden landing craft were sunk in Douglas Harbour. Later, in January 1943, two more barges were sunk and a third damaged in the same area by *PT 120*.

When, on 15 March, the US naval forces in the South-West Pacific became the Seventh Fleet, the PTs became designated as Task Group 70.1 (Motor Torpedo

Boat Squadrons Seventh Fleet) under Commander Morton C. Mumma Jr. He was responsible directly to the Fleet Commander, which did much to simplify PT operations and avoid the kind of clashes between friendly vessels that occurred sometimes during the Solomons campaign. By now, further PTs were arriving at Milne Bay, including Squadron 8 under Lieutenant Commander Barry K. Atkins, and Squadron 7 under Lieutenant Commander John D. Bulkeley of Philippines fame. A main base was established across the Bay at Kana Kopa.

For months there were extreme shortages of supplies, including spare parts, tools and even fuel, caused mostly by the problem of transportation in a country of swamp and jungle that had one of the highest average rainfalls in the world, and where every item of equipment had to be shipped in by the Allies themselves. In order to maintain patrols, for instance, generators had to be transferred from boat to boat as one returned from duty and another went out.

Nevertheless, the PTs were able to play their part in the total destruction of a large Japanese convoy in the Bismarck Sea early in March 1943. The eight destroyers and eight merchant ships were carrying 7,000 troops and supplies to reinforce the enemy positions at Lae and Salamaua. Their successful arrival would have posed a serious threat to the lightly held Allied positions along the coast. Wave after wave of Australian and American aircraft were sent in to attack the convoy, and by the night of the 3rd, when it was within range of the Tufi-based PTs, only one destroyer and one large merchant ship remained afloat, both of them in a damaged state. The PTs were led by Lieutenant Commander Atkins, who had now taken over command of the advance base from Lieutenant Baughman. They sank the cargo ship, *Oigawa Maru* (6,493 tons), and also torpedoed the destroyer, although it had to be finally finished off by aircraft the following morning. Then came the unpleasant task, during the next two days, of sinking the many small collapsible boats adrift in the Huon Gulf in which thousands of Japanese troops had escaped when their ships went down. They still had their personal weapons and could not be allowed to reach the shore to join up with the existing Japanese forces. Very few were willing to be taken prisoner.

This setback to the enemy, primarily the result of Allied superiority in the air, and the fact that the Japanese were already so heavily committed in the Solomons, proved that it was no longer possible for them to run surface ships from Rabaul to New Guinea. The only way in which they could get the bulk of their supplies through was by coastal barge, as in the Solomons, and these became the major target for the PTs. Their traffic was so reduced that the enemy were literally starved out.

But barge hunting was a hazardous operation. The Presidential Unit Citation awarded to Motor Torpedo Boat Squadrons 12 and 21, one of only two such citations made to the PTs (the other was to Squadron 3 for its work in the Solomon Islands), gives some idea of the conditions under which they operated:

For outstanding performance during the Huon Peninsula Campaign against enemy Japanese forces from October 1943 to March 1944. Highly vulnerable to damage from treacherous reefs and grounding during close inshore patrols,

Motor Torpedo Boat Squadrons Twelve and Twenty-one spearheaded a determined waterborne attack on the enemy, boldly penetrating hostile waters and disrupting barge traffic vital to the maintenance of Japanese strongholds in the New Guinea area. Dauntlessly exchanging gunfire with heavily armoured gunboats and barges, airplanes and shore emplacements, the boats of Squadrons Twelve and Twenty-one have successfully diverted hostile artillery fire to themselves in protection of Allied Land Forces; they have steadily destroyed the enemy's ships carrying troops, food and combat supplies; they have captured Japanese personnel, landed in hostile territory, and effected air and sea rescue missions. Tenacious and indomitable in the face of superior fire-power and despite frequent damage to boats and casualties among personnel, the officers and men of Squadrons Twelve and Twenty-one have fought gallantly and served with distinction in crushing enemy resistance in this strategically important area.

These two squadrons of 80-foot Elcos – 12, commanded by Lieutenant Commander John Harllee, and 21, commanded by Commander Selman S. Bowling – arrived between August and October 1943 to replace the older boats of Squadrons 7 and 8 which were gradually being withdrawn. Squadron 21 was notable as being the first to have a 40mm gun on every boat; also, its officers were some of the brawniest of any unit, for while in America, Commander Bowling had made a point of recruiting the best athletes he could find, including football players, swimmers, lacrosse players and rowers, of professional or top amateur standing.

During the period before their arrival, the older boats had more than proved their worth. They had followed the land campaign as the Allied forces advanced slowly up the coast, establishing forward bases on the way, first at Douglas Harbour and then at Morobe, from where they could more easily patrol Huon Gulf. At the end of June, led by Lieutenant Commander John Bulkeley and Lieutenant Pat Munroe, they covered the landings on Kiriwina and Woodlark Islands, and at Nassau Bay on the New Guinea coast, an operation planned to coordinate with the South Pacific landings in the New Georgia group. During the Nassau Bay landing they were used for the first time as troop carriers, each of three 80-foot boats carrying seventy men, and *PT 68*, which was a 77-footer with Lieutenant Commander Atkins as the unit commander on board, leading the way to intercept any enemy craft that might move down from Salamaua. While operating from Tufi, the PTs had sunk a submarine and eighteen barges, with two possibles. In the first two months at the new base at Morobe, no barges were sunk at all, partly because the traffic had not yet developed to the extent it would later, but also because the PTs were concentrating on the submarines that the Japanese were now employing to make the run from Rabaul to Lae. But then operations began to pick up again and up to the end of September, when the new squadrons took over, forty-four barges were sunk or destroyed, with seven possibles, one damaged and one cargo ship sunk. Patrols were now extending northward along the Huon Peninsula into Vitiaz Strait and the tactics employed in barge hunting had been refined.

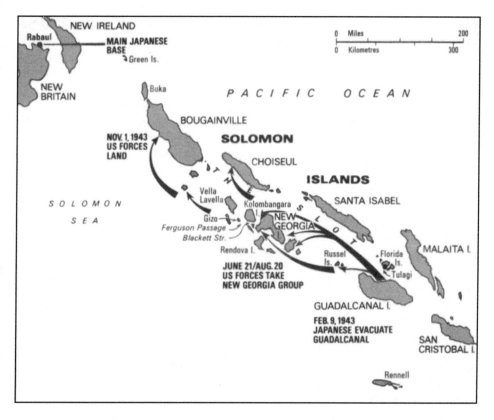

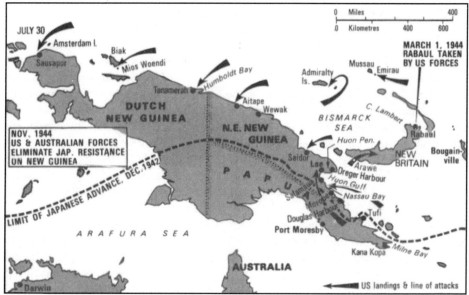

New Guinea and the Solomon Islands.

For instance, Ensign Frank H. Dean Jr, 'Skipper' of *PT 114*, had evolved the method of lying in wait for barges at suspected unloading points, rather in the manner of the MTBs in the English Channel. Bulkeley, meanwhile, was one of those who was particularly successful in making depth-charge attacks on barges if they could not be sunk by gunfire. All these tactics, learned the hard way by trial and error, were of the greatest value to the new crews.

By the time Squadrons 12 and 21 became fully operational, the Japanese garrisons at Lae, Salamaua and Finschafen had fallen to American and Australian troops, and after eighteen months of occupation the enemy had been cleared from Huon Gulf. Now began one of the grimmest periods of fighting of all, as the Japanese made a determined stand in the Huon Peninsula and tried to reinforce their positions with bargeloads of troops and supplies from New Britain, and from bases further up the New Guinea coast. This meant the PT patrols were greatly extended and the boats often had to go 100 miles or more to reach the enemy shipping lanes. With the Japanese sending in more and more barges, the number of actions was greatly increased, so that during November, forty-five barges were sunk and six damaged. But some of the PTs were also lost, mainly by grounding on uncharted reefs as they had to work very close inshore to intercept barges which were trying to slip undetected down the coast.

On 25 November, Bowling established an advance base at Dreger Harbour with boats of the two newly arrived squadrons, and the Morobe base was abandoned. Dreger Harbour eventually took over from Kana Kopa as the main PT supply and repair base in New Guinea. For the moment, however, it reduced by 65 miles the distance that the PTs had to travel before reaching their patrol areas. But even this did not last long, for the US Army landings at Arawe on the south-west coast of New Britain on 15 December, and at Saidor on the New Guinea coast on 2 January 1944, again extended the patrol distances. It became the practice for boats leaving Dreger Harbour to fill up with petrol at Arawe or Saidor before starting their patrol. At about this time, several boats of Squadrons 7 and 8 joined Squadrons 12 and 21 at Dreger Harbour, and three new Squadrons, 18 (Lieutenant Henry M.S. Swift), 24 (Lieutenant Commander N. Burt Davis Jr) and 25 (Lieutenant James R. Thompson), were formed. As a result of all their activities to the end of February, when the enemy were forced to withdraw from Huon Peninsula to Mandang, in Astrolabe Bay, 119 barges were sunk or destroyed. On 8 February, Commander Mumma was succeeded as Commander Motor Torpedo Boat Squadrons Seventh Fleet by Commander Bowling, and Lieutenant Paul T. Rennell took over command of Squadron 21.

It was soon after the Arawe landings that one of the outstanding fights took place between PTs and enemy aircraft. The PTs had begun regular nightly patrols off Arawe, and on the morning of 26 December, two craft which had been on such a patrol, *PTs 110* and *138*, stopped at Arawe to pick up wounded soldiers to take them back to Dreger Harbour. They were immediately attacked by fifteen to twenty Japanese dive-bombers. So sudden was the raid, made by aircraft flying directly out of the sun, that the first bombs fell before the PTs could return fire. Both boats were damaged and several of their crews wounded.

Before the planes departed, one was brought down by the 20mm gunner on *PT 110*, Stephen P. Le Febure. This was a foretaste of a similar attack made twenty-four hours later by up to thirty-eight dive-bombers and fighters on *PTs 190* and *191* that were 25 miles north-west of Arawe and returning to Dreger Harbour after an uneventful patrol. The planes attacked in small groups and dropped at least forty 100-pound bombs, as well as strafing the boats.

The PTs separated as soon as the attacks began, heading at speed for a fog bank some 12 miles away while radioing for fighter cover. It was forty minutes before the American planes arrived. During that time, in spite of repeated attacks, *190* (Lieutenant Edward I. Parley) was undamaged, and even *191* (Ensign Rumsey Ewing), which bore the brunt of the attack and which was hit a number of times, was still able to return to base under her own power. The gunners on both boats brought down four of the enemy aircraft.

Early in the action, Ensign Ewing was wounded and his second officer, Ensign Fred Calhoun, took over *PT 191*. Although himself wounded he stayed at the wheel, watching as each bomb fell and turning the boat out of its path. A direct hit was thus avoided, but bomb fragments splintered the boat, tearing a large hole in the side and putting one of the guns out of action. As often happened during such an engagement, the engine room got the worst of it. Hot water was spurting out of a broken manifold and the confined space was filled with petrol fumes. In spite of flying bomb splinters and bullets, Victor A. Bloom, the Motor Machinist Mate, managed to tape over the leaks, keeping the engines running, and prevented a potential fire by shutting off the fuel-tank compartment and blanketing it with carbon dioxide. He then went to give first aid to two injured members of the crew. For his skill and presence of mind in a highly dangerous situation he was awarded the Navy Cross.

By the end of March 1944, operating from new bases at Saidor, at Seeadler Harbour in the Admiralty Islands, following the US Army landings there on 29 February, and at Talasea in New Britain, the PTs were carrying out patrols as far east as the dividing line between South-West Pacific and South Pacific waters at Cape Lambert, only 40 miles from Rabaul. There were four distinct areas of operation: the New Guinea coast; the Admiralties; and northern and southern New Britain. The number of enemy craft sunk continued at the same high rate, but the PTs by no means had it all their own way.

One of the boats lost at this time was *PT 337* (Ensign Henry W. Cutter), which was hit and set on fire by enemy shore batteries in Hansa Bay on the night of 6/7 March while attacking barges moored close to the beach. The chief Motor Mechanic, William Daley Jr, was badly wounded but managed to escape on a life raft with Cutter and the rest of the crew. They tried to paddle away but found the current against them and when the boat suddenly exploded two hours later, they were still only 700 yards away.

Unable both because of the currents and enemy gunfire to land in the bay, Cutter set course back to Saidar. Daley died just before dawn, which left three officers and eight men. The raft was only a balsa-wood oval of 7 by 3 feet so was not large enough for all of them. Most of the time they took turns in the sea, trying to guide it by swimming. Dawn of the 7th saw them only a mile off the entrance to Hansa Bay. All day they paddled and swam, a sitting target for any enemy aircraft that might spot them. They drifted close to Manam Island, 6 miles from the bay, but every time they tried to land, offshore currents pushed them out to sea again. They had no food or water, and in the hope of finding supplies and possibly a native canoe in which to come back for the others, Ensign Robert Hyde and Allen Gregory left to swim for the island. They were not seen again. Then James Mitchell left to make an attempt to reach the shore. During the night, several of the crew became delirious. One of them, Morgan Canterbury, suddenly pushed himself off the raft and had swum away before anyone could stop him. Shortly after dawn three others, Ensign Bruce Bales, Evo Fucili and Edgar Schmidt, also set off for the shore. By this time the others were too weak to move.

On the morning of the 8th, the raft was still drifting less than a mile from the island, kept tantalizingly away from the shore by the unpredictable currents. Then Mitchell returned with the information that Japanese troops were working on the beach; he had seen them while still 75 yards from the shore, and so had been compelled to return to the raft. That ended any plan for going ashore on Manam Island – the Japanese were not known for their respect of prisoners of war. As it was, nothing was ever heard again of the men who had tried to swim ashore, apart from Mitchell. A document captured later referred to one officer and two enlisted men taken prisoner by the Japanese. But they were not reported as prisoners of war.

All day the raft continued to drift helplessly. A boat put out from the shore after dark and came close, but was driven away during a sudden squall when the waves rose up to 8 feet. The following morning those still left on the raft – Cutter, Mitchell, Harry Barnett, Henry Timmons and Francis Watson – found an overturned Japanese collapsible boat, righted it and managed to clamber aboard. By now, scorched during the day and chilled at night, all of them were suffering from exposure, were covered with salt-water sores and, worst of all, were tortured by thirst. That day they had their first taste of food since setting out from base three days earlier – a crab, which was found clinging to the overturned boat, and a dry coconut floating in the water. It helped a little, but did nothing to relieve the terrible thirst.

The agony continued all through the night and on into the morning of the 10th, when they were sighted by Army aircraft that had been combing the area in search of them. Emergency supplies were dropped, and the following morning the five men were picked up by a Catalina and taken to Dreger Harbour. Their five-day ordeal was over.

The experiences of the crew of *PT 337* were by no means unique. But they serve to give an example of the conditions under which the men of the 'little-ship Navy' fought in this most inhospitable of waters. For most of the time the PTs were operational, they had a clear superiority over the type of small craft that the Japanese had available. But if they were hit or grounded on one of the endless coastal reefs, the chances of survival were not high. The survivors of *PT 337* were lucky; many other crews were not.

While operations in the Admiralties and off New Britain tended to decline in the spring of 1944 as the Japanese gradually gave up positions they were unable to hold, mainly because of an inability to get reinforcements through, the PTs based at Saidor had their work cut out to combat heavy barge traffic along the eastern coast of New Guinea. It was dangerous work, for the Japanese were grimly determined to defend their positions here, and the number of shore batteries had been increased. In April, Squadron 24 was reinforced by the arrival of Squadron 10 under Lieutenant Commander Jack E. Gibson, the first of the Solomons squadrons to be transferred to New Guinea. Patrols extended up the coast to beyond Hansa Bay, a total of 185 being carried out until the end of June, by which time the Allied armies had advanced to a point where Saidor in its turn was too far behind the main area of operations to be continued as an operating base.

The occupation of the Admiralties, Emirau Island, and western New Britain had achieved the main intention of isolating and neutralizing the large enemy garrison at Rabaul. At the end of April, South-West Pacific Forces launched their biggest ever by-passing operation by landing at Humboldt and Tanahonerah Bays, 500 miles north-west of Dreger Harbour, and at Aitape, 400 miles north-west of Dreger Harbour, thus isolating the 50,000 troops of the 18th Imperial Japanese Army in the area between Wewak and Hansa Bay. The Japanese fought back strongly by moving westward against Aitape, defended by the 32nd Infantry Division. Again the enemy depended heavily on barges, the only naval vessels by now available to them, to maintain supply lines, and again the PTs were brought in to deal with this barge traffic. Soon after the landings, Squadron 7, under Lieutenant Commander Robert Leeson, arrived at Aitape, followed by Squadron 8 (Lieutenant Edward I. Parley). Squadron 18 moved up the coast from Saidor to Humboldt Bay, to be joined later by Squadron 12 (Lieutenant Commander Robert J. Bulkeley Jr).

Sinking the troop-laden barges was gruesome work, for the great majority of the Japanese resisted capture and preferred to drown themselves deliberately, rather than be taken aboard the PTs. During the five nights following the first action on 28 April, east of Wewak, fifteen barges and a picket boat were intercepted and destroyed, and a further eight damaged. But the main activity was off Aitape, where the Japanese were particularly determined to maintain their coastal supply line and to protect their barges with shore batteries. The PTs were out almost every night and the actions were usually violent. During the five months they were at Aitape, they claimed 115 barges sunk or destroyed, as well as damage to many coastal installations, and even the destruction or damage of over a dozen trucks on coastal roads. Eleven PTs were hit by enemy fire but only one, *PT 133*, was destroyed, and casualties were remarkably light – three men killed and seven wounded.

By early June, as the American and Australian forces gradually tightened the net round the Japanese and extended their landings into north-west New Guinea, at Wakde and Biak Islands, it became necessary for the major repair and supply base at Dreger Harbour to be moved forwards. A new base was chosen at Mios Woendi, a small coral atoll 10 miles south of Biak. With its deep-water lagoon and flat, sandy beach, sheltered by palm trees, it was the finest base site that the PTs found in New Guinea. Barge-hunting operations continued from there in June and July, but the number of targets was now dwindling. Unable to find a means of dealing effectively with the PTs, and having lost so many hundreds of barges, the Japanese, who were by now systematically withdrawing from the territories they had once conquered with such ease, preferred to carry out their evacuation overland, though this meant a hazardous trek through swamp and jungle, harassed during daylight hours by air attack, and the abandonment of most of their equipment.

The last PT advance base to be established in New Guinea was on Amsterdam Island, 250 miles west of Mios Woendi, following the US Army landing at Cape Sansapor on 30 July, which gave the Allies final domination of the north coast of New Guinea. During August and September, Squadrons 24 (Lieutenant Commander Davis) and 25 (Lieutenant Commander Richard E. Johnson) operated from there, but found relatively few targets, claiming only eleven barges, two 100-foot luggers and a 200-foot minelayer sunk. (The minelayer, torpedoed by *PT 342* on the night of 21 September, was one of the largest vessels sunk in the New Guinea campaign.) The two squadrons returned to Mios Woendi in October.

Operations from Mios Woendi had picked up in August, when twenty-six barges were destroyed. But this number dropped again to eight in September, by which time the Japanese evacuation was almost completed. The squadrons based on Mios Woendi – 9, 10, 12, 18 and 21, joined later by part of Squadron 36 (Lieutenant Commander Francis D. Tappaan) and the first two Higgins squadrons to arrive in the South-West Pacific, 13 (Lieutenant Commander Alvin W. Fargo Jr) and 16 (Lieutenant Commander Aimer P. Colvin) – continued to carry out combat patrols until 16 November. By then, US forces had already landed on Morotai Island, roughly midway between New Guinea and Mindanao, as a preliminary to the major offensive to liberate the Philippines.

The PTs had been in operation during the New Guinea campaign for twenty-three months, building up from the original six boats and one small tender at Porlock Harbour, to a force of fourteen squadrons and eight tenders. They had been in nightly action along the 1,000-mile New Guinea coastline, as well as in the coastal waters of New Britain and the Admiralty Islands. Against a fierce opposition which at no time let up, they and the aircraft which had kept up the pressure by day, had taken a terrible toll of the Japanese. Not only was the entire coastline littered with the wrecks of hundreds of sunken and burnt-out barges, but in the former encampments of the enemy were the bodies of thousands of soldiers who had refused to surrender, or refused the chance of doing so by their officers, and who had died from lack of supplies.

CHAPTER 12

The Growing Offensive

Early in 1943, the MTBs based on Malta achieved their first major success. Four boats, *264* (Lieutenant H.W. Sheldrick), *260* (Lieutenant H.F. Wadds), *313* (Lieutenant A.D. Foster), and *267* (Lieutenant A.P.G. Joy), with the Senior Officer of the 20th MTB Division, Lieutenant Peter Evensen, on board *264*, left the island at midday on 19 January on patrol towards Tripoli. After eight hours one of *267*'s engines broke down, so Lieutenant Joy had to turn about and return to Malta on two engines. The remaining three boats carried on at 28 knots, and half an hour later made landfall 25 miles east of Tripoli, before changing course towards Tripoli, running parallel to the coast.

Approaching the harbour at 10 knots on silent engines, they came upon a hospital ship just leaving, ablaze with lights and with the Red Cross signs lit up. The movement of this ship prevented the MTBs slipping into the harbour, which was their intention. They cruised around for an hour, then, while making another attempt to close inshore, they sighted three tugs towing a submarine.

Evensen immediately ordered *MTB 264* to attack with torpedoes, but these missed and blew up on the shore, so the boats closed to engage with guns. When one of the tugs was hit and set on fire, both this tug and the others promptly abandoned the submarine and headed for the safely of the harbour. *MTBs 260* and *313* chased them in, but had to withdraw when the shore batteries opened up. The tug which was on fire was further hit and ran aground south of the harbour entrance.

Meanwhile, the submarine had kept up accurate cannon fire and scored a number of hits on *264*. Evensen came in for another attack, intending to drop depth charges, but found that the submarine was grounded on a sandbank; the tugs had been trying to pull her off. There was not enough water in which to drop depth charges, so Evensen decided in favour of a torpedo attack by the other two boats. At this point a destroyer was seen emerging from the harbour at top speed and at the same time the shore batteries were firing uncomfortably close. The MTBs hastily withdrew about 10 miles, waited a while until the firing had subsided, then crept in at slow speed for another attack. When the submarine was again sighted at 02.20, *MTB 260* fired her starboard torpedo at 400 yards; there was an explosion as it hit squarely aft of the conning tower and the submarine completely disappeared. As the shore batteries were opening up again, the MTBs retired under cover of smokescreens, arriving back at Malta shortly before midday of the 20th. When Tripoli was captured three days later, the Italian submarine, *Santorre Santorosa*, was found abandoned on shoals a mile outside the harbour with severe torpedo damage.

Although Malta at this time still faced a serious situation, desperately short of aviation fuel, food and ammunition, the war on land was proceeding satisfactorily. Kept supplied by the Navy and assisted by RAF attacks, General Montgomery's land forces had followed up their victory at the Battle of El Alamein by completely breaking through the Axis defences on 4 November 1942, and were now maintaining the offensive which was to drive Rommel finally out of Egypt and Libya. And the enemy now faced attack from another quarter as a result of the British and American landings in French North Africa on 8 November. Operation Torch was the first major Allied offensive overseas, with General Eisenhower the Allied Commander-in-Chief and Admiral Sir Andrew Cunningham the Naval Commander.

Following landings at Algiers, Oran and Casablanca, the British and American forces pressed on as fast as they could to Tunis and Bizerta, for it was only by capturing these great naval bases that the Allies could launch an assault on Sicily and Italy. The Axis were just as determined to hold Tunisia, having been forced out of Egypt and Libya, and set about moving in all available men, supplies and equipment from Sicily. The immediate problem for the Allies was to reduce this movement of supplies, which, as Eisenhower warned, threatened to lead to a rapid deterioration of the situation. The Luftwaffe had retained air control over the Sicilian Narrows, operating from Sicily, and the Germans had a degree of control of the sea as well. Amongst the forces brought in to play against this apparent superiority were the small boats of Coastal Forces.

At the beginning of 1943, Coastal Forces in the Mediterranean had been built up to comprise four MTB flotillas, the 7th, 9th, 10th and 15th, seven ML flotillas and eight HDML flotillas. The MTBs were amalgamated into two main flotillas, the 7th (Lieutenant R.A.M. Hennessy) and 10th (Lieutenant Jermain), operating from Malta, but they had taken little direct part in the North African landings. In January, the 10th Flotilla was ordered to Bône on the Tunisian coast, about 100 miles west of Bizerta, and nightly patrols started towards the end of the month. Bône was originally intended as a temporary base, but later it became the main Coastal Force headquarters and repair centre until after the invasion of Italy.

In command at Bône was the man who was to do more than any other single person to build up Coastal Forces in the Mediterranean into a formidable fighting unit – Robert Allan. Before the end of the year he had been promoted first to Lieutenant Commander and then to Commander, at twenty-eight the youngest Commander in the RNVR. His many decorations included the DSO, OBE, Croix de Guerre, Legion of Honour, the American Legion of Merit and several Mentions in Despatches.

In order to support the effort to stop German supplies reaching Tunisia, the Malta-based MTBs also switched their area of operations to the east coast of Sicily and off the island of Pantelleria, where German and Italian motor torpedo boats were based. On the evening of 15 February, three Vosper boats left Malta to patrol south of Maritimo Island: *67* (Lieutenant T.J. 'Tim' Bligh), *77* (Lieutenant J.B. Sturgeon) and *82* (Lieutenant P.R.A. Taylor RNR), with the Senior Officer,

Lieutenant Hennessy, on board *77*. In view of the distance the boats had to travel, they all carried an extra 1,000 gallons of fuel in upper-deck tanks, the first time this experiment had been tried out. Another two Elco boats that had only just arrived in Malta that afternoon, *307* (Lieutenant John G. Muir) and *315* (Lieutenant Mabee RCNVR), left an hour later with the intention of making rendezvous 15 miles south of Maritimo.

An enemy convoy of one merchant vessel and two destroyers was expected to be the target, having been reported approaching Maritimo from the north-east. But after driving through the night at 20 knots, *6*'s steering broke down at 23.20 and all the boats stopped while repairs were carried out. It was at this point that reports came through of another convoy of four merchant ships and three destroyers located to the north of the unit. Even before the plots could be worked out, Bligh in *61* had sighted the first of these vessels, 1½ miles to starboard. The boats got under way on single engines, *61* steering by hand-rigged tiller, and approached the convoy which was in an ideal position broadside on ahead of them.

What followed was a chapter of frustrations and missed opportunities. Having ordered the MTBs to attack independently with torpedoes, *77* swung at top speed across the bows of the convoy's port column to attack the leading merchant ship on the port side. Miraculously she was not seen and was in a perfect firing position at 400 yards when Hennessy ordered the port torpedo fired. He thought at the time it had hit, but later reports showed this was not the case. Meanwhile, the convoy had now woken up and every ship was firing at the MTBs, the destroyers with 4-inch high-explosive shells that were bursting 50 feet in the air. *MTB 77* turned and fired her second torpedo at another vessel, but the firing mechanism failed at the last minute, although in the heat of the battle it was not realized until much later that the torpedo was still in the tube. The only success came when a burst of heavy calibre shells from one of the destroyers missed *77* and hit the bridge of the merchant vessel instead.

MTB 82 followed up *77*, but her torpedoes also missed. In the meantime, Bligh had taken his boat to the rear of the convoy to create a diversion, one of the tactics for which he was to become a legend in the Mediterranean. *MTB 61* had been converted for use as a gunboat, carrying no torpedoes, and it was the height of unbelievable frustration when, finding himself close to a destroyer and mistaken for an enemy S-boat, all that Bligh had to fire with was a 20mm gun, which could cause little damage. Luckily, only superficial damage was caused to *77* and *82*, and none to *61*. The official report stated that the MTBs should have fired both torpedoes to make sure of a hit, but it was felt that the operation proved the potential for MTB attacks in the Sicilian Channel. The two Elco boats also had their share of frustration – they were about to attack a single merchant vessel when a Wellington bomber flew overhead and sank the ship with a torpedo.

By the end of February, although the first of the 'D' Type MTBs and MGBs that were to provide the bulk of Coastal Forces from then on in the Mediterranean were on their way from Britain, and the bases were becoming more organized, the crews were getting depressed at the lack of targets. They turned their attention to mine-laying instead, reluctantly at first, then with more enthusiasm as it led to the sinking of an increasing number of enemy ships.

In the meantime, the S-boats had continued their own successful operations in the Sicilian Narrows against Malta-bound convoys, and on the night of 13 March torpedoed and sunk the destroyer *Lightning* off Sicily. But the same month saw the MTBs perfecting their technique for attacking F-lighters and Siebel ferries which the Germans were using with greater frequency along the coast in a last desperate effort to keep Tunisia supplied. While the Allied land forces relentlessly closed in along the diminishing coastline held by the enemy, the RAF and Fleet Air Arm squadrons made daily sweeps from Malta, while at night, MTBs and MLs from Malta and Bône increased their patrols in coastal waters. At the end of the month came the first really successful MTB operation, and with it the balance of small-boat warfare began to swing in favour of the Allies.

The weather on the night of 31 March/1 April was highly unsuitable for small boats, with a strong wind blowing and heavy seas. But after an enemy convoy was reported off Cape Zebib, making for Bizerta, four MTBs set out from Bône to make an interception, led by Lieutenant Jermain in *376*, with *266* (Lieutenant R.R. Smith) and *315* (Lieutenant L.E. Newall RNZVR); *265* followed for part of the way, but reported a man overboard and went back to search for him. Soon afterwards *316* developed engine trouble and also had to turn back, leaving only two boats to make the attack.

Reaching the interception point at the height of the storm, with the wind howling through the rigging, they cut engines and waited. Just over half an hour later they sighted the convoy, estimated to consist of three merchant ships with an escort of two destroyers and a number of S-boats.

In such bad weather, it was relatively easy for the MTBs to slip unseen at 10 knots between the convoy and land. They let the escorts pass, then fired torpedoes at the second and third vessels. Both ships exploded and sank almost immediately. There followed a brief engagement with a destroyer, which Smith tried to attack with depth charges. Then, having expended their torpedoes, the MTBs turned and headed for home. They had a long, weary battle through the heavy seas, in which both boats suffered a bad pounding, before arriving at Tabarka at 11.00 the next day. The crews were tired and soaked to the skin, but highly satisfied with the night's mission.

In April, two important events occurred in the ever-increasing build-up of Coastal Forces. The first of the 'Dogs', the 'D' Type Fairmiles, came into operation – the 32nd and 33rd MTB Flotillas, and the 19th MGB Flotilla – together with more Vosper and Elco MTBs, and five more ML flotillas to operate as an anti-submarine strike force along the North African coast. And the first boats of the American PT Squadron 15, Higgins 78-footers commanded by Lieutenant Commander Stanley M. Barnes, arrived at Bône, where they came under the overall command of British Coastal Forces. Until the Sicily landings in July, this squadron of twelve boats, later increased to eighteen, was the only representative of the US Navy in offensive action in the Mediterranean. It was later joined by further squadrons, and the PTs saw service in these waters until the end of the war, cooperating with MTBs and MGBs.

By the time the PTs arrived at Bône on 27 April, the MTBs had already begun to score successes against what were to be their most persistent targets in the Mediterranean – German F-lighters. But the Germans were still getting some supplies through to Tunisia, mainly because the Luftwaffe still controlled the Narrows by day and British destroyers could not operate until after dark. It was decided therefore to experiment by using the MTBs in daylight. The man picked for this hazardous task was Stewart Gould, fresh from his achievements in MGBs in the English Channel and now commanding the new 32nd MTB Flotilla at Bône. He was warned not to take undue risks. Before the operation, he left base on the night of 25/26 April in *MTB 639* (Lieutenant G.L. Russell), accompanied by *MTB 635* (Lieutenant R. Perks DSC), to go up the coast to Sousse to join *MTBs 633* and *637* which were also to take part.

It was meant to be a routine passage, but while crossing Bizerta Bay the two boats suddenly came across two F-lighters. Gould promptly attacked them with torpedoes and when these missed (they often ran under the shallow-draft lighters), he engaged the leading vessel with gunfire, while *635* attacked the second. Within minutes both caught fire, the crews jumped overboard and they later sank.

The unexpected success seemed to augur well for the main mission. Gould joined *633* (Lieutenant H.E. Butler DSC) and *637* (Lieutenant E.F. Smyth) and, two days later, 28 April, they were off the Tunisian coast in mid-morning, keeping a watchful eye out for the enemy. The weather conditions were perfect, which made their position even more vulnerable. Two Italian minesweepers were sighted, attacked and sunk, followed shortly afterwards by a German R-boat. The enemy had been taken completely by surprise at seeing the 'night hunters' out by day. The MTBs next strafed several Junkers transport planes they had spotted on the beach and another plane was brought down as it landed on the coast at Ras-el-Amar. So far, the mission had been a great success.

Gould decided to move further offshore and soon after midday sighted a convoy of one merchant ship and two destroyers, heavily escorted by thirty German aircraft. The MTBs moved in to attack, but themselves came under heavy fire from the aircraft, which concentrated on Gould's boat. All the torpedoes that were fired missed and after Gould's boat was set on fire some 10 miles off Cape Bon, the crew were compelled to abandon ship. Lieutenant Smyth brought *637* alongside the blazing boat and took off the wounded and others left on board, while *633* picked up the survivors from the sea. Then, still under attack from aircraft and shore batteries, the two boats weaved away at top speed. They managed to avoid damage and Oerlikon fire from *633* brought down an enemy fighter, but Gould was mortally wounded and died on board Smyth's boat.

The previous night the PTs had been out on their first patrol, working with experienced MTB commanders, many of whom had already seen a great deal of action in the English Channel, and from whom the Americans had much to learn. They got their first blood on the night of 8/9 May when *PT 206*, with Barnes on board, set off in company with *MTBs 316* and *265* on patrol between Cape Bon and Ras-el-Mirh. Sighting a small Italian merchant ship about 400 yards from the shore at 22.45, Barnes crept quietly forward and fired a torpedo at 350 yards range, speeding away again as the ship exploded. Later that same night, *PT 203* (Lieutenant Robert B. Reade), with *MTBs 61* and *77*, was also patrolling off Ras-el-Mirh when one of the British boats ran aground 300 yards from the beach. There was no chance of getting her afloat again as the shore guns had opened fire from the fort at Kelibia, so after the crew had set fire to the boat to prevent her falling into enemy hands, Reade brought his boat inshore and, under gunfire himself, picked them up and retired to safety.

Two nights later, the PTs had their first successful action against German S-boats. Under the command of Lieutenant Edwin A. Du Bose, *PTs 202, 204* and *205* were returning from an uneventful patrol off Cape Bon and were skirting the shore to give a wide berth to Allied destroyers stationed in the Bay of Tunis, when they suddenly found themselves in the middle of an engagement between a British destroyer and a force of S-boats. *PTs 202* and *204* laid a smoke screen and managed to turn away before being sighted. But *205*, commanded by Lieutenant Richard O'Brien, which was last in line, exchanged fire with an S-boat, eventually leaving the enemy craft burning fiercely. In the confusion, the destroyer mistook the PT for a German boat and chased her for nearly an hour before O'Brien managed to escape by putting in to Bizerta which had just been evacuated by the enemy.

Caught between British forces to the east and British and American forces to the west, Axis resistance in Tunisia was rapidly coming to an end. As Allied troops entered Tunis and Bizerta on 7 May, it was thought that the enemy would attempt a large-scale evacuation by sea, so Admiral Cunningham gave the order for Operation Retribution, not in a spirit of revenge but to prevent any of the enemy getting away to fight another day. Coastal Forces took part with all the available destroyers of Cunningham's fleet in day-and-night patrols along the coast to intercept any escaping craft. 'Let nothing pass' was the order of the day. But in the event, the Germans made very little effort to rescue their trapped forces and hardly any got away. On 13 May, the Axis Commander-in-Chief, Colonel General Jurgen von Arnim, surrendered. The way was now open for the next great step in the Allied plan – the invasion of Sicily.

The first essential was to clear the Sicilian Channel of the large number of mines that had been laid there over the previous three years, work that was carried out by MLs, minesweepers and trawlers. By 15 May, a passage through the Mediterranean was clear and two weeks later the first convoy since May 1941 made the direct run from Gibraltar to Alexandria.

Meanwhile, plans were being made to regroup the various MTB and MGB flotillas. Bône was established as the major repair and training base in the Western Mediterranean, under Lieutenant Commander Allan, while Bizerta was used for operations only. The 18th and 23rd MTB and 19th MGB Flotillas, together with the 15th PT Squadron, now equipped with radar, were to use these bases, while the 7th and 32nd MTB and 20th MGB Flotillas were to operate from Malta. At this time, small convoys of Coastal Force craft were arriving almost every month from Britain. One such arrival early in May included a group of commanders who were to become as well known in the Mediterranean as Hichens, Dickens and others in home waters. As well as seven MLs there were eight 'Dogs' in the convoy, four of them MTBs and four MGBs: *MTB 670* (with Lieutenant Commander R.R.W. Ashby DSC, the man who had escaped from Hong Kong, on board as Senior Officer of the 33rd Flotilla), *MTB 667* (Lieutenant C. Jerram), *MTB 654* (Lieutenant Tom Fuller RCNVR), *MTB 655* (Lieutenant E.T. Greene-Kelly), *MGB 657* (Lieutenant Douglas Maitland RCNVR), *MGB 658* (Lieutenant Cornelius Burke RCNVR), *MGB 648* (Lieutenant Bailey) and *MGB 663* (Lieutenant T. Ladner RCNVR). The four Canadians, Burke, Fuller, Ladner and Maitland, had all come over to England early in the war and joined Coastal Forces, taking part in much of the fighting in the narrow seas. Their experience was to prove invaluable in the Mediterranean, where the war of the little ships was now beginning to hot up.

The invasion of Sicily, the greatest amphibious operation of the war at that time, was to take place on 10 July. In order to mislead the enemy into expecting attack either against Crete and the Aegean Islands, as a prelude to Greece, or against Sardinia, troops were moved from Beirut to Cyprus. The RAF also began operating sorties against enemy bases on the Greek islands, and British submarines moved into the Aegean and Adriatic to carry out patrols and to attack enemy shipping in these waters. Meanwhile, Coastal Forces extended their patrols along the coast of Sicily and as far north as Sardinia in search of targets, as well as intelligence of enemy movements. And before the main invasion, there were a number of islands in the Sicilian Channel to be liberated.

Galita was freed early on without any resistance after a landing by coastal craft from Bône, in which the local population went wild in their welcome of the Allied forces. The gaunt island of Pantelleria, which had been fortified as a base for the Luftwaffe and motor torpedo boats, was another matter, however, requiring an invasion on a small scale that served as a dress rehearsal for the Sicilian operation. While MTBs and PTs patrolled offshore on the lookout for S-boats, Allied troops landed there on the morning of 11 June. There was only light resistance and the island had surrendered by midday. Two days later, the remaining islands of Lampedusa and Linosa followed suit.

It was at this time that both the British and American coastal craft came to be used for clandestine operations by Special Services and the Office of Strategic Services, such as landing agents and supplies on Crete and Sardinia, an activity that continued until late in the war. It filled in the lull in operations that came with the ending of the Tunisian and start of the Sicilian campaigns, but with the invasion of Sicily, Coastal Forces were in the thick of it again. The boats from Bizerta moved up to Malta, and all the available MTBs, MGBs and MLs were brought into operation for the landings on 10 July – the former to cover the flanks of the eastern assault force by nightly patrolling the Straits of Messina and off the approaches to Syracuse and Augusta, while the MLs escorted the convoys of landing craft to the beaches and guarded them at anchor. The PTs were temporarily withdrawn from operations under British Coastal Forces to operate with the US Task Force landing to the south-west, between Licata and Gela.

In the event there was little action for the small boats during the first two days. Syracuse and Augusta fell quickly, and Bobby Allan moved his bases there, so that the boats would not have to return to Malta each day. It now became vital to secure control of the Messina Straits, to prevent the enemy getting supplies through from Italy and, later, to stop them from evacuating Sicily. It was while on patrol here on the night of 14/15 July that three MTBs of the 24th Flotilla from Malta, *81* (Lieutenant L.V. Strong), *77* (Lieutenant J.B. Sturgeon) and *84* (Sub Lieutenant G.R. Smith), with Lieutenant Christopher Dreyer on board *81* as Senior Officer, saw action against two U-boats making passage through the Straits, *U 561* and *U 375*.

The three MTBs were lying closely together in mid-Channel with engines cut when the surfaced submarines suddenly bore down on them. They were too close for the MTBs to be able to fire torpedoes. The boats furiously back-pedalled in reverse and, still going astern, *81* fired a torpedo at the second submarine at a range of between 80 and 100 yards. It hit squarely on and the submarine, *U 561*, blew up with a shower of wreckage. The other submarine crash-dived just as *77*, in an ideal firing position, had a double misfire; *84* was just too late to catch the target. They were looking for survivors when a group of S-boats passed by at high speed. Dreyer signalled this information to another MTB patrol operating further south, comprising the larger 'Dogs' which were better equipped to attack the heavily armed enemy craft.

There were three boats in this patrol, *655* (Lieutenant Fuller), *656* (Lieutenant Tate) and *633* (Lieutenant A.B. Joy), with Lieutenant Greene-Kelly on *655* as Senior Officer. They sighted two of the enemy craft at 23.40, an hour and a half after Dreyer's action with the submarines, and attacked and destroyed both after the expenditure of a considerable amount of ammunition. Seven Italian MAS boats were later sighted, but they managed to escape with their superior speed.

With flotillas of MTBs and MGBs now based at Augusta, Coastal Forces kept up their pressure against the enemy boats, engaging in a number of successful actions during the following ten days. It was not all one-sided. Shore batteries on the mainland were a dangerous threat and sunk one MGB, *641*, off Messina on the same night as Dreyer's action. *MTB 316*, with all her crew, was lost in an action with the Italian cruiser *Scipione Africano* on the night of the 16th. Aircraft were still a danger and during a bombing raid on Augusta on the 21st, *MTB 288* was sunk at her moorings.

But on the 23rd, Palermo fell. The American PTs, which had seen little action so far, set up a base there and on the following night began patrolling the northern approaches to the Messina Straits. *PT 216* (Lieutenant (Junior Grade) Cecil C. Saunders) sank the 8,800-ton Italian merchant vessel *Vimindale* by torpedo, and other boats shot up the tug that was towing her until she too sank.

On 26 July, Mussolini fell from power and the Axis dream began to crumble. It was only a matter of another week before the armistice with Italy was signed. As resistance in Sicily declined, an all-out effort was made to prevent the Germans evacuating to Italy, much of the work of patrolling the narrow seas between the island and the mainland being carried out by Coastal Forces, now established in Sicily in some strength.

On the night of 29/30 July the PTs hit back at targets that had so far proved too elusive for them, the Italian MAS boats (now either taken over by the Germans or still operated by Italian fascists), and the German F-lighters. Previous engagements had shown the MAS boats to be faster than the PTs, and that the heavily armed F-lighters were more than a match for the PTs in terms of gun-power, carrying as they did nothing heavier than 20mm guns until early in 1944, when 40mm cannons were mounted. The F-lighters could only effectively be sunk by torpedo, a difficult operation in view of their shallow draft which required a special torpedo setting. Nevertheless, in an action that night with two of them, escorted by four MAS boats, *PTs 204* (Lieutenant O'Brien) and *217* (Lieutenant Norman De Vol) sank one and so severely damaged one of the escorts that she had to be sunk by the other MAS boats.

Sicily was completely occupied by 18 August. But although the Germans had lost 30,000 in killed, wounded and captured, and the Italians over 300,000, a large proportion of the German forces had managed to get away across the Messina Straits, in spite of destroyer and Coastal Force patrols. The 3-mile-wide channel was dominated by shore batteries and the Germans also had fast and heavily armed patrol craft to help cover the evacuation.

There was only a brief respite for Coastal Forces before they were called upon to take part in the invasion of Italy. This began with a naval bombardment near Reggio on 2 September, followed by artillery fire across the Messina Straits on the 3rd, the day on which the Italian armistice was signed. Landings followed on 8 September, between Catona and Reggio, for which the escort included some Coastal Force craft. But their main effort was reserved for Operation Avalanche, the landing at Salerno on 9 September.

Part of this assault called for the capture of the islands of Ventotene, west of Naples, Ischia and Capri, and of Sardinia. It was not known how the Italians would react and the special US force which set off from Palermo to land on Ventotene on 9 September included fifty seasoned paratroopers in six MLs of the 31st Flotilla, five MTBs, two Dutch gunboats and an assortment of American patrol boats. One reason for the size of the force was that Mussolini was thought to be on the island; another was that it was to act as a diversion to the main Salerno landing, and, complete with acoustic devices and radar reflectors hung from captive balloons, to deceive the Germans into thinking an assault was being made north of Naples.

As it turned out there was very little opposition on the island and Mussolini had left for Sardinia some days before. The MTBs moved on to accept the surrender of Capri, including an MAS flotilla, on 12 September, while another force of four MGBs captured the island of Procida on the 15th. Ischia surrendered the following day. Then on the 18th, Sardinia fell to the grand force of two MGBs, *660* and *662* under Tim Bligh's command, which transported an American general, an Italian colonel and their aides to accept the island's surrender. They missed capturing Mussolini by a few hours.

Coastal Forces crews were not the only ones to show this kind of audacity. Whether or not it was the very fact of being in small boats which made for a more closely knit unit and a greater degree of purpose, these were qualities that the crews of the German S-boats certainly did not lack either. After their initial successes in the Mediterranean, they had been having a hard time of it. From their forward base at Derna they were pushed back to Pantelleria, then to Porto Empedocle on the west coast of Sicily, Palermo and finally Naples, where the remaining flotillas, the 3rd, 7th, 22nd and 24th, were formed into the 1st S-Boat Division under Kapitänleutnant Max Schultz. Finally, with the surrender of Italy and the Allied landings, they became for a while water gypsies, travelling from port to port, never sure in those early, confusing days what kind of welcome they would receive from the Italians, whether friendly or hostile.

This was the problem uppermost in the mind of Oberleutnant Schmidt, commander of *S 54*, when he put in to Venice on 29 July. It was a beautiful day, the inner harbour was swarming with gondolas and sunbathers were out in the Lido. But when the S-boat moored in the harbour, she was immediately surrounded by militia and frostily ordered by an Italian officer to surrender. The Venetians wanted nothing more to do with the Germans.

It seemed a hopeless situation, one small boat against a city. But Schmidt demanded to see the Mayor. When this man arrived, Schmidt declared he had no intention of striking his flag, and what was more, as he was in the van of a powerful battle fleet and demanded that those Italians who were friendly to the Allied cause should give up their arms. Otherwise he would radio to the fleet to bombard their beautiful city and reduce it to ruins. The bluff worked. Over 5,000 Italians gave up their assortment of rifles, grenades and bazookas, and Venice was handed over to Schmidt and his twenty-six men. As the days passed tensely, Schmidt was asked what had happened to the battle fleet. He replied airily that he had ordered it away as it was no longer needed in Venice. Then, after they had been there a week, units of the German Army arrived and Schmidt thankfully handed over his task to them.

But these events were a light relief to the grim fighting that was to come as the Germans first pulled back from the toe of Italy under the weight of the Allied onslaught and the blow of their partner's surrender, then hardened their resistance. On 13 September, they attacked and occupied the large island of Rhodes, off the Turkish coast, and with Crete and other islands also in their hands they were in a position to seal off the entire Aegean from the Allies. It was at this point that Coastal Force operations became more widespread and entered the busiest period of the Mediterranean war, with their activities dividing into three main theatres: the Tyrrhenian Sea off the west coast of Italy, the Adriatic and the Aegean.

CHAPTER 13

Hit and Run in the Aegean

With the 'D' type Fairmiles and new American-built Vospers coming into operation in increasing numbers, the older Elco boats continued to give good service, although armed with nothing heavier than Oerlikons. They were formed into the 10th MTB Flotilla, under Lieutenant Commander Peter Evensen. In September 1943, while Allan took his boats to begin operations off the west coast of Italy and the Commander (later Captain) of Coastal Forces in the Western Mediterranean, Commander A.E.P. Welman DSO DSC, began investigating the possibility of establishing bases in the Adriatic, Evensen was ordered to take his flotilla east. This meant a 1,000-mile passage from Messina to Alexandria, which was covered without mishap, and in October they moved up to operate in the Aegean from the island of Casteloriso.

The key to the situation in the Aegean was Turkey. If the Allies could hold the islands and establish control of the Aegean shipping routes, it was hoped that Turkey might be brought into the war on the Allied side. Small British garrisons were established on some of the islands in September, including Leros, Kos, Kalimno, Symi, Naxos, Levitha and Stampalia, and it was hoped after the Italy landings to capture Rhodes, the gateway to the Dodecanese.

But the Germans were equally determined not to risk the effect it might have on Turkey and the other neutrals by letting go of the Aegean. Large numbers of forces, including troops, vessels for seaborne operations, and in particular fighters and bombers, were moved to Greece, and the Germans forestalled the Allies by themselves capturing Rhodes. They quickly followed this by taking other Ionian Sea islands, including Corfu, and then moved against those held by the British. With the Luftwaffe dominant in the skies, these islands fell one by one in October until only the main garrison on Leros remained. With insufficient forces available, the Allies had to give up their plan for Operation Accolade, the opening of the Aegean, and operations for the next six months were confined to small-scale Commando raids and sabotage, and guerrilla warfare by resistance groups, in all of which Coastal Forces played an important part.

Many of the smaller islands were not garrisoned by either side and could be used by the small boats for hiding up in by day. Other lightly garrisoned islands changed hands several times as they were raided first by one side, then the other.

The first successful action by the 10th MTB Flotilla came during the early hours of 19 October when three boats, *315* (Lieutenant Leonard Newall DSC RNZNR, with Evensen on board as Senior Officer), *309* (Lieutenant R. Campbell RCNVR) and *307* (Lieutenant John Muir), while on patrol between the islands of Kos and

Kalimno, which the month before had fallen to the Germans, torpedoed and sank a 600-ton coaster and an F-Lighter. But overall, things had continued to go badly for British forces in the Aegean. Leros surrendered on 16 November, then Samos was evacuated, and the garrison on Casteloriso was reduced to just sufficient men to keep it operating as an advanced MTB base. From then on, operations in the Aegean became a matter of harassing the enemy in order to keep as many German troops tied up in the area as possible.

Typical of this period and the problems that the small boat crews had to cope with was an operation during the period 7-26 December by *MTBs 315* (Lieutenant Newall) and *266* (Lieutenant J. Breed RNZNVR). It was Newall's first operation as Senior Officer. Having been in Alexandria for repairs, the two craft set out for Casteloriso on the evening of the 7th, arriving the following morning. During the passage *266* had lost her starboard rudder (this was later found to be due to negligence on the part of the Coastal Forces base at Alexandria and the subject of disciplinary action), but the crew managed to plug the exposed rudder gland on arrival at Port Vathi and for the remainder of the period operated on two rudders. After refuelling, the boats left Port Vathi on the evening of the 8th and sailed westwards on silent engines to patrol between enemy-occupied Rhodes and the Turkish mainland, retiring to Arabah Island before daybreak.

Owing to the swell caused by a force 4 wind and the poor shelter that the island provided, it was decided the following night to investigate Port Sertchech, some 7 miles down the coast, as a possible laying-up place during the day. This was found to be ideal in every way: good shelter in most weathers, deep water close to the shore, and commanding a good view of Rhodes from a nearby hilltop. It was arranged for a fuelling caique to be moved down to Port Sertchech from Arabah Island.

As Lieutenant Newall wrote:

For the following four nights, patrols were carried out in the vicinity of Rhodes harbour and Symi, and the north and western coasts of Rhodes Island were closely investigated. But there wasn't the slightest sign of activity anywhere, except for a regular hourly searchlight sweep to seawards by a light near Tholo on the northern coast. During the day, periodic visits were made to the look-out position at Sertchech but no sea or air traffic was observed. On the morning of the third patrol, when about to return to our hideout position, it was discovered that *266 's* centre shaft had become uncoupled from the engine while she had been running on the wing engines. This was rectified after securing at Port Sertchech.

At 10.30 on the llth, an enemy report of a 3,000-ton merchant vessel proceeding from Cape Krio towards Rhodes was received and we proceeded to a position just to the east of Cape Alupo in order to intercept if she passed outside Turkish territorial waters. At 13.00 she appeared in sight about half-a-mile offshore and was identified as the Turkish vessel *Dumpulinar*. She proceeded eastwards, keeping well inside territorial waters.

The Aegean Sea.

In the early hours of the 13th, when returning from a sweep down to the south-western point of Rhodes, *315* ran her port Vee-drive and it was decided to return to Port Vathi the following night for repairs.

Just as they were about to leave for Port Vathi, however, the Greek secret agent in the neighbouring island of Loryma arrived. Newall had come across him the night before while the man was on his way to Rhodes to see what information he could pick up. Now he told Newall that a tug towing two caiques had left Symi forty minutes earlier, heading for Rhodes. The two MTBs set out at once and intercepted the vessels 4½ miles off Kum Burne. The tug was 80 tons, the caiques about 100 tons each. Newall continued:

We attacked with depth charges and guns. Although well armed, the tug put up no resistance and was soon left in a sinking condition. Gunfire, including mortar bombs, was then concentrated on the caiques but since they did not appear to be sinking very rapidly, each boat went alongside one of the caiques and placed a demolition charge aboard. During this manoeuvre, *266* took on board one prisoner.

For some time we had been held in the searchlights from Rhodes, and since the shore batteries were warming up to their task and *315* was definitely reduced to two engines, I decided to retire and proceed to Port Vathi, eventually arriving at 01.00 the following morning.

During the 14th and 15th, the boats were refuelled and a new Vee-drive fitted to *MTB 315*. Then they set out to return to Port Sertchech, but the weather was rapidly worsening and *MTB 266* began to have more trouble with her defective centre engine stern gland. The boats returned to Vathi, but the gland could not be repaired. The only solution was to jam the centre shaft in such a way that it would not trail when running on the wing engines, the idea being to patrol on the wing engines and use the centre only in an emergency.

At 17.00 on the 17th we again sailed for Sertchech but the contrivance used for jamming the centre engine of *266* carried away and we returned to Vathi intending to try a different method the next day. However, at 01.15 on the 18th a signal was received from the Commander-in-Chief, Levant, to examine Symi Harbour, and considering this to be an emergency I decided to proceed there at 30 knots with both boats, and after the operation to use the remaining stern gland packing to stop *266*'s leak.

The two boats returned to Vathi on the 24th, then, acting on orders, took several Army officers from the Casteloriso garrison to Limassol, remained there during the daylight hours of the 25th, and eventually returned to Alexandria early on the 26th.

The Commander of Coastal Forces in the Eastern Mediterranean, Commander R.E. Courage, commenting on the breakdowns to *266*, wrote: 'It is remarkable that commanding officers and crews of Coastal Force craft do put so much faith in the work done on their boats by base repair staffs, when the latter are often no more skilled than themselves. No larger ship with more experienced personnel would be so trusting.'

In his report, Newall drew attention to the difficulties caused by the weather:

Camouflage was not always possible owing to the wind, and at night, patrols had to be confined largely to the sheltered waters between Rhodes and Turkey. Neither of the two enemy reconnaissance planes which passed overhead during the first week there appeared to notice us, and it was not until our return to Sertchech on December 18 that the enemy seemed to have any idea that we were in the vicinity. On that day, two more planes passed overhead and may very easily have seen the boats since they were not under camouflage. During the afternoon of the 18th, the agent came round from Loryma and arrangements were made for a report of any further enemy movements to be passed on to the MTBs. From that point of view, Sertchech is admirably handy.

Newall's examination of the harbour at Symi helped to lay the groundwork for an audacious Combined Operations raid on the island in July of the following year. It was typical of such raids during this period. The object was to liquidate or capture the enemy garrison, destroy the military installations, capture or destroy any enemy shipping found, and then leave the island within twenty-four hours. The landing and evacuation of the 224-man force was to be carried out by eight 'B' Type MLs, four HDMLs, two schooners and *MTB 309*.

As Symi was beyond striking distance from the nearest Coastal Force base at Casteloriso, it was necessary to concentrate the whole force at an advanced base without the enemy's knowledge. The Gulf of Dorio on the Turkish coast was chosen, and the coastal craft adopted the method of lying-up under camouflage that had already become such a feature of Aegean operations. The raid, known as Operation Tenement, had been under consideration for some time, but it was not practical as long as the enemy had destroyers in the Aegean. However, of the four known to be in the area, one had been damaged by a submarine, another by the RAF and the remaining two by a Royal Marine raiding force; all were docked in Piraeus for repairs. The raid was planned to take place between 13 and 15 July 1944.

Even with the destroyers out of the way, there were still difficulties. First of all the force had to concentrate without the enemy knowing; then the concentration had to be made in Turkish waters, close enough to the objective for the return journey to be made under cover of darkness; and finally the troops had to be collected from such widely dispersed areas as Palestine, Alexandria, Cairo and parts of the Aegean. The detailed plan was not made until 6 July, when RAF reconnaissance had been completed and the Force Commander, Brigadier D.J.T. Turnbull DSO, had arrived in the forward area. Intelligence had reported that the garrison was manned by between 195 and 200 enemy troops. They appeared to be in a high state of tension, firing spasmodically day and night as if to keep up their spirits. But expecting that any attack, if made, would be carried out during the hours of darkness, they had adopted a system of standing to by night and standing down by day. It was decided therefore to make the raid in daylight, and to select the beaches so that even if the enemy became warned of the landing, they could not send troops to oppose it in under two hours. The time chosen for the attack on the garrison was 07.00 on the morning of 14 July (06.00 by the enemy's time, as they were one hour behind).

The Senior Officer of the coastal craft was Lieutenant Commander D.M. Russell. He was on board *HDML 1386*, one of three boats which landed an advance party on the north-western side of the island the night before the raid.

The military force was divided into three groups, all of which included Greek troops of the Sacred Squadrons as well as Commandos and demolition experts. They were to concentrate at different points on the Turkish coast on the evening of the 13th – the main force under Brigadier Turnbull in Losta Bay, the west force under Captain C.M. Clynes at Dersek, and the south force under Captain J.S.F. Macbeth at Sertchech – and then make three separate landings on Symi. When the boats had completed the disembarkation, five of the MLs were to sail round to the harbour and at 07.00, zero hour, commence a bombardment of the castle in which the garrison was housed. Another three MLs and the MTB were to stand guard offshore and intercept any attempt that the enemy might make to send reinforcements to the island.

At five minutes before midnight, the first boats of the main force arrived at Marina Bay and were met by the advance party. Although it was completely dark as the moon was not due to come up until 01.00, the landing proceeded smoothly. Then it was discovered that the last boat, *ML 349*, was missing. As this contained all the mortars and machine-guns, there were some anxious moments until it was discovered she had put into the adjoining bay by mistake. 'This caused a 45-minute delay which could be ill afforded in view of the extremely difficult and steep approach march to our position,' Turnbull wrote later.

Another mishap occurred to this last party during the hurried disembarkation when two of the Greek officers fell out of a rubber raft bringing them ashore and were drowned – they had little chance as they were fully equipped with heavy packs and had disappeared before anyone could get to them. One of the Vickers machine-guns was also lost, which seriously weakened the force's firepower. But the landing of all stores and personnel was completed by 01.50.

The west force landed without incident east of Fanouri, but the south force, landing at midnight in Fanoremini Bay, encountered some resistance from an enemy patrol while going ashore on the rocky beach and it was 02.00 before the operation was completed.

Describing the approach marches to the enemy garrison, Turnbull wrote: 'These were over very difficult terrain, with big rocks and boulders and no paths. Owing to the impossibility of landing large carrying-parties, all ranks had to carry extremely heavy loads in addition to their equipment. Conditions were of a kind to test the best mountain-trained troops.'

But the positions from where the attacks would be made were all occupied by 05.00. From his command post, Turnbull could see down into the harbour , and noticed two Italian motor torpedo boats and three barges just leaving. At 06.40, firing was heard at sea as the Italian craft were sighted and attacked by the covering force of MLs and *MTB 309*. Shortly afterwards the two MS boats returned to the harbour. One of them was on fire and was abandoned by her crew, while the other tied up at the jetty.

By this time, the main force had begun to attack the castle with mortar fire while the MLs commenced a bombardment from the sea. This was the signal for the west force to attack Fanouri; the enemy there soon surrendered and all their defences and ammunition dumps were destroyed. Meanwhile the south force had already attacked and captured the monastery at 06.30 and was now moving towards the harbour. At 07.30 they captured Molo Point. Greek troops with the main force advanced towards the harbour and boatyard, met up with the south force and the port was soon cleared. The MS boat at the jetty was attacked with grenades, boarded and captured. Then the second MS boat, which had been reboarded by her crew after the fire had gone out, came into the harbour and surrendered after a short fight.

At this stage it was a three-hour journey to get ammunition up from Marina Beach and patrols were pinned down by accurate fire from the castle. An attempt to bring supplies round to the harbour in dories failed when two of the small craft were hit and sunk by 20mm fire. The castle was now the only point of opposition on the island. It was surrounded on three sides, but the attackers had run short of ammunition and were unable to get supplies from the landing area. A state of deadlock had been reached so Turnbull decided to try to bluff the enemy into surrendering.

The German petty officer who had been in command of one of the MS boats was sent to the castle under escort to inform the defenders that they were completely surrounded and that as the rest of the island was in Allied hands it was useless to continue resistance. After an hour he returned with the news that the enemy were prepared to talk, so Lieutenant Fox was sent back with him. Nothing happened for another hour, but then a party of Carabinieri from buildings adjacent to the castle surrendered under a Red Cross flag. This party was sent to the castle with Lieutenant Commander Ramseyer to continue the negotiations. Eventually, at 15.00, the enemy garrison surrendered and came marching down into the town. Ten minutes later, a German air attack was made which, as Turnbull commented, might well have influenced the garrison not to surrender. But it was too late.

The Commandos proceeded to demolish the enemy's installations, including two 15-ton ammunition dumps, an explosive dump, the wireless station and telephone exchange, fuel dumps, the boatyard and nineteen caiques that were in it at the time. The arms captured included one 77mm gun, seven 20mm Breda guns and a large number of machine-guns, mortars, rifles and pistols. Also, of course, the two MS boats were captured complete and found to be serviceable.

Allied casualties, apart from the two Greek officers who had been drowned, were six wounded. The Germans had five killed, five wounded and forty-one taken prisoner; ten Italian fascists were killed, ten wounded and ninety-one taken prisoner; three Quislings were also taken prisoner. Only a few of the enemy had managed to escape into the hills, from where there was desultory firing during the afternoon.

Owing to a breakdown of the naval party's W/T receiving apparatus, it was not known whether the message requesting the Coastal Forces craft to return as soon as possible after dark to evacuate the island had been received. The MLs did return, however, and at 23.00 the force began to evacuate from Symi harbour, with the prisoners under escort in the two MS boats. One patrol was left on the island to continue demolitions and also to distribute food to the civilian population. But the following day, the enemy carried out a heavy aerial bombardment and landed a reconnaissance party to report on what had taken place. The British patrol was successfully withdrawn during the evening and several hours later the Germans landed a force of 300 men, escorted by five ships and a dozen aircraft, to reoccupy the island.

The MLs which had taken part in the raid were amongst a number assigned to the Aegean earlier in the year from Alexandria. The first to see service with Aegean Raiding Operations, as they were called, was *ML 1226*, commanded by Sub Lieutenant J.E. Hickford, which had landed a party of Commandos under Major Patterson on the island of Niseros on the night of 6/7 March. After picking up equipment from another island, the ML returned to Niseros on the 7th to find that Major Patterson had captured two German lighters and set sail in them with the rest of his party for Deremen. Hickford was to embark the

Commando interpreter, together with the Mayor of Niseros, his family and five wounded Germans.

The Mayor's party – three men, three women and a child – came on board while the boat lay anchored off the island's monastery and were put in the wireless room. The Germans were too badly wounded to go below and were laid on the deck. Hickford weighed anchor soon after midnight and set course for Deremen. He wrote:

> At 01.46, a schooner under full sail and burning navigation lights was sighted off Cape Krio. Action stations was sounded and I proceeded to close and board her. The boarding party under Sub Lieutenant Newman were satisfied she was a Turkish vessel with correct papers, and after an exchange of food and cigarettes we parted amicably.

The ML resumed her original course, then at 02.45 another schooner and three lighters in line ahead were sighted close inshore to Kuchi Island.

> I closed to investigate and the leading lighter attempted to escape inshore at maximum speed. I increased and closed her and boarded her. The crew of eight Germans and a naval officer immediately surrendered. The boarding party searched them for weapons. They had none and were forced into the bows and covered by Able Seaman Flewin with a 9mm Lanchester and a Greek from the Niseros party with a stripped Lewis. Stoker Challis investigated the engines and reported he could control the lighter from the wheelhouse. I then left the three of them on board and told them to follow us.

The remaining lighters were coming up astern at high speed, so Hickford left the boarded vessel and turned to intercept them. The schooner meanwhile had been lying off at about 300 yards and although the ML had kept her covered with the 3-pounder, it was thought she might not be armed. Suddenly, the two lighters opened fire with light automatics, and immediately the schooner also opened fire with a heavy gun, thought later by Hickford to be an 88mm, and a cannon aft.

This fire was returned and the schooner and one of the lighters hit. But then a shell from the schooner's heavy gun hit the ML on the starboard side of the wheelhouse where ammunition was stored, there was an explosion and a sheet of flame flared up. The 3-pounder ceased firing. Hickford took evasive action towards Mordala Island, followed by the schooner which continued to fire until she had fallen back out of range. When the damage and casualties were checked, it was found that one of the crew was dead and another severely wounded, with his left leg severed at the thigh, and also his right wrist. He was given morphine and a tourniquet applied to his right arm, but it was impossible to apply one to his left side. He later died. The nearest German prisoner to the 3-pounder was also dead. The starboard side forward of the wheelhouse was completely wrecked and there were holes along the hull. When a strong smell of carbide was noticed, Hickford discovered that a shell had penetrated the transom and caused calcium flares to ignite. The fire was brought under control with Foamite and Pyrene extinguishers.

Further boats were sighted during the passage to Deremen, but with his guns out of action, Hickford took avoiding action by keeping down moon of them and remained unseen. The ML entered harbour as the dawn rose.

Meanwhile, the three men who had been left on the boarded lighter found themselves in a difficult situation when the ML left. As soon as the battle began, one of the German prisoners had dived for a concealed gun and started firing. The two seamen and the Greek civilian had been forced to take shelter behind the wheelhouse. A gunfight developed, then, as the other vessels approached, the three men dived into the water and swam for the island. They were machine-gunned from the lighters. Only Flewin managed to reach the shore, to be picked up later by a Greek caique and eventually returned to the Coastal Forces base. Nothing more was seen of the other two and they were presumed dead.

This was the kind of operation conducted in the Aegean during the spring and summer of 1944 – continual harassment of the enemy, quick raids on islands then away again, small boats that sheltered amongst friendly islands by day to slip out at night when the moon was high to hunt the enemy on Homer's ancient seas, fighting hand-to-hand battles like the buccaneers of old. It was the most that could be done since, with the loss of Crete, the Allies could not base air and coastal forces close enough to the Aegean to be able seriously to challenge the enemy's control of that sea.

Although the main objectives were not achieved – those of inducing Turkey to enter the war and establishing a supply route through the Aegean for armaments going to Russia, thus saving many of the Arctic convoys that took such a heavy toll of men and ships – these operations did keep large numbers of the enemy occupied in defending their island bases. It was a war of nerves, guerrilla warfare by sea, in which the Germans never knew when or where the Allies would strike next.

Eventually, after the landings in Normandy and Southern France, the Germans were compelled in August 1944 to begin evacuating the Aegean. British forces landed on Kithera on 16 September, the first Greek territory to be liberated. A Coastal Forces base was established on the island and more craft arrived from other Mediterranean areas. Many of their activities from then on until the liberation of Athens were concerned with cloak-and-dagger missions to aid the partisans, as well as raiding parties to speed up the enemy's withdrawal.

CHAPTER 14

Battle Squadron

The expansion of Coastal Forces activity into the Aegean and Adriatic made it necessary for boats to be transferred to these areas from Malta and Messina, with an inevitable falling off in the number of operations that could be carried out along the west coast of Italy.

After the landings in Italy, Commander Robert Allan had moved his mobile base up from Messina to Maddalena, the former Italian naval base in Sardinia. From here the 20th MGB Flotilla began operations by the end of September 1943, patrolling the north-western waters particularly round Elba; they were soon followed by the 7th MTB Flotilla and the American PTs under Lieutenant Commander Barnes. Except when they were withdrawn for special operations with American forces, such as the invasions of Sicily, Italy and later Southern France, the PTs operated throughout as part of British Coastal Forces. In mid-October an advance base was established at Bastia, in Corsica, and from here the entire Gulf of Genoa came within patrolling distance.

As the Germans were driven slowly towards Rome during the winter of 1943, their supply lines by road and rail from Genoa came under continual attack and they had to rely increasingly on waterborne transport from the north. This mainly took the form of F-lighters and cargo ships that made the run down the coast by night, behind protective minefields and under cover of shore batteries, making it too risky to send in destroyers to stop the traffic. And so the job was left to the MTBs, MGBs and PTs, which with their shallow draft could usually pass safely over the minefields.

Experience had shown that the strongly built F-lighters could only be effectively sunk by torpedo as they were virtually invulnerable to the gun-power the small boats carried at that time. The F-lighters on the other hand were heavily armed with 6-inch and 8-inch guns, which made it necessary for the MTBs to get their torpedoes away quickly before coming under fire themselves. This led to the development of a technique for tracking a target by radar to assess its course and speed, then sneaking quietly in from the most favourable angle of approach and firing torpedoes before the enemy knew they were being attacked.

The PTs were the best craft for tracking the enemy, equipped as they were with a much more effective kind of radar. But the MTBs carried better torpedoes than the Americans – faster, more reliable and of higher explosive power – and the MGBs carried heavier firepower with their 6-pounders. And so joint patrols were instituted, in which a PT acted as scout and tracker while the MGBs held off any attack that was being made, and the MTBs came in to fire their torpedoes.

The technique of using MTBs and MGBs together on operations was not new, having orginally been developed during the early days in the English Channel. But Coastal Forces in the Mediterranean went one step further by reorganizing the 'Dog' flotillas to include four each of MTBs and MGBs. In one of these flotillas, the 56th, every commanding officer was a Canadian, with another Canadian, Lieutenant Commander Douglas Maitland, as Senior Officer. This flotilla became something of a legend in the Mediterranean. Soon after its formation it took part with other Coastal Force units in the Anzio landings on 21 January. In conjunction with the PTs under Stanley Barnes, the Canadian boats made a 'dummy landing' further along the coast as a diversion, using the usual techniques of record-playing the sounds of a landing over loudspeakers and setting off fireworks to simulate a battle. It was while this was in progress that an F-lighter and two S-boats passed by, further offshore. The six 'Dogs' set off in pursuit, *MGBs 657* (Maitland), *658* (Cornelius Burke), *633* (Tommy Ladner), *640* (Campbell McLachlan), *659* (Peter Barlow), and *MTB 655* (Pickard). Coming up fast in line ahead in the wake of the enemy, the MGBs delivered a fierce broadside which soon silenced the German gunners, and set the F-lighter and one of the S-boats on fire. Pickard's MTB which should then have made a torpedo attack had been hit and had fallen out of line. But just as Maitland turned back to look for him, the F-lighter blew up with a tremendous explosion.

It was the first time one of these craft had been destroyed by gunfire and the significance was not lost on Commander Allan. German opposition had stiffened considerably, with the F-lighter convoys now being escorted by S-boats and large landing-craft mounting high-velocity 88mm, as well as 40mm and 20mm guns. The MTBs found it difficult to get near enough to make a torpedo attack, and even when they did the torpedoes usually passed underneath the shallow-draft lighters. But the Canadians had shown that an attack by gunfire could be successful, pointing to a new method of approaching the problem. Allan began devising plans which led to the formation of Coastal Forces' 'Battle Squadron', one of the most spectacular and successful small-boat units of the war.

This force was built around three British LCGs (Landing Craft Gun), each mounting two 4.7-inch and two 40mm guns manned by Royal Marine crews. These formed the Battle Group (the actual craft used were LCGs *14, 19* and *20*). They were screened from possible S-boat attack by an Escort Group, comprising the Canadian-commanded 'Dogs', *MTB 634* and *MGBs 662, 660* and *659*. A Scouting Group of *PTs 212* and *214*, under the command of Lieutenant Edwin A. Du Bose in *272*, was to search ahead for targets and also act as a screen against any enemy destroyers in the vicinity. And finally there was the Control Group of *PTs 218* and *208*, with Commander Allan in *275* commanding the entire operation. He was virtually in the position of admiral of a battle fleet – a battle fleet in miniature – going into action against a somewhat similar opposing force but in which events would move a great deal faster than if they had been big ships.

One of the most successful operations by the 'Battle Squadron' took place on the night of 24 April. Allan led the Control Group in *PT 218*, with *209*, and Du Bose the Scouting Group in *PT 212*, with *202* and *273*. The LCGs were escorted by

PTs 211 and *276*, *MTBs 640*, *633* and *655*, and *MGBs 657*, *660* and *662*. The MTBs were commanded by Tim Bligh and the MGBs by Douglas Maitland. The force left Bastia at various times in the afternoon, because of their different speeds, and made rendezvous in the vicinity of the Vada Rocks at 20.00.

At this same time, a German convoy of eight F-lighters and a tug was setting off from Leghorn to take supplies further down the coast to San Stefano, while a smaller convoy of two patrol trawlers, each towing a barge, left shortly afterwards from Porto Ferraio, northward bound for Leghorn.

The first radar contact was picked up by the Scouting Group at 22.05, just off Vada Rocks, and a few minutes later Allan picked up another contact off Piombino Point on his own radar screen. The first was the southbound convoy and the second appeared to Allan to be an escort group heading to make rendezvous with the convoy; it was in fact the northbound convoy. In any event, Allan decided to pass ahead of this and attack the main target.

The F-lighters were close inshore when Allan located them shortly after midnight. As starshells lit up the enemy craft, many of the first rounds fired by the LCGs landed on the cliffs. But others found their targets, and within minutes four lighters and the tug had been blown up and sunk. Then the Battle Group turned away to intercept further radar contacts which had appeared to seaward, leaving the MGBs to close the beach and search for any further targets. One F-lighter was found, undamaged but abandoned by most of her crew; this was set on fire by the MGBs and later blew up. After picking up survivors, the MGBs were ordered by Allan to return to Bastia.

In the meantime, the LCGs had located three more F-lighters, two of which were hit and sunk almost immediately, but the third returned a high rate of fire which narrowly missed the LCGs. *PT 218*, from which Allan was controlling the operation, pulled ahead and drew most of this fire, which also landed dangerously near but did not hit the boat; no damage or casualties were suffered by any of the Allied craft. Then the third F-lighter was hit and withdrew under a heavy smokescreen. Fearing she would escape, Allan detached the MTBs to finish her off. They did inflict further damage, but the craft did not sink and eventually beached south of San Vincenzo.

An hour later the Scouting Group made contact with the two patrol vessels towing barges that were the northward-bound convoy. As the LCGs were too far away to make an interception, Allan gave the PTs permission to attack with torpedoes. They came under fire from the enemy craft before manoeuvring into an attacking position, but one of them, *PT 202*, fired a five-star recognition cartridge which happened to be handy and the enemy stopped firing. The PTs made a final run-in unopposed, fired their torpedoes and one of the vessels blew up, sinking almost immediately. The second opened up heavy fire again, at which the PTs withdrew under a smokescreen.

The 'Battle Squadron' was then ordered to return to Bastia, but the operation was not yet over. At 04.00 on the morning of the 25th, Bastia reported that an unknown number of enemy boats was stopped in a position 3 miles due west of Capraia. Allan considered that it was probably an S-boat force lying in wait for his return. He warned the LCGs of the suspected presence of S-boats, giving them a lookout bearing to starboard, and at the same time altering course to port. The Scouting Group were also informed of the enemy position and ordered to proceed round the north of Capraia, while the Close Radar Screen (*PTs 211* and *276*) was ordered to intercept round the south of the island.

The enemy force was in fact made up of three German torpedo boats, small destroyers, which were laying mines off Capraia. They were engaged by the PTs of the Scouting Group which fired their remaining torpedoes. One of the enemy boats, *TA 23*, was damaged by an explosion. Whether it was the result of a torpedo hit or striking a mine was not known, but as she was in a sinking condition and could not be saved she was later torpedoed and sunk by one of the other German craft.

None of the MTBs or PTs managed to make further contact with the torpedo boats. But it was a fitting conclusion to what had been a brilliantly successful operation, in which eleven enemy vessels had been sunk without any corresponding damage or casualties to the Allied craft.

In May, Coastal Forces were stepped up by the arrival at Bastia of the 7th MTB Flotilla, made up of new Vospers and American-built Higgins, and the American PT Squadron 22. A further squadron, 29, started operating from a new base at Calvi, on the west coast of Corsica, from where they could move in closer to the French coast and the Italian coast west of Genoa, and the American PT Squadron 15 was divided up between Bastia and Calvi. Lieutenant Commander Barnes, who had been awarded the Navy Cross for his heroism and leadership during the Tunisian and Sicilian campaigns, was in operational command of all three American squadrons.

Equipped with modern Mark XIII torpedoes, which could be fired from light racks instead of the old heavy torpedo tubes, and mounting 40mm guns, these boats were much more effective than the previous PTs. There were fewer incidents of torpedoes running erratically – or even turning and heading back for the boat that had fired them, as had happened in the past. From May to July, the American boats operating alone claimed two corvettes, eleven F-lighters, one cargo ship and several small craft sunk, and one motor torpedo boat, *MAS 562*, captured. Further craft were sunk in joint operations with British craft. Then, on 1 August, the PTs were withdrawn from operations to prepare for the part they were to play in the invasion of Southern France, scheduled for 15 August.

Meanwhile, the effectiveness of the British MTBs was also improved by the arrival of the Mark VIII Two-Star torpedoes with magnetic pistols. This device exploded a torpedo without contact with the target being necessary, and was to revolutionize attacks on shallow-draft vessels like F-lighters. The 7th MTB Flotilla, under Lieutenant A.C.B. Blomfield, was the first to use the new torpedoes. On the night of 9 May three of these boats, *MTBs 378, 377* and *376*, with Lieutenant R. Varvill as Senior Officer, and *PT 203*, torpedoed and blew up two F-lighters. This was followed up by a further success the following night when Blomfield led *MTBs 420* and *421*, together with *PT 214*, against a merchant vessel and escort of five R-boats off Vada Rocks. One certain and one probable hit was scored against the merchant vessel, and one probable hit against one of the escorts. Then on 27 May, off Spezia, Varvill again led *MTBs 421, 419* and *420*, and *PT 218*, against a force of five F-lighters escorted by an S-boat. Three of the lighters were torpedoed and blown up – each of them hit by one of Varvill's torpedoes fired both together, a remarkable feat, and the third by a single torpedo fired by *420* (Lieutenant E.S. Good) – and a fourth was forced to beach. Resuming patrol, an hour later the MTBs sighted a 1,500-ton merchant ship escorted by a sloop or small destroyer. *MTB 419* (Lieutenant A.H. Moore) scored a hit with his one remaining torpedo against the merchant ship, which broke in half and sank. Good's boat was hit by the escort, but he managed to bluff his way out by firing recognition cartridges. As a result of firing five Mark VIII torpedoes – the four Mark XIIIs fired by the PT all missed – the bag for the night was three F-lighters and one merchant ship.

While the 7th MTB Flotilla continued to maintain these successes, other coastal craft, including the PTs and the four ML Flotillas now based in the area, joined the 56th MTB/MGB Flotilla in Operation Brassard, the landing on Elba. This was planned for 17 June, thirteen days after units of Fifth Army had entered Rome following nine months of hard fighting up from Salerno.

Because of the large number of mines laid off Elba by the Germans, it was considered too risky to use deep-draft vessels for the landing, so nearly all the surface support was provided by Coastal Forces. Again the PTs were out with their sound apparatus to simulate dummy landings on the night of 16/17 June, while the actual landing on the south coast was made by Senegalese troops of the French 9th Colonial Infantry Division. Then the MLs began the arduous task of minesweeping while the Canadian-commanded 'Dogs' patrolled the approaches to the island.

On the second night after the landing, while leading four boats on patrol between Elba and the mainland, Maitland ran into an enemy force of a destroyer, a torpedo boat and an F-lighter, standing off the island in preparation for making an evacuation. *MTB 655* (commanded by Lieutenant Pickard with Maitland on board) made a run-in to fire her torpedoes, which missed and exploded on the shore. Almost simultaneously the destroyer turned and headed straight for the three MGBs, gathering speed as she came. There was a sharp interchange of fire, but the destroyer's heavier guns won out. *MGB 658* (Lieutenant W.O.J. Bate RCNVR) was badly damaged, with three men killed and Bate and another four men wounded. At one point in the action the steering jammed and the gunboat was almost rammed by the destroyer.

Elba was quickly overrun within two days. The subsequent establishment of heavy guns on the island denied the Germans use of the coastal waters to the south and was a great help to the Allied advance up the Italian coast.

Ever since the Adriatic had been opened up for Coastal Force operations, flotillas had been periodically transferred there from the Italian west coast area. Just before the Elba landing, the 57th MTB/MGB Flotilla had joined those which had already gone. Now with the Elba operation completed and with the remaining craft preparing for the next big operation, the invasion of Southern France on 15 August, the 56th MTB/MGB Flotilla was also transferred to the Adriatic.

CHAPTER 15

With the Partisans

Just after six o'clock on the warm, still evening of 2 April 1944, two boats slipped quietly from Komiza Harbour, on the island of Vis in the Adriatic, and headed towards the Yugoslavian coast. Both boats were 'D' Type Fairmiles. In the lead was *MTB 651*, commanded by Lieutenant K.M. Horlock, with the Canadian Senior Officer of the 61st MGB Flotilla on board, Lieutenant Commander Tom Fuller DSC RCNVR. Following behind was *MGB 647*, commanded by Lieutenant Mountstevens.

The boats of Coastal Forces operating amongst the islands of the Adriatic off the Dalmatian coast had already begun to find lucrative targets in the schooners which the Germans were using for the coastal transportation of supplies. Several had been sunk the previous month. But on this night, Tom Fuller was to carry out, on his own initiative, a different method of fighting in small boats that was to develop into an entirely new Coastal Forces technique.

The two boats made their way south along the coast until they reached Zalaz Cive shortly before midnight. Here Fuller spoke to the local Partisan leader and picked up four American special agents who had an Italian prisoner with them. 'It was our intention to proceed inside Zulana Harbour and strafe the local German garrison,' Fuller wrote. 'However, on the information of our American friends that the Germans had 155mm and anti-tank batteries there, we decided otherwise and proceeded along the coast east of Zulana.'

An hour later, they sighted a small 30-ton schooner. The normal procedure would have been to challenge her, take the crew prisoner and then sink her with gunfire. But Fuller had other ideas. The Coastal Forces base at Vis was short of certain supplies, so it would be a pity to waste those that the schooner was obviously carrying. He brought his boat up close, boarded the enemy vessel, captured the crew and took her under tow back to Vis. The cargo was found to include explosives, a jack-hammer drill and compressor, landmines, cigarettes and cigars, and mail for the German garrison at Korcula.

The following night the same two boats again set out together on patrol. Fuller later reported:

We proceeded to Blitvenica Island, arriving at 20.14. 'It was too early to enter the area, so we decided to kill time by looking for a W/T station on the island and landing a shore party. The lighthouse keeper, Antonio, rowed out to us in his small boat, but unfortunately we could not take him with us as he had several children ashore who would have starved. We found nothing in the way of a W/T station, so we left at 21.04 and proceeded to Murter Island.

Off Prisnjak Island, they sighted a 1,000-ton merchant vessel, wrecked and firmly aground, with two small schooners standing off. These were both boarded and captured, and again towed back to Vis, where their cargoes of firewood, wheat and ammunition added to the booty of the previous night.

These exploits set the pattern for a new kind of operation. The following night, Horlock went out in *MTB 651* with *MGB 661* (Lieutenant R. Cole) and captured another schooner carrying wheat. The next night Fuller was out again in *MGB 661* (Cole) with *MGB 647* (Mountstevens) and captured a 400-ton schooner laden with food. Three nights later the prize was two schooners and a motorboat, with another schooner and a motorboat sunk. And on the night of 14 April, *661* (Cole, with Fuller on board) and *MGB 646* (Lieutenant Knight-Lacklen) destroyed a tug and the 400-ton tanker it was towing, and captured a 250-ton lighter. In the one month of April, the four boats had captured no less than eight schooners, a lighter and a motorboat, and had sunk a schooner, a motorboat, a tug and a tanker. The captured vessels were turned over to the Partisans, who had accompanied the boats to help them navigate amongst the islands, and whose piratical and blood-curdling yells when boarding the enemy craft had ensured a minimum of resistance; these were then armed and added to their 'Tiger' fleet.

Commenting on Fuller's exploits, the Captain of Coastal Forces in the Mediterranean, Captain J.F. Stevens, who had relieved Captain Hubback the previous year, stated:

> The most notable feat of these operations has been the extremely successful boarding tactics, which have enabled a number of useful prizes to be taken, in several instances without a shot being fired. The tactic of keeping very close inshore – a matter of yards – has enabled our craft to gain surprise and the enemy vessels have then been boarded rapidly after a hidden approach from astern. All commanding officers have been warned to be very strictly on their guard against decoy or Q-ship schooners.

His report prompted the following comments by Admiralty chiefs:

> The tactics evolved date from the 18th century and earlier and are evidently as effective now as then. It is clear that, to be consistently successful, the piratical tactics adopted require good seamanship and a high standard of cooperation between COs and crews of the flotilla boats, together with complete confidence in the SO.

And, with a hint of envy from one desk-bound Admiral: 'These forces have brought their boarding and cutting out tactics to an exceptionally high standard. Some people have all the fun – and deserve it.'

Fuller was awarded a Bar to his DSC for these actions, Cole a DSC and Mounstevens was Mentioned in Despatches. Later, after other flotillas in the Adriatic had also gone into the piracy business, a competition was held to see who could achieve the minimum time to board, capture, take in tow and have

under way at 10 knots a vessel in prize. Fuller won, with a record time of twelve minutes.

Coastal Forces had first moved into the Adriatic the previous year, following the Allied landings in Italy. Their original purpose had been to attack enemy shipping along the east coast of Italy, as Allan's flotillas were doing on the west coast. Brindisi was selected as the first Coastal Force base, where the 20th MTB Flotilla (commanded by Lieutenant H.A. Barbary) and the 24th MTB Flotilla (commanded by Lieutenant David Scott), both of which had already been operating with some success from Taranto against enemy installations on the Albanian coast, arrived at the end of September. They soon moved farther up the Italian coast to operate from a base established at Bari, but there were few targets along the east coast within patrolling range of the small boats. This realization coincided with another important factor at that time: the decision by the Allies to increase their help to Marshal Tito's Partisans who were fighting a guerilla war in the Balkans, and in so doing were keeping as many as fifteen German divisions contained in the Balkan peninsula. It became necessary to get agents, Commandos and supplies across the Adriatic from Italy into Greece, Albania and Yugoslavia. This task was given to Special Service MLs, operating under Lieutenant Commander Morgan Giles, with Lieutenant Commander Merlin Minshall being responsible for liaison with the Partisans and Brigadier Fitzroy Maclean on the Dalmatian coast.

Minshall set up his office at the Partisan Dalmatian headquarters on Hvar Island. He first had to overcome considerable suspicion on the part of the Communist Partisans, who had earlier seen the Allies helping the Royalist Chetniks of General Mihailovich, some of whom were actually cooperating with the Germans against the Partisans. The confused situation had been sorted out when Brigadier Maclean established contact with Tito, and the Allies decided to transfer their help to the Partisans. By mid-December Minshall had gained their confidence and to the accompaniment of cloak-and-dagger intrigue, the MLs began their gun-running operations, together with Partisan schooners which were also used to bring across supplies. Most of the arms and ammunition were those salvaged from the enemy after the fighting in Sicily, which admirably suited the Partisans as they were already using equipment captured from the Germans and Italians.

At the same time, the MTBs also turned to the Dalmatian coast as a more favourable hunting ground than the east coast of Italy, and as another way in which the Allies could help the Partisans. After investigations during October, Komiza Harbour on the island of Vis, which was held by the Partisans, was chosen as an advanced Coastal Forces base, and in November the Bari MTBs began to operate both from there and from Hvar amongst the islands off Dalmatia. As in other Mediterranean areas the Luftwaffe commanded the skies by day, during which time the craft had to hide up under camouflage. There were constant air-raid alarms, and to add to these difficulties this was a period of violent storms which damaged many of the craft. In spite of this, regular nightly patrols were maintained and by December the MTBs were beginning to achieve successes against German coastal craft.

One of the first of these actions was on the night of 18/19 December, after two MTBs, *297* (Lieutenant J. Donald Lancaster, now Senior Officer of the 20th Flotilla) and *637* (Lieutenant Robert C. Davidson) which had been helping the Partisans in a raid on the Dalmatian coast north of Brae, became separated. Davidson was carrying out a diversionary bombardment when he came upon a Siebel ferry and two small landing craft loaded with troops and drums of fuel. At first they were thought to be friendly and Davidson gave the Partisan challenge. When they did not reply, he closed them at increased speed and then saw they were German. He opened fire with all guns, which was heavily returned by the enemy, causing hits along the hull and in the engine room of the MTB, and casualties amongst the men on the bridge. Shortly afterwards, however, the Siebel blew up when the fuel drums were hit and exploded, and the other two craft also caught fire and sank. In the meantime Lancaster, who was continuing his patrol alone, came across a camouflaged torpedo boat hidden under the cliff at Krilo Point and sank her with two torpedoes.

Three nights later, 21 December, the MTBs achieved their biggest single success in the area up to that time. It had been reported that the ex-Yugoslavian cruiser *Dalmatia*, now taken over by the Germans and renamed *Niobe*, was aground off Silba Island. Two MTBs – *298* (Lieutenant the Hon. F.M.A. Shore) and *226* (Lieutenant P.H. Hyslop) –under the command of Lieutenant Lancaster were sent out from Hvar. It was evident that if they were to return from attacking the cruiser before daylight, when there was the ever-present danger of being spotted by enemy aircraft, they would have to maintain 25 knots all the way. *MTB 226* was in need of repair and Hyslop's engine-room staff had a constant struggle to keep up that speed to stay with the leader.

The cruiser was sighted at 01.00 as the MTBs passed through the narrow channel dividing the islands of Skarda and Ist. 'If *Dalmatia* was to be torpedoed, a silent approach and a surprise attack was necessary,' Lancaster wrote later.

The MTBs reduced speed to a few knots and crept towards the stranded cruiser, which had a small destroyer and several S-boats with her. At a range of 500 yards, still not yet sighted, the MTBs fired their torpedoes and withdrew. A series of violent explosions followed which indicated that all four torpedoes had found their mark. The enemy craft in the vicinity opened fire, but neither of the MTBs were hit as they returned through the channel the way they had come, arriving back at base at 07.15. The cruiser became a total loss and German reports showed that one of the torpedoes had also hit and sunk a tug that was alongside at the time.

This success did something to mitigate a disaster which had occurred earlier in the month at Bari. A sudden raid just after dark by twelve German bombers, coming in over the sea at wave height in order to escape detection by radar, had resulted in the destruction of seventeen cargo ships of a convoy that was just then unloading, and serious damage to other craft, including a number of MTBs and the Coastal Force base ship, HMS *Vienna*. It was not only this damage which was such a blow to Coastal Forces, but one of the sunk cargo ships had been carrying new Packard engines and spare parts for the 20th MTB Flotilla. Because of this serious depletion in the strength of Coastal Forces in the Adriatic, arrangements were made immediately to bring reinforcements round from the west coast of Italy. The first four 'Dogs' arrived shortly before Christmas. One of them was *MGB 662* commanded by Tim Bligh, later promoted Lieutenant Commander, who, as Senior Officer of the 57th MTB/MGB Flotilla, was to be responsible for some of the most successful actions fought by Coastal Forces, not only in the Adriatic but in any theatre.

At about this time, as British and Partisan activity along the Dalmatian coast increased, the Germans decided that it was necessary for them to occupy the offshore islands. Korcula was attacked and captured on 23 December and forces were concentrated to take other islands, including Hvar, Brae, Lagosta and finally Vis, early in 1944. In anticipation of this, Lagosta was partially evacuated and many of its installations destroyed. Partisan headquarters and Minshall's liaison office were moved to Vis, while Brae and Hvar were left only lightly defended. But Vis was to be held in strength by the Partisans, supported by a garrison of Commandos, in view of its importance as a Coastal Forces base, as a terminal point for the delivery of arms to Tito, and as a springboard for any large-scale operations which might be found necessary in the Balkans. Lieutenant Commander Giles took over command of naval operations as Senior Naval Officer, Vis, while Commander Welman continued to run the Coastal Force bases on the Italian mainland, which were now established at Brindisi,

Bari and Manfredonia. The Vis garrison was commanded by Brigadier T.B.L. Churchill CBE MC.

Coastal Forces operations in January were interrupted by bad weather and the only success was on the night of the 13th, when Hyslop in *MTB 226* torpedoed a small merchant ship in Sumartin Harbour during an attempt with *MTB 651* to intercept German troops invading Brae. But then, with more German shipping concentrating in the area for their occupation of the islands, things began to look up. Between 29 January and 9 February alone, five enemy schooners, one tanker, one tug and one motor pinnace were sunk in five operations, in which the Senior Officers concerned were Tim Bligh, Lieutenant G.M. Hobday and Lieutenant David Scott DSC.

Typical of these was the operation carried out in the early hours of 31 January. *MTBs 85* (Lieutenant Hyslop with David Scott on board as Senior Officer), *297* (Lieutenant J. R. Woods RCNVR) and *295* (Lieutenant Shore), left Komiza Harbour shortly after midnight for the island of Dugi Otok, the first visit to be paid there by Coastal Forces. It was reached without incident and at first light, after refuelling from the drums they carried, the boats moved close inshore and the crews set about camouflaging them.

In the afternoon Scott made contact with the local Partisan leader and was told to his surprise and alarm that the Germans had landed on the other side of the island that very morning. And what was worse, they were now reported to have control of the mouth of the harbour in which the MTBs were lying up. Scott wrote:

> While we were digesting this fact a very out of breath Partisan arrived with the news that four E-boats were entering the harbour. We immediately got under way and lay together under the lee of a cliff. Had the E-boats appeared they would have got a rude shock as we could have dealt with them one at a time as they appeared round the Point at very short range. Fortunately for both parties, as we were only twelve miles away from Zara aerodrome, the enemy apparently passed across the entrance.

In the evening, the MTBs escorted a convoy of eight Partisan schooners out of the harbour and past the entrance where it was thought the Germans might have set up a gun emplacement. Luckily they had neglected to do so. Leaving the Partisans to their own devices, the MTBs proceeded northward to carry out a patrol to the south of Silba Island where the Partisans said traffic passed between the hours of eight and midnight.

Scott continued: 'It was decided in view of the fluid situation in the islands and the lack of confidence expressed by the Partisans, who had already burnt every schooner that could not move, that it would be unwise to lie up by day, and it was my intention to return to Komiza on completion of the patrol.'

Silba was reached shortly after 20.00 and the MTBs moved into position in the enemy shipping lane and cut engines. After two hours, the sound of diesel engines was heard approaching from the distance. It grew louder, and then two shapes loomed out of the darkness to port.

The MTBs got under way on silent engines and slowly moved closer to the shapes, which became identified as one large and one small schooner, heading north. Scott challenged the vessels by firing three times with his revolver. When there was no answer, he assumed them to be the enemy:

> We decided to get as close as possible to sweep the decks with machine-gun fire to neutralize any opposition from the guns that such schooners were known to carry. During the last stages of our approach the schooners, which were by now alongside each other, commenced to call out in German and asking us if we were 'Deutsch Schnellboote'. A non-committal reply was made and we approached to within half a boat's length. An over-excited citizen then called out 'Deutsch' three times, to which we replied by opening fire from all the guns of MTBs *85* and *298*. When we ceased fire, it was found that the crews had renounced Adolph Hitler and cries of 'Amigo Italian!' could be heard.

The survivors were taken prisoner, consisting of six Italians and two Germans, and *MTB 298* sank what was left of the schooners by dropping depth charges. In view of the fact that there were wounded amongst the prisoners, the MTBs took the chance of returning to Vis by daylight, where they arrived safely on the morning of 1 February.

Having now occupied a number of the Dalmatian islands, including Korcula, Brae and Hvar, the Germans turned their attention to Vis, the most important Partisan and Allied stronghold. But at this point a bitter quarrel broke out between the Wehrmacht and the German Naval Command as to who should be primarily responsible for the operation. This led to a postponement of the intended attack, first to March and then to April. It was during the first days of April that Coastal Forces based on Vis began to affect German coastal traffic really seriously, particularly by the series of brilliant captures by Tom Fuller, and Dönitz, Commander-in-Chief of the German Navy, became insistent that the island should be seized. The Wehrmacht, by this time, were doubtful if it was worth the commitment of so many valuable forces, especially as they were not convinced that they could continue to hold the island afterwards. The arguments were presented to Hitler. Although he tended to agree with Dönitz about the strategic importance of Vis, he felt that if the Army lacked conviction about the undertaking, it was not worth doing.

Meanwhile, a lack of targets caused the number of MTB and MGB actions to decline in May, and only one lighter and one 250-ton oil barge were sunk. The Special Service MLs also sunk another lighter which they happened to come across during one of their gun-running missions. Then, at the end of the month, Tim Bligh, who had earlier gone back to Bastia, returned to the Adriatic with the 57th MTB/MGB Flotilla of which he had just taken command, and by the middle of June the first of his boats were operating from Komiza. On 24 June, while on patrol in *MGB 662*, with *MGB 659* (Lieutenant Peter Barlow) and *MTB 670* (Lieutenant Eric Hewitt), Bligh celebrated his new command by sinking the German torpedo boat *T7*, which had been patrolling the Adriatic for some time but which no Coastal Forces craft had been able to come to grips with before.

During June and July, the Allies increased the number of their Commando raids on enemy-occupied islands in order to relieve pressure on the Partisans fighting in the Bosnia region. Coastal Forces provided cover for these bitterly fought operations which caused heavy casualties on all sides.

Although a few schooners and small lighters were sunk during this period, most of the MTB and MGB patrols failed to result in any contact being made with the enemy, and the Coastal Force crews were becoming frustrated at the lack of targets. This was especially felt by Doug Maitland's Canadian-commanded 56th Flotilla which had arrived in the Adriatic in July, fresh from their successes off the west coast of Italy. Their arrival in these waters coincided with that of an old enemy, the heavily armoured and armed German F-lighters. Bligh was the first to come across these in the Adriatic, on 7 August, while on patrol in his *MGB 662*, with *MTBs 670* (Hewitt) and *667* (Jerram), when two F-lighters were intercepted off Vir Island at 22.00. Knowing how difficult they were to torpedo, Bligh decided initially on a gun attack. In so doing, although one of the lighters was set on fire, his own boat was badly damaged, with one man killed and nine wounded. Then Hewitt turned on the second lighter and sank it with a torpedo, the first 'Dog' in the Mediterranean to sink a moving F-lighter by this means. The MTBs fired their remaining three torpedoes at the other burning lighter, but even though it was lying stopped with all guns silent, events returned to normal and all of them missed. The lighter was eventually sunk by further gunfire.

On the night of the 17th, the Canadians had their first chance against the F-lighters, when one of these was sighted in a convoy that also included two large schooners and a number of small landing craft and S-boats. Interception was made in the Mljet Channel by Maitland in *657*, Burke in *658* and Ladner in *653*. In a running gun battle, the two schooners, one S-boat, one oil-lighter and one Pil boat were sunk, and at least four other vessels, including the F-lighter, damaged. The MGBs suffered only slight damage.

The most successful action came on the night of 11/12 October, by which time the Germans were withdrawing both from the Dalmatian islands, and from Greece and the Aegean islands. It was, in fact, one of the most decisive actions ever fought by Coastal Forces anywhere.

Four 'Dogs' – Bligh in *MGB 662* with *MTBs 634* (Lieutenant Walter Blount DSC), *637* (Lieutenant R.C. Davidson DSC) and *638* (Lieutenant D. Lummis) – had left Komiza Harbour on the afternoon of the 10th to patrol off Zara and then lie up the following day at Ist. The weather was fine, with a slight force 1-2 NE wind and nil sea or swell. Blount, who had been to Ist before, was sent on ahead at 19 knots to contact the Partisans and get the latest information on enemy shipping. The other three boats settled down to a steady 17 knots in arrowhead formation.

After arriving at Ist, Blount reported back that an enemy convoy of four or five ships, mostly F-lighters, had been seen to enter Zara three or four days before and was expected to leave shortly, northbound. No other shipping had been seen for the past three days, so it was thought certain that something would be passing near Vir Island that night. In addition, three Partisan 'Tigers' – armed schooners – were patrolling the Maon Channel to the north where they had recently sunk one, and captured one, enemy schooner.

Bligh led his unit, now rejoined by Blount, through the very narrow but deep channel between Ist and Mulat at 19.45 and course was set on silent engines to Vir Island.

'At 20.40 the unit closed the coast of Vir and lay stopped in wait for the expected northbound convoy,' Bligh later reported. 'The weather by now was dark and thundery, with vivid flashes of lightning to the south. But apart from two panics caused by sighting the spire of Zara church, all was quiet.'

Little happened that night, except some distant firing which came occasionally from both Ist and Mulat where German boats were harassing the Partisan garrisons. The expected convoy did not appear, and although in the early hours of the morning the unit moved off to try to locate two destroyers which the Partisans reported had been seen between Skarda and Ist, these were not found. At sunrise the unit proceeded to Ist and later in the day held a conference with the local authorities, when it was decided to repeat the previous night's patrol. The 'demonstration' of the night before, which it was found had included S-boats firing torpedoes at Mulat breakwater, as well as destroyers' gunfire aimed at the 'Tigers', was thought to have been for the purpose of clearing the path for a big convoy that coming night.

The unit left again for Vir at 18.25 and several hours later were moving into position. Bligh wrote later:

At about 22.20 *MTB 634*'s starboard outer engine pushed a conrod through the crank-case and most of the engine-room crew were overcome with fumes.

At about 22.45 all the boats started rolling, as if a lot of ships had passed to seawards, so at 23.00 the unit proceeded northwards – a guess that eventually proved correct. Visibility was now very low, due to widely scattered cloud, but I was not prepared for the shock of suddenly seeing enemy ships on the port bow, at about 400 yards range.

Bligh at once ordered the unit to stop, then head into the shore just north of Vir light. The targets were now seen to be four F-lighters, one of which was altering course towards the unit. She appeared to be an escorting 'flak' lighter which had probably sighted the boats and was coming to head them off.

Blount was ordered to make a snap torpedo attack on this target while Bligh led the others ahead at 8 knots to engage the remaining craft by gunfire. Blount wrote later: 'I prepared to attack with torpedoes, but the range had closed to 100 yards by the time the sight was on and I decided it was too close, so I altered back to starboard and opened up with all guns on the "flak" lighter who was now firing at *MGB 662*.'

As the MTB turned, less than 50 yards now from the enemy, she was hit in the port ammunition locker, which exploded and went up in flames. While the fire was being extinguished, her guns raked the lighter, which burst into flames from stem to stern. By the light, every detail could be seen, including an 88mm amidships, a quadruple 20mm aft, and many 20mm in sponsons down the starboard side. Her bridge collapsed and she appeared to be breaking in two.

Meanwhile, fire from the 'flak' lighter had hit *MGB 662* as she was moving away to attack the other enemy craft and at once killed one of the pom-pom loaders. Fire was returned from all guns. And then:

> It is scarcely possible to describe the next ten minutes. The visibility was such that the leading boat in the line had a completely different picture from the fourth boat, and the slight offshore breeze was blowing smoke from the MGB's gunfire across the line of our ships and the enemy convoy, which was, of course, much more of an advantage to us than them as we had the inshore position and knew where to expect them, while the only ship that they could see was *MGB 662*.

Having drawn ahead of *MTB 634* and the 'flak' lighter, Bligh found himself engaging a whole host of targets on his port side, including F-lighters and S-boats. Very heavy 88mm and 20mm fire was coming his way, all of it high, from a variety of vessels, which had a blinding effect on the gunners and those on the bridge.

> Nevertheless, I saw a Pil boat hit by the 6-pounder and blow up, starting a petrol fire on the surface of the water. In the light of *MTB 638*'s starshell ahead, I saw F-lighters being hit by my pom-pom and Oerlikon. I saw an E-boat in the light of the petrol fire hit, set alight, and blow up – a victory achieved by the bridge .303 Vickers – and on the port quarter I witnessed an inspiring display of 6-pounder gunnery. An F-lighter, at about 400 yards, was steering away from us, unilluminated and almost invisible, even through binoculars, yet the 6-pounder fired nearly thirty rounds that scored hits in about a minute. A brilliant display of gunnery that was an inspiration to all the three boats astern and a source of courage to the Senior Officer. The 6-pounder also hit and sank a Pil boat with an inert cargo.

By this time, the MGB had crossed the northern end of the convoy and was lying stopped, waiting for the other boats to rejoin, and trying to ensure that none of the enemy got away.

Davidson in *MTB 637* had engaged another of the F-lighters after Bligh's order to go 'single line ahead, speed eight knots', but was screened on the port beam by *MTB 638* and could only fire with pom-pom. Then another target appeared ahead, bows-on to another burning F-lighter, and Davidson opened up with all guns at a range of 75 yards:

At this range none of our guns could miss. She immediately caught fire. The after superstructure resembled Wembley Stadium on a dark night, except for the Nazi flag. The gunners reduced it to a blazing wreck, and another target seen abeam of this blaze was being engaged by *MTB 638* with accurate fire.

At 23.17 two large objects were observed on the port beam, and turned out to be upturned vessels.

As previously arranged, Lummis's *MTB 638*, which was last in line and a little back from the others, had illuminated the scene with starshell as soon as the action started. Then, moving forward, she had sunk a Pil boat with Oerlikon fire, engaged an F- lighter at 200 yards and left her burning fiercely, set another F-lighter on fire and scored hits on an S-boat which appeared on the starboard quarter. *MTB 638* sustained one 20mm hit during this engagement.

Blount in *MTB 634* had also fired at the F-lighters under attack from the two other MTBs, then an S-boat which had appeared bows-on was engaged by his port .5-inch turret, and seen to explode and disappear.

Describing the scene, Bligh wrote:

Everywhere on the port side there were burning ships and explosions. There were visible many more ships than the original four F-lighters. The sight was fantastic.

At 23.14 the situation was resolving itself and a sweep was carried out round to the west and south to discourage any of the enemy from returning to Zara. An active F-lighter could be seen to seaward of the scene of action, steering south, but he turned inshore and I was confident that we would easily find him again; I somehow felt that none of the enemy would try to push any further north and was mostly concerned with the southern flank.

At 23.46, when about one mile from Vir Light, an F-lighter was seen close inshore; it turned over and submerged and was thought to be the one that was damaged by 662's 6-pounder. I was looking for the other F-lighters and decided not to investigate. It was probably a wreck anyhow.

At 23.53 targets were sighted at Green 20° and 637 was ordered to illuminate with starshell. This was done well, and 662 opened fire with all guns on an F-lighter and a Pil boat or E-boat lying close inshore, near Vir Light. The enemy now opened heavy fire from a position abaft the beam, almost certainly one or more F-lighters lying very close to the beach, well north of Vir Light and completely invisible. All boats returned fire at the flashes, but only damage can be claimed except that they shut up until we were going away to the northward, when they fired vigorously at nothing to the south-west. It was thus decided to go away and lie off until the moon got up and the light improved, and then come back and torpedo the remaining enemy. This was a risk as the enemy may have crept close to the coast and got away, but I decided to place complete confidence and reliance in my radar set and its experienced operator, A/B Henry J. Beadles, and to lie off stopped at about 4,000 yards. I felt certain that we should be able to pick up any F-lighter that tried to move, but had to admit that if a Pil boat wanted to get away, well, then it could; but I did not want to risk losing any boats by taking them into a dark coast with a belligerent group of well-armed vessels lying on the beach, when there was a big improvement of visibility due in two hours time.

Various echoes were plotted during the next two hours but they turned out to be ghost or aircraft echoes in the centre of the channel. It was now planned to approach the coast just north of Vir Light on a north-easterly course with torpedoes ready for immediate firing. *MGB 662* was to illuminate the coastline with starshell and the first MTB to sight an F-lighter was to fire torpedoes and say so at once on the intercommunication; no other MTB was to fire torpedoes until the result of the first attack was observed. By spreading out the unit, danger from enemy fire was reduced and perfect intercommunication ensured that good control was maintained.

During the waiting point, several little explosions were seen on the coast between Vir Point and Vir Light.

At 01.51 the moon was giving moderate light and it was decided to carry out the third attack of the night. All went according to plan until 02.21 when *662* opened fire with starshell. Then the first hitch occurred, in that under the light of the shells nothing of any size could be seen. After twenty minutes searching with starshell by both *662* and *634*, and some pom-pom fire from all boats, at the two small objects north of Vir Light that had been seen, and nothing having happened from the beach, it was decided to close very near the coast and run down to the southwards.

At 02.51, when about fifty yards off the coast line, the unit was brought round to south-west and set off down the coast at eight knots. At 02.54 a very large F-lighter was sighted dead ahead, at 450 yards, with bows into the beach, a perfect torpedo target. *MGB 662* at once altered round to starboard, ordering *634* to sink the target with torpedoes, and lay off ready to engage with covering gunfire. *MTB 634* fired at 02.56, scoring hits with both torpedoes, and the unit, in loose formation, was stopped to the eastwards of the smoking wreckage.

At 03.10, *662* decided to close the small piece of F-lighter still visible to try to identify it. Smoke was being carried away from the shore by a light breeze and *662* went through this 'screen' to the southwards at 03.14. At that moment I had the shock of my career to find myself at about fifty feet from a beached convoy of two F-lighters and some small craft. Fire was opened at once with all guns and the unit called up to close me with despatch. These beached craft were heavily damaged by gunfire from all boats, and the one F-lighter that was not burning was sunk by a torpedo from *657* at 03.37.

It was learnt later that *634* watched their target after the smoke had cleared away from the torpedo explosions and were surprised to see that an F-lighter was still in the same place as before their attack; in fact it was another one right behind and parallel to it.

During the whole of this third attack the enemy could not have fired more than twenty rounds in all.

It was now decided to withdraw. Two of these last F-lighters had been torpedoed, hit, and the third was well ablaze. Any small craft that were alongside the lighters had been sunk. There seemed no object in staying and it was desired to get out of the channel before the RAF came over; accordingly at 03.55 the unit proceeded to Ist. All the way across the burning F-lighters were seen to be blowing up continuously.

When all the reports were put together and assessed, it was considered that the four boats between them: had sunk six F-lighters, four Pil boats and one S-boat; had probably sunk another F-lighter; and had damaged three S-boats by gunfire, with one of them possibly sunk. Casualties were one killed, two seriously wounded and one slightly wounded, and there was very slight damage to *MTBs 634* and *638*. It was a remarkable achievement, in which the unit had been lucky in contacting the enemy at the crossing place of two convoys – one coming up from Sibenik and Zara and the other coming down from the north. But, as Bligh concluded his report: 'This was the first really decisive victory of D boats over the old enemy, F-lighters, which had 88mm and 20mm guns. It was made possible by low visibility, land background, uncertainty of identification by the enemy, absurdly close ranges, excellent gunnery, and admirable coolness on the part of the commanding officers.'

CHAPTER 16

Preparation for the Great Invasion

Vital as the events taking place in the Mediterranean were, it was in Western Europe that the main Allied assault was now centred. The Normandy landings in June 1944 involved Coastal Forces in their greatest single operation of the war, and once again established the English Channel as the focal area for small-boat fighting, in which American PTs played their part together with British boats.

During the previous eighteen months, while the main activity had shifted temporarily to the Mediterranean, Coastal Forces in Home waters had continued to maintain their guard over coastal convoys in the narrow seas and off the English east coast. They had taken the fight against enemy shipping into an area which now extended from the Channel Islands right up the German-occupied coast to the Norwegian fjords, and had steadily built up their numbers, until by the time of the great invasion they constituted a formidable armada of twenty-eight flotillas of MTBs/MGBs, twenty of MLs, and eleven of HDMLs.

The end of 1942 had seen the tide turn against the enemy in the battle of the coastal convoys, with the little ships of Coastal Forces playing a major part in breaking the back of the S-boat menace. There could be no let-up, for the Germans continued to fight with a tenacity born of growing desperation. But from the beginning of 1943, the emphasis in Coastal Forces was on attack rather than defence. It became a major undertaking for the S-boats to make sorties into the North Sea for the purpose of mine-laying or attacking British convoys. When they did it was usually in large numbers, widely dispersed, in the hope that some might slip through the offshore patrol screen. They rarely did, but the resulting battles between the small boats were amongst the fiercest fought of the war.

For most of the time the S-boats were required for escort duties with their own convoys, so that by the spring of 1943 the British and German roles had become largely reversed, with the German craft in the same defensive position in which the British MTBs had been during the first two years of the war. These heavily escorted convoys proved as difficult to attack as the Germans had earlier found it was to attack British convoys. Allied to the fact that enemy shipping, particularly in the Dover Straits, was greatly reduced, this led to an inevitable falling off in the number of MTB and MGB actions in 1943.

Nevertheless, successes were achieved, due in large part to better boats coming into service to replace the old ones, especially the large 'D' boats and the improved Vosper and British Power Boat Company craft, and a greater degree of sophistication in Coastal Forces methods of operation. It had been realized as far back as 1941 that night fighting in small boats required new and specialized techniques – the training establishment at Fort William (HMS *Christopher)* in Scotland had been formed primarily with this in mind. But something more was required, to allow crews to train together and to benefit from instruction in the kind of tactics that the pioneers had learned the hard way in the days of trial and error. Accordingly, in mid-1942, a working-up base was established at Weymouth (HMS *Bee)* under Commander R.F.B. Swinley, and by 1943, not only were new crews being trained there but existing crews were seconded from operations to take part in the courses provided, where they found, perhaps to their surprise, that they still had much to learn about gunnery, signals, torpedo drills and general tactics. Among those posted to Weymouth at various times to give instruction, and to pass on their own knowledge and experience, were commanders whose exploits had already become famous, such as Peter Dickens, Ronald Barge, Philip Lee, Patrick Edge, Mark Arnold Foster and Peter Scott.

There were changes too in the organization of Coastal Forces, which although not ideal, went part of the way towards solving the problems that had hampered the work of Rear Admiral Kekewich in his difficult and somewhat anomalous position. Two Admiralty departments now became responsible for Coastal Forces. On the materials side, concerned with the development of boats and their equipment, Captain F.H.P. Maurice was appointed Director of Coastal Forces Material, while operations came under Captain D.M. Lees DSO, as Deputy Director Operations Division (Coastal). In Nore Command, which had responsibility for the three Coastal Force bases on the east coast at Great Yarmouth, Lowestoft and Felixstowe, a Captain of Coastal Forces (Captain H.T. Armstrong DSO and Bar, DSC and Bar) was appointed in February 1943, with a small staff, to coordinate operations and training.

All these appointments reflected the greater degree of importance that the Royal Navy had come to attach to Coastal Forces – a far cry from the early days when they were little understood and even dubbed 'Costly Farces' by some humorists. There was much greater coordination with other services concerned in coastal warfare, particularly with Fighter Command and Coastal Command's Strike Wing, in which short-range aircraft worked with destroyers and MTBs from Nore and Dover Commands in operations against enemy convoys.

In taking the war across the North Sea to the German-occupied coast of Europe, it was the longer-range 'D' boats that were the most successful, able as they were to hunt in areas where least expected. One such operation took place on 12 March off the Hook of Holland, where three nights earlier Yarmouth-based MTBs had sunk a 6,500-ton tanker and two of her escorts, but had also lost one MTB (commanded by Lieutenant F.W. Carr) in an action against destroyers. As on that occasion, the boats were led by Lieutenant Commander Kenneth Gemmel, who was later to take command of a British flotilla operating with the Norwegian flotilla already in the Shetlands, against the coast of Norway, and was to be awarded both the DSO and DSC.

The memory of what had happened on the previous mission was very much in the mind of Gemmel and his crews as the three MTBs approached the same spot and immediately sighted a convoy of three big merchant ships surrounded by smaller escorts. It was at a longer range than usual – some 3,000 yards – that they fired their torpedoes, although from a perfect firing position. Two ships were hit. One broke in half and sank quickly, the other caught fire first, then sank more slowly by the stern. The MTBs turned away and headed back for home. From start to finish the enemy was unaware of their presence. The Admiralty thought it best to keep the Germans guessing and so for some time Gemmel's action was kept secret.

It was on that same night that Lieutenant Arnold Foster DSC, leading three MTBs from Dover and assisted by a force of MGBs from Ramsgate under Lieutenant G.D.K. Richards DSC (one of the greatest of the gunboat commanders who was killed in action later in the year), torpedoed and sank another heavily escorted German merchant ship which had left Boulogne on one of the enemy's rare attempts to make a dash through the Straits.

At the original instigation of Robert Hichens, before he was killed, the decision was taken in the summer of 1943 to equip all the 'D' class Fairmiles and most of the newer MGBs as MTBs, by installing torpedo tubes. The wheel had thus turned full circle, for just as the early MTBs had found themselves hampered by a lack of guns, which led to the development of the MGB, now the gunboats sometimes found themselves in a position to make torpedo attacks but with no torpedoes to fire, while the MTBs they were escorting were unable to get into such satisfactory firing positions. The ideal appeared to be a combined MTB/MGB – which was exactly the type of craft with which the Germans had entered the war. As the boats were gradually converted, they proved the value of this arrangement by increasing the percentage of the successes against the enemy, particularly as the enemy convoys were now strongly escorted by S-boats, which often made it necessary for a single boat to fight a gun duel as well as make a torpedo attack.

But as in all the small-boat fighting, it was the men rather than the equipment on which the results finally depended. This had been amply proved by Peter Dickens's successes of the previous year, even with unreliable and outdated boats whose performance had been gradually improved as a result of the heroic efforts of the base staffs. Now, as Senior Officer MTBs at Felixstowe, with mostly Vosper 72½-footers in his own 21st Flotilla, he continued to show that there was still a place for the smaller but faster craft, if handled in the right way. With the help of Lieutenant I.C. Trelawny DSC, who commanded the llth MTB Flotilla, he perfected his tactics of stalking and the unobserved approach to achieve some of the most successful results of the year.

One such operation took place in the early hours of 14 May. It was a perfect night for MTBs – sea calm, visibility limited so that there was a good chance of getting close before being seen – when Dickens left harbour in *MTB 234*, accompanied by *244* (Lieutenant K. Hartley), *247* (Sub Lieutenant G.J. Macdonald DSC, RNZVR) and *252* (Sub Lieutenant V. Ohlenschlagar).

By 01.40 on the morning of the 14th, the boats had reached their position 3 miles off the Hook of Holland, stopped and cut engines, and set hydrophone and RDF watch for any convoy that might pass. Dickens later wrote:

My leading stoker then staggered onto the upper deck and reported that exhaust fumes had leaked into the engine room and that the motor mechanic and stoker had fainted. They were dragged out and all three laid out on the upper deck to recover. The motor mechanic and stoker did not regain consciousness for about three minutes, when they were violently sick and had splitting headaches. In view of this I decided to remain in my present position which covered the approaches to the Hook and any passing traffic so as to give time for the engine-room crew to recover properly.

After about two hours, a confused sound was heard on the hydrophone. The MTBs started up at 9 knots, and at 03.41 four large ships with S-boat escorts were sighted fine on the starboard bow. They were not merchant vessels as expected but warships that were thought at first to be torpedo boats but later turned out to be minesweepers.

Macdonald and Ohlenschlagar were ordered to make an attack after Dickens and Hartley had separated and come in from different angles to create a diversion. But as the MTBs began to move into position, they suddenly found that the range which was thought to be 2 miles was only 500 yards – they were right on top of the convoy. An S-boat challenged Macdonald with the letter 'P'. Macdonald replied with 'R', which confused the enemy and made him hold his fire for a vital few moments.

This gave a chance for Dickens and Hartley to come in to make a torpedo attack, reversing the roles originally planned, but all according to the tactics Dickens had devised. Unfortunately the two MTBs had not yet had time to separate and in the confusion of the moment, for they had just been seen and were coming under heavy fire, both fired their torpedoes at the same target, which was the second ship in line. As this blew up with a vivid red flash, the MTBs made smoke and disengaged. It was at this point that one of those incidents occurred which could have been serious but which in fact had its lighter side, as Dickens now recalls:

Having fired our torpedoes, Hartley and I disengaged to the east and had turned 90 degrees so that we were going parallel to the enemy, pretty close, and straight towards the shore at full speed. I was between Hartley and the enemy. I wanted to turn right away and get behind the smoke for we were being hit, but could not because Hartley for some unaccountable reason was holding his course. I waved and shouted madly to no effect, and it only came out afterwards that the strap of his binoculars had caught in the spokes of the wheel so that the coxswain could not turn it. Not knowing the reason why and reasonably assuming the steering had been hit, he exerted all the pressure he could, thus half strangling Hartley until, thank goodness, the strap finally broke.

Shortly before 04.00 Dickens made contact with the other two boats of Macdonald and Ohlenschlagar, which had also disengaged after knocking out the S-boat's after gun. Having found out that they had not yet fired their torpedoes, Dickens took them back to the attack. They came across the wreck of the ship that had been torpedoed and by then was sinking by the stern. Her bows had been blown clean off. But what was more important was that another of the big minesweepers was slowly circling the wreck. Macdonald went in alone to make an attack, but both his torpedoes missed. Then Ohlenschlagar had a go. Although he was sighted and came under heavy tracer fire, he kept going and fired at 400 yards. One torpedo misfired, but the other found its mark. The second target blew up in a sheet of flame and appeared to break in two.

At that moment a third ship appeared, but with no torpedoes left, Dickens had to break off and head back for base. Two German minesweepers had been sunk, compared to only superficial damage to three of the MTBs (241 was not hit at all) and one casualty, Ordinary Seaman J. Pollard on Hartley's boat, who was slightly wounded by shrapnel in the arm.

The claims at first made by Dickens were for two torpedo boats, which were much the same size as the minesweepers they were later found to be. The German propaganda machine made use of this misidentification in the following broadcast from Berlin two days later:

Yesterday the British Admiralty spread the false report that during an engagement between German and British naval forces off the coast of Holland, two German torpedo boats had been sunk. It is declared officially that on the night of 13/14 May no German torpedo boats were either attacked or damaged, and certainly not sunk.

This is what actually occurred off Scheveningen: a formation consisting of six British MTBs attempted to operate on the German sea routes off the Dutch coast and was, before reaching their destination, spotted by forces of the German naval coastguard and engaged. During this short-distance engagement the British MTBs, whose gunnery was inferior, received several direct hits. Two boats caught fire which soon spread over the entire length of the British boats. A third capsized owing to heavy damage received below the waterline after having been fired at heavily by both sides. In clear moonlight it could be seen that she sank. Apart from a number of losses of personnel, the German boats suffered no damage and were able to remain in position until daybreak. They have reached their base at dawn on 15 May in full numbers.

The monitoring officer of this German news broadcast added his own wry question: 'As Lieutenant Dickens and his team presumably returned to base by swimming, has any consideration been given to granting them survivors' leave and applying for the long-distance record?'

Dickens and his flotilla continued to achieve such successes and in the summer he was awarded the DSO. Then, in the autumn, after a brief spell at Weymouth to instruct others in the tactics that had become his hallmark, he was given command of a Hunt-class destroyer. But the tradition he had established at Felixstowe was ably continued by Trelawny's 11th Flotilla.

Coastal Force activities in the English Channel showed a marked decline in the summer and autumn, not only because of the fewer ships that the Germans put to sea, but also because of unfavourable weather conditions. Three Newhaven-based flotillas of SGBs, 'D' Type MGBs, and 70-foot MTBs, had begun to operate in a new area off the Normandy coast, but the German radar-controlled batteries mounted high up on the cliffs made this a difficult and very dangerous hunting ground.

As regards the enemy's offensive tactics, the S-boats were now rarely able to achieve success. But the Germans were well aware of their value in holding down large British defensive forces and in the autumn they decided to step up their operations in the North Sea with a number of well-planned mass attacks. The first of these on the night of 24/25 September resulted in the loss of one British trawler by torpedo, and in two ramming incidents in which *S96* was sunk and two MLs, *145* and *150*, were very badly damaged. Honours were fairly even. Then, on 24 October, three S-boat flotillas set out again on another mass attack against a northbound convoy off the Norfolk coast. This became a major battle, spread out over many hours and a large area of the North Sea, with as many as sixteen separate encounters between the German boats and the British patrols of destroyers and coastal craft.

The convoy of merchant vessels and trawlers was sailing towards the Humber and escorted by five destroyers, *Pytchley, Worcester, Eglington, Campbell* and *Mackay*. Coastal Force dispositions for the night had been made with an eye to a possible attack. On anti-S-boat patrol in units some 10 miles offshore were *MGBs 609* and *610* under Lieutenant P. Edge, *MGBs 607* and *603* under Lieutenant R.M. Marshall, *MGBs 315* and *327* under Lieutenant J.A. Caulfield, and *ML 250* and *RML 517*, under Lieutenant Commander Robert Elford. *MTBs 439* and *442*, under Lieutenant C.A. Burk RCNVR, were on stand-by in Lowestoft.

The S-boats, up to thirty of them, left their bases on the Dutch coast at nightfall and just before midnight, when about 12 miles off the convoy route, broke up into divisions of four or six boats each. By this time their presence had been detected by RAF bombers returning from a raid and the convoy was alerted. The S-boats had apparently used the direct route from Ijmuiden north of the Ower Bank, and as they would probably return that way, Nore Command plans were laid accordingly to cut off their line of retreat.

Pytchley was the first to make contact with the enemy. From her position guarding the seaward flank of the convoy the destroyer picked up a unit of six S-boats by radar at 23.18 and went into action against them 4 miles north of 56B buoy. She drove them off to the north-east, severely damaging one in a 'well-fought action which undoubtedly saved the convoy from being accurately located'.

When the report of *Pytchley's* contact had been received, *MGBs 609* and *610* (Unit R) were ordered towards the vicinity of the S-boats, while *MGBs 607* and *603* (Unit Y) went to intercept their line of retirement to Ijmuiden, together with the two fast MTBs which left Lowestoft to cover the northern end of Brown Ridge. *Eglington* was ordered to remain with the convoy while the remaining three destroyers were 'fleeted' north to help the MGBs.

It soon became clear that the S-boats had split into numerous groups which were approaching the outer war channel at a number of points east of 57F buoy. This would have posed a dangerous threat were it not for the fact that by good fortune the convoy was two hours ahead of its timetable. When the S-boats reached the shipping route, therefore, they were well astern of the convoy and the only anxiety was for the trawler *William Stephen*, which was straggling some miles behind.

At 00.27, *Worcester*, reaching the eastern end of her patrol, engaged four S-boats and drove them off with Oerlikon fire, scoring hits on one. Less than an hour later the same destroyer engaged another group of three boats and this time scored a direct hit with a 4.7-inch shell. The boat blew up and the blazing wreckage was passed as *Worcester* chased the others northwards. Returning to the channel half an hour later, *Worcester* sighted several more S-boats stopped at the scene of the action, picking up survivors. These were engaged and driven off.

Mackay meanwhile had also been engaged in two actions against different groups of S-boats at 00.40 and 01.48. While driving them off, the enemy made smoke and dropped a number of delayed-action depth charges, which the destroyer easily avoided.

The trawler *William Stephen* had dropped back 5 miles by the time these actions developed. With S-boats both ahead and astern of her, she ran into a group shortly before 01.00, was torpedoed and sunk. Fifteen survivors were picked up and made prisoner.

It was now time for the Coastal Forces craft to intercept the enemy boats which had been driven northwards by the destroyers. Caulfield's MGBs, Unit V, had seen the first actions of *Worcester* and *Mackay* from a distance to the south and had also felt the underwater explosion of the torpedoed trawler. At 01.20 they made contact with three S-boats leaving *Worcester*'s second action and scored hits on these. An hour later three more were sighted on a north-easterly course at high speed, but owing to their large turning circle, the MGBs were unable to manoeuvre quickly enough to engage these.

In spite of their one success in sinking the *William Stephen*, the S-boats failed to make any contact with the main convoy, and what was more, they had had a rude surprise in the fierce reception that greeted them. But the most dramatic incident was yet to come. The MGBs under Lieutenant Marshall, Unit Y, made contact with the S-boats chased away by *Mackay* soon after 02.00. They were only doing 15 knots as one, *S63*, had been badly damaged, and were taken completely by surprise when the MGBs came for them at high speed with all guns firing. *S88* took terrible punishment from this concentrated fire and was soon ablaze from stem to stern. It happened that Korvettenkapitän Lützow, commander of the 4th S-boat Flotilla, was on board this craft and was killed by a direct hit on the bridge.

The remaining boats increased speed and made smoke in an attempt to escape. The MGBs turned to port to cut them off and Marshall in *607* found an S-boat close on his port bow. He increased speed to engage, but the enemy boat suddenly turned to starboard and came towards him with the apparent intention of ramming. Not to be outdone, Marshall put his helm hard to port so that it was he who rammed the enemy, striking him full amidships at full speed. The force of the collision bounced both boats clear of one another. Marshall stopped to take stock of the situation and found, somewhat to his surprise, that his boat was not badly damaged. His casualties were heavy however – five dead and six wounded – caused by a blast of gunfire from the S-boat just before ramming. And most of his guns were out of action.

The S-boat on the other hand was already on fire and as the second MGB, *603*, commanded by Lieutenant F.R. Lightoller, came up to see if Marshall needed help, the enemy boat was seen to sink. Shortly afterwards, the burning *S88* blew up with an explosion that sent debris hurtling 200 feet into the air. Nineteen survivors were picked up and made prisoner. While this was being done, the explosion of another boat going up was seen about a mile off.

In the meantime, all the other Coastal Force craft had been engaged in running battles with further groups of S-boats, in which heavy damage was suffered on both sides. The two MGBs of Unit R, under Lieutenant Edge, were involved in a cat-and-mouse game of stalking one group to prevent them breaking through the cordon. When they did turn north to make a run for it, the two forces converged and in the brief but concentrated action that followed one of the S-boats was severely hit and seen to disappear in a cloud of smoke. The MTBs of Lieutenant Burk, Unit J, had a more difficult time and his own boat was badly damaged by a hit on the bridge which killed the first lieutenant.

As the boats returned to their bases, some of them crippled and only able to move slowly, the events of the night were gradually pieced together. It seemed that the damage inflicted by either side in sixteen separate actions was probably about even. But none of the British craft were lost, as against at least four of the German. As an Admiralty report stated:

> This major E-Boat operation was frustrated with considerable loss to the enemy and the results were a triumph for the Nore organization. Nevertheless it was lucky the convoy was early; it would appear that after *Pytchley* had prevented the first group locating it, the only E-boats which had a chance of finding it and making an attack were those driven off by Unit R.

The successful beating-off of such a large enemy force kept the S-boats well clear of the east coast for a while. As the year ended, Coastal Forces were very much on the attack, harrying enemy shipping from the north – where the Norwegian 54th and now the British 58th MTB Flotilla under Gemmel operated from Lerwick against the Norwegian coast, to encourage the Germans in their belief that the Allies were planning a large-scale invasion of Norway – to the south where the MTBs and MGBs of Plymouth Command were now fighting regularly in the Channel Islands and off the coast of Brittany.

One of the long-standing complaints of the German S-boat crews had been that although their boats were faster than most of those of the British, they suffered from inferior armament. During the winter of 1943/4, however, a number of S-boats were rearmed with 40mm in place of their 20mm guns, which brought an aggressive new spirit amongst the German forces. In the past they had always avoided contact with their opposite numbers whenever possible, not from any lack of bravery or determination, but acting on German Naval Command policy. Unless they were defending their own convoys as escorts, their primary targets were Allied merchant ships, using either torpedoes or mines, and not the small craft of Coastal Forces which they usually hoped to avoid by their superior speed. These tactics had become less and less successful as Coastal Forces developed interception techniques to force the S-boats into combat, and on such occasions the German craft usually found themselves outgunned and at a distinct disadvantage.

Now, with heavier guns, the S-boats showed less reluctance to engage in a direct confrontation and the time came, on the night of 14/15 February 1944, when they actually sought out and hunted a group of British MTBs.

The events of the night began when a group of six S-boats crossed the North Sea with the intention of laying mines off the east coast. They were picked up by shore radar at 23.07 and driven off by the Harwich-based corvettes *Mallard* and *Shearwater*, which were on patrol. As they sped away, the S-boats were seen to jettison their mines. Meanwhile, five MTBs under Lieutenant Derek Leaf DSC had been sent earlier to the south end of Brown Ridge to try to intercept the enemy boats on their home run. The MTBs were 71½-foot BPB craft, able to stand up to long spells at high speed, but even so, they were too late: the enemy were already ahead of them. So Leaf decided to make for Ijmuiden, to be waiting on their doorstep when they returned to base.

Approaching the Dutch coast, however, the MTBs came upon an enemy flak ship and two trawlers. A combined attack was made, in which the flak ship was torpedoed and sunk by *MTB 455* (Lieutenant M.V. Round RNZNVR), while Leaf's boat, *MTB 444*, repeatedly hit one of the trawlers with gunfire and left it burning. In coming in to make another attack, Leaf ran straight towards another enemy ship which he did not see until the last minute. The MTB was heavily hit both above and below the waterline. Leaf, his Petty Officer and two ratings were killed and two others wounded.

This was not realized at the time by the other boats, however, and when three of them regrouped and *444* and *455* could not be seen, Lieutenant C.A. Burk RCNVR, commanding *439*, took over as Senior Officer of the unit and set off to search for the missing boats. Almost immediately, Burk had the nasty shock of discovering by radar that six S-boats were shadowing his unit 1,000 yards off on the port quarter, an almost unheard of occurrence. The enemy craft were allowed to close to 600 yards, at which point further radar contacts, probably more S-boats, were picked up ahead. Burk decided to attack the shadowing boats first, rather than all groups at once. The unit altered course to port, increased to full speed and crossed the bows of the leading S-boat at 100 yards. Fire was opened at this and the second boat in line. Both were hit and the leader silenced and left stopped with a fire burning aft. During this engagement the MTBs were repeatedly hit by small-arms fire.

Burk then turned to attack the second group of six S-boats, but during this manoeuvre *MTB 441* (Lieutenant W. Fesq RANVR) lost contact with the others. While trying to rejoin them he came across two boats which he thought were MTBs but which, after challenges were flashed, turned out to be S-boats. Fire was exchanged and *441* broke away. There were so many radar echoes at this time that Fesq had no means of telling which were friendly and which were enemy craft, so he turned and headed back to base.

The other two boats meanwhile found themselves outnumbered by no less than seventeen S-boats. Fire was exchanged while running at high speed, but the MTBs sustained little damage and only three men were slightly wounded. Eventually they broke off and set off for base, having already established W/T contact with *441* and *455*, which were also returning and not in need of help. No contact could be made with *444* as the wireless on Leaf's boat had been put out of action.

What happened after Leaf was mortally wounded was described by Sub Lieutenant P.P. Bains, the first officer of *444* who took over command:

As all the electrical equipment had been put out of action, I decided it was useless to try to regain contact with the remainder of the unit and so steered a north-westerly course to avoid further enemy boats until 04.15, when I altered for base and increased speed to 30 knots. Smoke and a distinct smell of burning was coming from the W/T compartment (where the telegraphist had been one of those killed; the others were the helmsman and Oerlikon and pom-pom gunners). This was drenched with Pyrene as the source could not be discovered but the smell and smoke persisted all the way back to Lowestoft. A serious leak in the forward mess-deck was discovered, and as soon as the hands could be spared, a chain of buckets was formed. This managed to keep the water down below danger level. There had also been a fire in the engine room which had been put out by the motor mechanic and stokers.

The loss of Derek Leaf, one of the most brilliant of the MTB leaders, was a serious blow to Coastal Forces. It had been he, as Senior Officer of the 3rd MTB Flotilla, who had devised the successful tactics of attacking trawlers from astern as a means of avoiding detection by their hydrophones, which appeared to operate best forward of the beam. Indeed, it was these tactics that had resulted in success on his last attack.

During the three years of night fighting by Coastal Forces, it had been the North Sea which commanded the lion's share of operations. Now it was the turn of the English Channel to come into prominence with the greatest operation of them all, the Normandy landings, in which Coastal Forces had many important roles to play.

As the invasion was to be launched principally by Portsmouth Command, in March a Captain, Coastal Forces, Channel, was appointed (Captain P.V. McLaughlin) to the staff of the Commander-in-Chief, Portsmouth, to take charge of all MTB and ML operations (MGBs were no longer designated separately). Such an appointment was long overdue and came more than a year after the similar appointment in Nore Command which had achieved such good results.

While Captain McLaughlin and his small staff, which included such experienced flotilla commanders as Christopher Dreyer and Peter Scott, made detailed plans for the part that Coastal Forces were to play in the invasion, American PT boats made their first appearance in the Channel, brought over originally at the urgent request of the Office of Strategic Services to land and pick up agents on the French coast. This led to the re-commissioning of Squadron 2, which had previously been wound up in the Solomons at the end of 1943. The first of the Higgins boats, under Lieutenant Commander John Bulkeley, arrived at Dartmouth in April. They were fitted with special navigational equipment to aid them in locating specific points on the French coast, and their officers and men trained in launching and rowing special four-oared boats, constructed with padded sides and muffled rowlocks, so that they could land men and equipment on a beach swiftly and silently on the darkest nights. The first of these cloak-and-dagger operations took place on the night of 19 May, when *PT 71* landed agents with equipment on a beach within 500 yards of German sentries. They continued up until November. The crews never knew the identity of their passengers and never once made contact with the enemy, which was as intended.

To take part in the invasion itself, further PTs were shipped across: Squadron 34 (Lieutenant Allen H. Harris), Squadron 35 (Lieutenant Commander Richard Davis Jr) and Squadron 30 (Lieutenant Robert L. Searles). Bulkeley was appointed as task group commander of all PT operations.

The main job of the British and American craft was to help defend the flanks of the spearhead attack on the shores of the Baie de la Seine and maintain guard over the subsequent flow of cross-Channel traffic. The most likely attacks were expected to come from destroyers, torpedo boats and minesweepers, of which the Germans still had large forces based in the Low Countries and on the Atlantic coast of France, and from S-boats based along the coast from Cherbourg to Holland. In the weeks before the invasion, ten flotillas of MTBs and MLs laid nearly 3,000 mines unobtrusively in areas close to the French coast, while at the same time other MTBs carried out their usual anti-S-boat patrols, and the MLs prepared for their wide range of tasks which were to include minesweeping, duties as escorts and navigational leaders, and shepherding in the landing craft.

Knowing that an invasion was imminent, although not its date or location, the Germans were preparing their own plans. The S-boats played an important part in these and Petersen, as commander of all S-boats in the Channel and North Sea, with his headquarters at Scheveningen, Holland, was involved in a direct battle of wits with McLaughlin and his staff at Portsmouth. In order to hamper the Allied preparations, Petersen increased his patrols until large numbers of S-boats were at sea every night.

Their biggest success came in the early hours of 28 April. A force of six S-boats from the 5th and 9th Flotillas had set sail from Cherbourg the evening before to attack an Allied convoy reported to be in the vicinity of Portland Bill. By the time the S-boats arrived they found they had missed the convoy, which had passed out of the danger area. The German craft were preparing to return home when, to their amazement, they came across a convoy of eight American tank landing ships sailing sedately at only 3½ knots in line ahead across Lyme Bay, off the Dorset coast, with only a corvette as escort, way ahead of the convoy and not guarding its flank. It seemed too good to be true. The S-boats raced into the attack before the Americans knew what had hit them. As the LSTs, packed with men and equipment, scattered in confusion, the S-boats sank two of them with torpedoes and severely damaged a third. The gunners on the other landing craft began wildly firing their machine-guns, often hitting friendly craft. By the time the corvette *Azalea* realized something was wrong and had turned about, the S-boats had sped away, completely unscathed, leaving a death toll of 441 military and 197 naval servicemen, which increased to a total of 749 over the following weeks as more bodies were recovered from the water or floated on to the shore.

News of the disaster came as a shock to General Eisenhower and his commanders who were planning for the great invasion of Europe only five weeks away. The American landing craft were in fact taking part in an exercise to practise amphibious landings on the beach at nearby Slapton Sands, chosen because of its similarity to the beaches of Normandy. If a few small German boats could slip through at night, apparently undetected, and create such havoc amongst just eight landing craft, what might they not do against a target of thousands when the real invasion took place?

If nothing else, the event once again proved the vital importance of coastal waters, both in offence and defence, and the value of small, well-armed boats which were difficult to detect at night. It was a lesson the Royal Navy had learned the hard way earlier in the North Sea and English Channel but a danger underestimated by the Americans – although the US Navy in the Pacific would have told a different story. Plans were put in hand to strengthen the forces defending the Normandy invasion fleet, including the deployment of more British and American motor gunboats. The Royal Air Force began a series of bombing raids against S-boat bases which severely reduced their numbers. And a news blackout was imposed on the fiasco to avoid a loss of morale among the American troops waiting to take part in the invasion, many of them as inexperienced in combat as those who had tragically lost their lives in Lyme Bay.

But in reality, such S-boat successes as Lyme Bay were exceptional. As Kapitänleutnant Rudolph Petersen summed up at the time: 'Owing to the superior radar, strong escorts and air patrols of the enemy, and the German dependence on good visibility (for their boats still lacked radar), each success must be paid for by many fruitless attacks.'

And as the Allies pieced together the events of that night, it became apparent that it was not so much a German success as a chapter of Allied errors. The destroyer *Scimitar* should have been part of the escort, but had been in a collision with one of the landing craft the night before and had put in to Plymouth for repairs. The destroyer *Saladin* was intended to replace her, but through an oversight had not reached the convoy. Shore radar contact with the S-boats had in fact been made and *Azalea* warned two hours before the attack took place, but still the corvette allowed the convoy to proceed slowly right into the enemy's path without any evasive action. Although the *Azalea* was under the orders of US Navy officers, it was her British captain who was censured for not taking more effective measures to defend the convoy. The heavy loss of life included men who had jumped from their sinking or damaged craft and drowned because there were too few life rafts, they had not been instructed properly in the use of life vests, and, in the case of the troops, they were encumbered by their heavy equipment and the helmets they were still wearing.

As stated in Captain Roskill's *Official History of the War at Sea*:

> The first five months of 1944 marked a very important stage in the development of our maritime control over the narrow waters; for it was then that we gradually established a sufficient ascendancy to ensure that, when the invasion fleets set sail for France, the Germans would not be in a position to molest them seriously. The degree of success accomplished could not, of course, be judged until the expedition actually sailed; but by the end of May there were solid grounds for believing that, even though the passage would undoubtedly be contested with all the means available to the enemy, his worst efforts would not suffice to frustrate our purpose. Such was the measure of the accomplishment of the astonishingly varied forces of little ships and aircraft which had so long fought to gain control of our coastal waters, and to deny a similar measure of control to the enemy.

As D-Day approached, so the work of Coastal Forces increased. Now it was not only a matter of laying mines to protect the flanks of the 15-mile-wide path of the invasion fleet across the Channel, but every effort had to be made to prevent S-boats from mining this path or the convoy routes of the invasion forces gathering in harbours along the south coast. There was a momentary alarm when, during an exercise on the night of 18/19 May in which MTBs were to act the part of S-boats to test the defences against these, two real S-boats approached the outer patrols. They were chased off, however, by two SGBs.

It is outside the scope of this book to describe the complex plans for D-Day in detail. Very briefly, Operation Neptune, which was the naval part of the overall invasion, Operation Overlord, called for two great task forces to make landings on either side of a line dividing Seine Bay. To the east was the British area, under Rear Admiral Sir Philip Vian, where three divisions of the British Second Army were to land at three points, 'Sword', 'Juno' and 'Gold', on a 30-mile front between the River Orne and the harbour of Port-en-Bessin. To the west was the American area under Rear Admiral A.G. Kirk, where the US First Army was to make two landings, 'Omaha' and 'Utah', on a 20-mile front. Two follow-up forces were to come in immediately behind the main assaults: Force L, commanded by Rear Admiral W.E. Parry, and Force B, commanded by Commodore C. D. Edgar.

Out of the total of 1,213 warships allocated to the assault phase of the operation, 495 were coastal craft, including SGBs, MTBs, PTs, MLs and HDMLs. With the Eastern Task Force there were ninety craft, including thirty American. With the Western Task Force there were 113, including eighty-one American. It was in the latter area that the SGBs and most of the PTs were to operate. A further 292 craft came under Home Commands, amongst which were thirteen Dutch, eight French and three Norwegian. The landing craft of various types which were to take part in the initial phase totalled 4,126.

D-Day was originally scheduled for 5 June. As instructed, a group of three PTs, which were to be among the spearhead forces, set out on the 4th to rendezvous with minesweepers off the Isle of Wight and began the crossing towards Seine Bay. Only after they left was the belated notice received that D-Day had been postponed until the 6th because of the bad weather forecast. The PTs were all set to make a landing on their own, a day ahead of time, with consequences in revealing to the Germans the location of the invasion that hardly bear imagining. Luckily they were intercepted by a patrolling destroyer when halfway across the Channel and sent back to Portland.

There was great anxiety and tension throughout that day, 5 June. It seemed impossible that the enemy could still be unaware of the Allied plans, considering the sheer size of the operation and the fact that the concentration of shipping of every kind imaginable in the Solent and Spithead was so great that scarcely an empty berth remained in those wide stretches of sheltered water. But there was no sign of enemy activity. As darkness fell on the waiting, darkened ships it seemed, incredible as it was, that the greatest invasion armada the world had ever seen might after all achieve that element of surprise that counted for so much.

CHAPTER 17

D-Day and After

Shortly after 04.00 in the morning of 6 June, Kapitänleutnant Fimmen, commander of the 4th Schnellboote Flotilla at Boulogne, was woken from a heavy sleep with the news that a large Allied invasion force was crossing the Channel towards Normandy. All his boats, which had earlier been withdrawn from anti-invasion patrol because of bad weather, were to put to sea at once.

The invasion itself came as no surprise. Talk amongst the S-boat commanders and crews during the past weeks had been about little else. But where and when would it take place?

Now they knew. The boats had been kept in a state of readiness with ammunition and torpedoes loaded. The crews hastily assembled and at 05.00 the heavy doors of the S-boat bunker were opened, to reveal the grey early morning light. The boats nosed their way into the harbour. And it was at this moment that the air attack started.

Waves of British and American bombers appeared out of the low cloud and bombs began to rain down in the vicinity of the harbour. Fimmen hesitated, then gave the order for the boats to return to the bunker. It would be suicide to stay at sea under such a bombardment. Even as the craft reached cover, the first bombs began to hit the roof of the bunker.

Earlier that morning, the 5th S-boat Flotilla at Le Havre had suffered a similar set-back while trying to leave harbour to attack the invasion fleet. Under heavy fire from Allied fighter-bombers, the craft of Kapitänleutnant Johannsen's flotilla fought back desperately, only partially helped by the somewhat demoralized coastal batteries. But the pressure was too great and they too had to return.

The boats of Kapitänleutnant Mirbach's 9th Flotilla at Cherbourg were the only S-boats that managed to put to sea on the morning of the invasion, but they were immediately repelled by a heavy wall of defensive fire before they could approach even the fringes of the mighty invasion fleet. In desperation they fired their torpedoes at maximum distance with no real chance of hitting anything – they did not – and turned back to harbour. Throughout the early morning and first day of the invasion, all the Channel S-boats were compelled to remain inactive in their bunkers while their frustrated crews, unable to help, anxiously followed the news of the battles that were taking place on the beaches.

The only German warships that were able to come at all near the invasion fleet that morning were three Mowe-class torpedo boats which put out from Le Havre. In one torpedo attack on the exposed flank of the 'Sword' force they managed to hit and sink the Norwegian destroyer *Svenner,* but then the sight of the overwhelming forces ranged against them became too much. They turned and headed back for base at full speed, luckily sheltered by a smoke screen which the British had themselves just laid as a defence against air attack.

That one incident was the only enemy action at sea against the initial landings, which began between 06.30 and 07.45 following repeated air attacks on coastal batteries and enemy communications, and the heaviest naval bombardment along the entire 50-mile front ever to be made from sea to land. Few of the German coastal batteries were able to fire at the oncoming transports, and those that did caused no damage. The Luftwaffe was entirely absent. It was only when the assault forces reached the obstacle-covered beaches that the hard land fighting began. Otherwise the invasion had gone according to plan, with the enemy first taken completely by surprise, and then demoralized by the sheer weight and strength of the Allied forces. As the first day drew to a close, with all the beaches taken and the leading troops already pushing inland while fresh waves of men and supplies landed, it became clear that the Normandy invasion had been more successful than anyone could have dared hope.

Such a state of affairs could not last for long, of course. As the advantage of the initial surprise waned and the existence of the cross-Channel supply route to the Allied forces became known, the Germans began their counter-attacks, increasing in intensity during the long weeks of bitter fighting that followed. The S-boats were out in force from Cherbourg to Le Havre, the ports on either side of the Allied bridgehead, on the night after the invasion. And so began the series of clashes with MTBs that were to rage nightly in the narrow seas until September, when German shipping was finally driven out of the Channel and through the Dover Straits into the North Sea.

It was primarily against the eastern flank that the Germans concentrated their attack. One reason for this was the highly effective defence on the western side that made it seldom possible for enemy craft to break through the screen into the American area. The PTs, for instance, had no contact at all with S-boats between the time of the invasion and right up until August when they were withdrawn from the Normandy area, some to be transferred to operate in the vicinity of the Channel Islands, while others were attached to Portsmouth to work with British Coastal Forces patrolling the eastern flank.

But the main reason was that most of the German destroyers and light craft were concentrated at Le Havre, the more heavily defended port. The losses amongst the Cherbourg-based S-boats were so high during the first week of the invasion that they were transferred to Le Havre. Cherbourg itself fell to American troops on 26 June and from then on the fight in the Channel centred on Le Havre.

During the early hours of 7 June, the S and R boats were out in strength and it was then that the first clashes with MTBs occurred. There were no less than seven encounters during the night, in which the 55th Flotilla under Lieutenant Commander D.G. Bradford DSC RNR and the Canadian 29th Flotilla under Lieutenant Commander Anthony Law DSC RCNVR bore the brunt of the fighting. The first casualty was an R-boat, which blew up after hitting a mine off

Le Havre. During a later engagement with Coastal Forces, *MTB 624* was holed in her petrol tank and *MTB 682* suffered superficial damage, with five wounded. A group of S-boats emerging from Cherbourg were intercepted by the frigate *Stayner* with *MTBs 448* and *478*, and forced to retire after a brief action. Other S-boats were more successful, however, and at 03.00 *LST 715* was torpedoed and set on fire in Seine Bay. All hands were saved but the craft became burnt out.

The weather held up operations for the next few nights and it was not until the early hours of the 11th that the enemy were again out in force. The frigate *Halstead* and a merchant ship were torpedoed in Seine Bay, and the US fleet tug *Partridge*, 25 miles off the French coast. But other attacks on homeward-bound convoys were beaten off by frigates and MTBs of the 55th Flotilla, with considerable damage to the enemy. In another action against S-boats, led by Lieutenant R.T. Sykes with a unit of the 35th Flotilla, Sykes's own boat was hit by gunfire along the hull near the waterline to such an extent that as he increased speed the bottom literally fell out and the boat sank. All the crew were rescued but there was one fatal casualty, a press correspondent who had been on board as a passenger. Later, another unit of the same flotilla, under Lieutenant Commander D.H.E. McCowen DSO, redressed the balance by sinking an S-boat of another group from Cherbourg.

In giving his appreciation for the work of Coastal Forces, the naval commander of the Eastern Task Force stated that it was largely due to their efforts that the area was kept virtually free from surface attack. During the first week of the invasion, apart from damage caused to vessels of both sides, the losses were three S-boats and one R-boat against two MTBs. But what was more important was that, among the mass of Allied shipping in Seine Bay, only two LSTs and six smaller landing craft were sunk. The only other success achieved by German surface forces was the sinking of three small ships in a convoy south of the Isle of Wight.

On 13 June, Beaufighters scored a notable success by sinking three S-boats and one R-boat off Le Touquet. This was followed up shortly after dusk the next day by an even greater disaster to the enemy, when, in a heavy raid by Lancasters of Bomber Command on Le Havre, eleven S-boats were destroyed and three damaged in their concrete bunkers, and three torpedo boats and many smaller vessels sunk in the harbour. Among those killed was Johannsen, commander of the 5th S-boat Flotilla. At one blow, the whole balance of the naval war in this area was changed. The 6th S-boat Flotilla was moved down from Boulogne at the end of the month to make up these losses, but the German boats caused no further damage to Allied craft during June.

The MTBs on the other hand had a chance to renew their attack after so many days of defensive patrols when the Germans began the final evacuation of Cherbourg. Two groups of the 14th MTB Flotilla were waiting outside the harbour for the departure of the last evacuation convoy. The first group of three boats, under Lieutenant G.H. Baker, caught the convoy as it was forming up and scored torpedo hits on two coasters, a trawler and a tug. Then the second group came in, led by the Senior Officer of the flotilla, Lieutenant D.A. Shaw DSC, and scored two more hits plus one possible, in which one ship was seen to sink. Whatever the total result of these attacks – it could not be seen if any vessels managed to escape close in along the shore – only one enemy vessel remained to seaward; this was eventually destroyed by gunfire by three 'D' Class MTBs under Lieutenant Commander McCowen.

In spite of the overwhelming odds against them, for the situation was now reversed with the Allies in complete command of the air over the Channel while destroyers, frigates and coastal craft were constantly patrolling to guard the cross-Channel convoys, the S-boats continued their nightly forays. They remained elusive targets, and although there were constant clashes off Le Havre between them and MTBs supported by frigates, the results were usually inconclusive. Small-boat losses were about even on both sides. On one night for instance the MTBs of the 55th and 29th flotillas, which were helping in the blockade of Le Havre, sank two R-boats by torpedo but shortly afterwards lost *MTB 632* in a gun action with minesweepers. On another night, a series of collisions in Seine Bay resulted in the loss of two British MTBs and one S-boat.

With the fall of Cherbourg there was a change in the boundaries of Portsmouth Command. Previously responsible for operations off the Cherbourg Peninsula, Coastal Forces from Portsmouth were now switched to the eastern flank to cooperate with those flotillas already working in the British Assault Area and maintaining a close blockade of Le Havre, and also to patrol along the coast off Cap d'Antifer to protect the cross-Channel supply route from S-boats that might come down from Boulogne or Dieppe, a task previously undertaken by Dover Command. These dispositions were entirely successful in preventing the S-boats from making any direct attack on the invasion forces, although the superior speed of the enemy boats and the heavier armament they now carried enabled them to evade the close actions needed for their total destruction. The Germans turned their attention instead to the use of R-boats to lay mines off Le Havre, and also to sweep those laid by the Allies, with a view to the eventual evacuation of their shipping from the harbour, which was becoming increasingly inevitable.

It was at this time that two German 'secret weapons' made their surprise appearance. First came the human torpedo, a contraption in which the pilot sat astride an unarmed torpedo with his head in a Perspex dome just above the surface of the water and guided a second armed torpedo, slung underneath, towards a target. A number of these were sent out early on the morning of 7 July amongst anchorages off the British landing areas. They might well have posed a dangerous threat to the crowded shipping, but in fact, slow-moving as they were, it was not very difficult to spot them from coastal craft. Once seen, there was no escape for the pilots. Most were sunk by gunfire, and the same fate overtook others sent out on succeeding nights. A few got through and had limited successes, but the likelihood of survival was so small that after a few weeks this kind of attack was rarely used.

The second of the 'secret weapons' – an ordinary motorboat armed with explosive charges in the bows, which the operator aimed at a target and then jumped clear at the last minute to be picked up by a similar but unarmed boat – was even less successful. The MTBs and MLs had a field day with them, dashing about to pick them off one by one, without having to worry about any return fire and using them virtually as target practice. These too were withdrawn from the scene, after ten of the boats and fourteen of the human torpedoes were sunk in one night's operation.

More serious than these sorry countermeasures, which did little but uselessly waste the lives of brave men, was the renewal of S-boat operations against their traditional targets – the south coast convoys. Less heavily guarded than those crossing the Channel, and with the Allies' main attention diverted to events across the water, these were more vulnerable to enemy attack. On the night of 26/27 July, for instance, S-boats damaged two ships in a convoy off Dungeness, and four nights later they torpedoed five off Beachy Head, of which one sank. In both cases the S-boats got away unscathed.

In the western area, meanwhile, where a flotilla each of SGBs (under Lieutenant Commander P. Baker) and 'D' Type MTBs (under Lieutenant Commander G.C. Fanner DSC) had been attached to Admiral Kirk's Task Force to reinforce his four PT squadrons, there had been few actions in the early days of the invasion and no contacts with S-boats. The biggest problem here was from mines, which had been laid in great numbers by German aircraft and coastal craft. The American and British boats spent much of their time picking up survivors from mined ships, carrying messages and ferrying passengers. (One craft, *PT 71*, commanded by Lieutenant William M. Snelling, took on one tour of the invasion beaches Generals Eisenhower, Marshall, Arnold, Bradley and Hodges, and Admirals Kirk, King, Stark, Moon and Wilkes – probably a record for the amount of gold braid carried in one boat.) After Cherbourg was captured, there was even less for these craft to do, so two of the PT squadrons, 35 and 30, were transferred to Portsmouth, while the remainder joined the Coastal Force units which were operating from Plymouth and Dartmouth off the coast of Brittany and in the Channel Islands. Bulkeley was given command of a destroyer and his post in charge of the PT squadrons was taken by Lieutenant Allen H. Harris. At the same time, Lieutenant Commander Peter Scott MBE DSC and Bar, was appointed as liaison officer between the British and American coastal forces.

The MTBs from Plymouth had already achieved some successes in the Channel Islands. One of the best actions had been on the night of 3/4 July, when four boats of the 65th Canadian MTB Flotilla, commanded by Lieutenant Commander J.R.H. Kirkpatrick DSC, had attacked a convoy off St Malo and sunk two merchant ships, and possibly a third, by torpedo. Then the Coastal Forces of Plymouth Command moved further west, even down as far as the Atlantic coast, while the PTs took over in the Channel Islands. Their exploits were so successful that enemy traffic amongst the islands was brought virtually to a standstill by the time the enemy garrisons on St Malo and the Île de Cezembre fell on 18 August. From that point on, the Channel Islands ceased to be of any military importance.

This success was achieved in spite of a bad start, when, during the first PT operation on 8 August, *PT 509* was destroyed by a German minesweeper off Jersey. The only survivor was the radio operator, John L. Page. While crawling along the deck of his blazing craft, which had drifted alongside the enemy vessel, he came under a hail of small-arms fire which wounded him in thirty-seven places, including a heavy bullet lodged in his right lung after ripping a hole in his back, while his right arm and leg were broken. Incredibly he was still alive when taken prisoner. At the former English hospital at St Helier he underwent four months of continual operations by a German surgeon, who removed dozens of bullets and fragments from every part of his body. He was eventually liberated from the island's prison camp when Germany surrendered the following year.

The battles off the Normandy coast in the meantime had been growing in intensity. By this time the number of S-boats still operational had been whittled down through loss or damage to no more than a dozen, and although they were still a factor, Coastal Forces' worst enemies were now the German shore batteries. It was even thought that the small MTBs, which were faster and less easy targets, would have been more useful than the 'D' boats which had now come to make up a large proportion of coastal craft in operation.

All efforts were concentrated on maintaining the close blockade of Le Havre as the Germans tried to move in supplies and reinforcements, and at the same time evacuate their shipping from the harbour. MTBs fought nightly in support of the blockading destroyers and frigates, to the point where the last week of August was the most eventful period ever for Coastal Forces in the narrow seas.

The actions on the night of 25/26 August were typical of this period. As had become the usual pattern, the Germans began by sending out from Le Havre a unit of S-boats to act as a diversionary force to draw off the MTBs, in the hope that a convoy forming up outside Fécamp could be brought into the blockaded harbour. The S-boats were chased by three MTBs under Lieutenant J.D. Dixon DSC who, as Senior Officer of the 35th Flotilla, had been in the forefront of recent fighting, in spite of being wounded in an action three weeks before D-Day. With their higher speed the S-boats managed to get away and eventually joined the convoy to act as escorts on the return run.

The Allied attack now centred on this convoy. The MTBs were joined by the frigate *Thornborough*, and during an engagement 400 yards offshore at about 02.00 on the morning of the 26th, one coaster was set on fire and an S-boat damaged. Meanwhile, under cover of this action, the French destroyer *La Combattante*, which had already sunk two S-boats earlier in the year, crept up on the convoy unobserved and in attacks lasting nearly an hour sank five coasters, one S-boat and forced another damaged S-boat to become beached. The one armed landing craft and one R-boat, which were all that was left of the convoy, turned back to Fécamp. At this point Lieutenant Shaw, with another unit of three MTBs, came in to cut off their retreat and sank both craft with torpedoes.

Thus no German vessels managed to reach Le Havre that night. And even though a group of R-boats with a trawler and an armed landing craft were able to sail from Dieppe to Fécamp, they were badly damaged in an attack by PT boats under Lieutenant W. Ryan USNR.

Two nights later the Germans evacuated what was left of their shipping from Le Havre, after heavily mining the harbour. As they sailed north-eastwards up the Channel, dodging by day into the harbours of Fécamp, Dieppe and Boulogne for protection, they were hounded all the way by MTBs, frigates and destroyers, which gradually reduced their numbers. By 1 September, all German shipping had been driven through the Dover Straits and into the temporary shelter of their bases on the Belgian and Dutch coasts. The Channel was cleared of the enemy for the first time in four years. The fight for the narrow seas had been won. During that last momentous week, Allied naval forces, including MTBs and PTs, had sunk nine armed landing craft, five coasters, two trawlers, two R-boats and one S-boat, with several more S-boats badly damaged and no longer serviceable. From D-Day until the end of August, MTBs alone claimed thirty-four craft sunk and nine possibles, for the loss of ten to themselves – three in action with S-boats and the remainder by mines. The S- and R-boats sank eleven Allied craft and damaged eight others. The number of S-boats lost from all causes up to the end of 1944 was no less than fifty-three.

The Allied armies on shore were also driving the Germans north. Dieppe fell to the Canadians on 1 September, the Second Army swept through northern France and Belgium to reach Antwerp by 4 September, and the garrison at Le Havre, which had resisted so stubbornly and been temporarily by-passed by the Allies, finally surrendered on 12 September. Most of the Channel ports were liberated by the end of the month, although the German garrison at Dunkirk held on and did not surrender until later in the war. But the main phase of the invasion of Normandy was now completed. With the Channel cleared, supplies could be landed anywhere along the coast without any need for naval support. The main activities of Coastal Forces were therefore transferred to the North Sea. It was at this point that the two PT squadrons, which had been of such help in the Channel operations, were disbanded and the boats transferred to Russia under lend/lease. The only PTs to remain in home waters were those engaged in operations amongst the Channel Islands, based now at Cherbourg.

During the invasion, while many of the east coast MTB flotillas had been transferred to the Channel area, some remained to continue patrols in the North Sea. It was feared that the Germans would have taken advantage of this reduction in the forces available to increase their attacks on east coast convoys, but they did not, partly because of their wariness of the few MTBs that still remained there, but mainly because, as experienced crews and boats were lost, no replacements were forthcoming.

Meanwhile, such MTB commanders as Macdonald, Wright (Lieutenant Commander D.G.H. Wright DSC) and Gemmel, back now from his winter in Norwegian waters, continued their attacks on enemy shipping off the coasts of Holland and Belgium, although there were now far fewer targets. The end of the Normandy campaign, however, brought renewed activity in these waters, with both the British and German flotillas reinforced by boats which had been serving in the Channel. For the Allies it was now a matter of time before the war could be brought to a final conclusion. For the Germans it was a last-ditch stand in which the S-boats fought to the bitter end.

The most decisive operation of this period in the North Sea came on the night of 18/19 September, when four S-boats, covered by three others, made the run from Ijmuiden to deliver supplies to the beleaguered German garrison at Dunkirk. The supplies were landed successfully while the three covering boats of the 10th S-boat Flotilla, commanded by Kapitänleutnant Karl Müller, engaged in diversionary tactics to draw off any British forces in the vicinity. They succeeded only too well and paid dearly for their devotion to this duty. Shortly before 23.00, they were detected by the radar-fitted frigate *Stayner* which was on patrol with two 'D' boats of the 64th Flotilla commanded by Lieutenant Commander D. Wilkie – *MTB 724* (Lieutenant J.F. Humphreys) and *MTB 728* (Lieutenant F.N. Thomson).

Stayner vectored the MTBs on to the course of the enemy craft, while herself preparing to give support with her guns. The MTBs attacked shortly after 23.00 and set fire to one of the S-boats following Müller in arrowhead formation, which had not turned away quickly enough. Then the MTBs turned their attention on the other two boats and it was during the engagement which followed that the German craft collided with each other. Whether it was because of this or the hits that had been received, Müller's boat began to sink and had to be abandoned.

The one remaining S-boat was then chased and reduced to a crawl after hits in her engine room. The MTBs came in for the kill, passing on either side of the S-boat and pouring gunfire into her until she burst into flames. But the enemy craft had been able to return the fire before sinking, hitting Thomson's boat, and it was at this point that the MTBs momentarily lost contact with each other when Thomson's R/T broke down. Sighting each other again, each MTB took the other for one of the enemy and opened fire. By the time they had broken off, hits had been scored on both boats.

Meanwhile, *Stayner* had finished off the first S-boat, completing the destruction of all three enemy craft. When the task of picking up survivors began, after the MTBs had realized their mistake and re-established contact with each other, over sixty prisoners were taken, including Müller himself.

Among the MTBs which had been transferred to the east coast from Dover Command after the fall of Le Havre was the 11th Flotilla, under Lieutenant F.W. Bourne DSC. In the early hours of 1 October, five of these boats were involved in an action against an enemy convoy off Ijmuiden which showed what kind of ordeals the MTB crews sometimes had to undergo in making a successful attack.

The five boats were: *MTB 351* (Lieutenant N.C. Morrow, with the Senior Officer on board), *360* (Lieutenant D.A. Hall), *349* (Lieutenant K.E. Harris), *347* (Lieutenant A.D. Foster) and *350* (Sub Lieutenant H.G. Franklin DSC). They left harbour at 14.45 on 30 September and arrived in position off Ijmuiden at 20.43. Sighting a dark object lying close inshore, they went to investigate and found it to be the wreck of the liner *Strasburg*, sunk earlier in the year, with two masts and a funnel showing above the water.

As the visibility, which had earlier been very good with a nearly full moon, was now closing down to 2 miles, they approached Ijmuiden harbour. Shortly before midnight they sighted a convoy of what appeared to be at least twelve ships. As they altered course to come nearer, two red flares went up from the enemy ships, indicating that the presence of the MTBs was known but they had not yet been seen. The convoy was now found to consist of two or three medium-sized merchant ships, one flying a balloon, escorted by an armed landing craft and several trawlers.

As *MTBs 351, 360* and *349* came in to make a zone attack, in which the torpedoes were launched in a fan-shaped pattern to cover the widest possible area, another landing craft was seen to starboard, at about 400 yards. The MTBs altered course to pass under her stern at 100 yards, still undetected by the convoy's screen. Then at 00.35 one of the merchant ships fired starshell which illuminated the three MTBs. The order to stand by was given by loud hailer and *349* fired her torpedoes at 800 yards at the bridge of the leading ship. The attack was followed up seconds later by *360*, but her torpedoes exploded prematurely about 150 yards ahead of *351*. Because of this, the targets were obscured from Bourne's boat and he could not fire. 'As the unit was under heavy fire from light automatic weapons and 3- and 4-inch shells,' Bourne later reported, 'the first division disengaged to starboard. While doing so, at 00.38 a heavy explosion occurred and a large cloud of smoke was seen in the direction of the leading motor vessel.'

At this point, *351*'s centre engine seized up, reducing her speed to 14 knots, while still under heavy crossfire from one of the screening trawlers and the landing craft. The MTB replied with twin Oerlikon fire on the nearest trawler which had turned to give chase, and succeeded in starting a fire on the stern and hitting the bridge. *MTB 349* was unable to fire as the target was covered by *351*, and in the meantime *360*, which had laid a smokescreen while disengaging, was repeatedly hit by heavy calibre shells, causing a fire to start under the bridge and in the W/T cabin. Her steering gear became jammed and she veered off to port, opening fire with her own twin Oerlikon and inflicting damage on another trawler. Hall then managed to alter course to the north so that he was keeping station with the convoy, a manoeuvre that effectively stopped the enemy fire as his boat was now taken as one of the escorts. All the main engines of *360* had been hit and badly damaged, and in making another attempt to clear the convoy, the boat again came under fire which finally stopped her. Burning furiously and in a sinking condition, she was abandoned by Hall and his crew.

The second division in the meantime, *MTBs 347* and *350*, had followed in to make an attack on the next merchant vessel in line, but found the target obscured by smoke from the gunfire and the burning wreck of *360*. At 00.40, *347* was heavily hit, a 3- or 4-inch shell tearing a large hole in the starboard torpedo tube, and other gunfire knocking the after Oerlikon gunner over the side, wounding two other gun crews, damaging the bridge and port torpedo tube, and setting fire to a pan of ammunition. The range of the enemy merchant ship was now

800 yards, but 347's torpedoes failed to fire because of the damage caused to the tubes. She disengaged, while 350 decided to go in to the attack alone. At 500 yards, Franklin fired his torpedoes at a track angle of 75 degrees to the enemy's observed speed of 10 knots.

Two large explosions were observed on the target, amidships and on the port quarter. By this time heavy tracer was blinding the commanding officer (Franklin), who disengaged to starboard between the line of enemy ships on a reciprocal course to the enemy, passing a small trawler at 25 yards range. This was severely mauled by the MTB's gunners and two fires were seen to start on the bridge and quarter. This trawler was followed by a tug and then a large enemy destroyer, possibly a Narvik. This was the end of the convoy and, observing a burning MTB away to northward (the wreck of 360), 350 turned to close and give assistance.

After driving off two trawlers which were close to and firing at the wreck, 350 began picking up survivors and by 01.00 had rescued five ratings.

Meanwhile Foster's boat, 347, was still being hit while disengaging to starboard. Shells tore into the engine room, put the steering gear out of action, swept the upper deck fittings away and holed the bottom of the boat. Incredibly, the only casualty was the motor mechanic, who had a shell splinter in his shoulder. Attempts were made by the engine-room crew, holding their breath because of the fumes, to plug the hole in the bottom with bunk cushions. This succeeded temporarily, but then the MTB, only able to make 4 knots and on hand steering, crossed the bows of a trawler. Fierce fire was exchanged and the enemy craft left burning. But her return fire had caused further damage to 347, including more leaks forward which were plugged with mattresses.

On the shattered bridge, Foster ordered the helm put hard to starboard to bring the boat on a reciprocal course to that of the enemy. The boat turned, and kept on turning – the rudders had jammed. Circling helplessly out of control, she collided with the next enemy in line, a minesweeper which was firing on both quarters at the other MTBs and which had not seen 347. Bourne wrote:

As the Oerlikons were being reloaded by the one remaining gunner and in view of the extreme proximity, the CO decided not to attract her attention with the .303.

While circling away the steering gear was freed and the boat brought to reciprocal of the enemy's course. As she drew nearer the minesweeper she was hit on the starboard bow by a large shell, presumably fired by one of the inshore escorts. A small fire started in the wheelhouse, but was extinguished at once. About this time three trawlers were seen to port, at a range of 1,000 yards. Two minutes later the next enemy in line, a small tug, was abeam at 75 yards. She was engaged and heavily hit on the bridge by the CO (Foster), who had manned the after twin Oerlikon. Fire was then switched to another dark shape, now abeam at 250 yards. The remaining rounds in the pans, about ten in all, were fired but no hits seen. This target was then silhouetted and seen to be a large destroyer. Fortunately she did not open fire. By the time 347's guns were reloaded, she was no longer visible and no other ships could be seen.

All these events had taken place within just over ten minutes. At 01.10, 347's engines stopped and the mechanics, although working desperately and having to hold their breath whenever they went into the engine room because of the fumes, found they could not be restarted. Foster realized the only way to get back was by a tow, but the chances of that seemed remote. About a mile away to the north he could see a burning wreck with three other craft lying off, but he had no way of knowing that this was actually 360 and the other MTBs looking for survivors as his radio had been put out of action, which also made it impossible to call up the other MTBs.

In case the distant craft proved to be those of the enemy, Foster set about preparing scuttling charges so that his boat would not fall into their hands, but by now 347 was sinking anyway. The wounded were put onto a raft, then the order given to abandon ship. At 01.30 she sank by the stern and disappeared.

All the crew of 347 were later rescued, except for the gunner who had been blown overboard at the beginning of the action; six of them were wounded. Of *MTB 360*, eight of her crew were killed and two seriously wounded. The three surviving boats were little damaged and only the Senior Officer, Bourne, was slightly wounded. It had been a heavy price to pay, but two enemy merchant vessels had been sunk by torpedo, and at least two trawlers and a tug damaged.

Towards the end of the year the main Coastal Force activity in home waters moved even further north, to where the 54th Norwegian MTB Flotilla was still operating from Lerwick against enemy shipping off the coast of Norway. Attacks were carried out in widely separated areas, often two or three on the same night to keep the enemy guessing. In thirty-four operations between 25 September 1944 and 15 February 1945, the Norwegian MTBs sank nine merchant ships (eight by torpedo and one by gunfire), six trawlers and other escort craft, one S-boat and two minesweepers.

By early 1945, with the war in Europe rapidly coming to its conclusion, a reduction in the overall strength of Coastal Forces was already under way. Building programmes were cancelled, older boats paid off and a number of bases closed down. But the final drama in the North Sea had not yet been played out.

In January, there came a sudden resurgence of activity by S-boats, operating mainly from Dutch bases against Allied convoys bringing supplies from the Thames area to the Scheldt Estuary. They came out in groups of six to eight, with as many as six separate groups in one night. In order not to hamper the work of the midget submarines, Germany's most recent 'special weapon', which was certainly more effective than the explosive motorboat or human torpedo, the S-boats were not permitted to lay mines but had to concentrate on making torpedo attacks. They achieved a limited success, sinking one LST off Margate on the night of 15/16 January and one more ship by the end of the month. But in clashes with destroyers and MTBs they usually came off worst – and on 23 January one was even sunk in the Thames estuary by British coastal guns.

The midget submarines did not come up to German expectations, however – of more than eighty captured or sunk, Coastal Forces accounted for twenty-three – and it became apparent that mines laid in Allied shipping routes by the fast and elusive S-boats were still the most effective weapons. Accordingly, towards the end of February, after a lull caused by the bombing of their bases, the S-boats were again out in large numbers, engaged mostly in minelaying in the Antwerp, Scheldt and east coast shipping routes, but also carrying out torpedo attacks wherever possible. One such occasion was on the night of 21/22 February, when two small merchant ships were sunk off the east coast and a third damaged. But it was the mines laid by the S-boats that caused the most damage – those laid in the first two months of the year led to the loss of fifteen ships, totalling 36,000 tons, and four more damaged, against a loss of only four S-boats.

This pattern continued in March, when the S-boats sank only two ships by torpedo off Lowestoft, but another eleven Allied ships were lost to the mines they laid. The MTBs were constantly on patrol to meet this threat, but although they invariably managed to drive off a direct S-boat attack, they found it as difficult as ever to come to grips long enough with the German craft to achieve a conclusive result.

Within a period of one week in April, however, in a series of fierce encounters between S-boats and MTBs that were made possible by the high degree of cooperation which existed by then between Allied air patrols and surface vessels, the S-boats were finally defeated. A major factor in this was the development by the RAF of an excellent airborne radar which could detect enemy craft almost as soon as they left harbour, and track them all the way across until the British boats made contact with them.

It began on the night of 6 April, when a unit of three MTBs under Lieutenant J. May, intercepted a group of five S-boats. In a collision, both May's boat and one of the enemy craft were sunk. An MTB commanded by Lieutenant Foster rammed and sank another S-boat, and severely damaged a third by gunfire. Then, unfortunately, he hit the wreckage of May's boat and his own boat had to be written off. The following night, Lieutenant Dixon sank two S-boats by gunfire in a brilliant action that caused no damage to his own force and won him a Bar to his DSC. Another S-boat was blown up by a mine off Ostend. Five nights later, the patrolling frigate *Ekins* and two MTBs intercepted a group of S-boats on their way to lay mines in the Scheldt estuary, and severely damaged one. The S-boats returned to base without accomplishing their mission – and there they remained for the rest of the war. The night of 12/13 April marked the final action between British and German motor torpedo boats in home waters.

For the first time in over five years, the S-boats were no longer a threat to British coastal convoys. They were beaten ultimately by the joint efforts of the Royal Navy and the RAF's Coastal Command. But it was to naval Coastal Forces that most of the credit was due. Only on one last occasion did the S-boats put to sea again. On 13 May, after Germany's unconditional surrender, two boats flying the white flag sailed from Rotterdam to Felixstowe, bringing with them German naval leaders who were to inform Nore Command of the location of enemy minefields. Amongst them was Kapitänleutnant Fimmen, who had taken over command of the 4th S-boat Flotilla after the death of Lützow. The two boats were escorted into harbour by ten MTBs, on board which were most of the senior officers of the east coast flotillas. After so many nights of fighting against each other, as well as coping with common hardships in the bleak and storm-ridden North Sea, crews of the opposing sides met face to face for the first time, while the British had a chance for their first real look at the elusive *Schnellboote*.

CHAPTER 18

The Riviera War

While the battle in the English Channel was drawing to its end in the late summer of 1944, another invasion took place on yet another front – Operation Dragoon, the Allied assault on southern France. Coastal Forces again had an important role to play, together with the PT boats which had been withdrawn from normal operations in the Ligurian Sea on 1 August to prepare for what was primarily an American operation.

The military plan in brief was to land three American divisions and a French armoured brigade on five beaches along a 45-mile stretch of coast east of Marseilles, between Cavalaire Bay and Agay, at 08.00 on 15 August. An airborne division was to drop inland before the main assault to hold up German reinforcements. The follow-up forces, consisting of seven French divisions, were to commence landing on the day of the invasion. Designated as the Seventh Army, the overall military force was commanded by Lieutenant General A.M. Patch, US Army, while Vice Admiral H.K. Hewitt USN, was in charge of the naval side of the operation.

Most of the PTs were to be used in their by now accustomed role of making feint landings to throw the Germans off balance and divert their forces from areas where the real landings were taking place. Another group was assigned to the task force whose job it was to land US Rangers on Cap Negre and the offshore islands of Levant and Port Cros to capture the heavy enemy coastal batteries that might have endangered the left flank of the main assault. Meanwhile, the four ML and three HDML flotillas, which had assembled at the Coastal Forces base at Maddalena, were to undertake a variety of duties, including sweeping mines ahead of the convoys and landing craft, patrolling the beaches and acting as air/sea rescue craft. The 7th MTB Flotilla was to help to guard the right flank against surface attacks by German craft from Genoa and Spezia, although few were expected with the very limited naval forces known to be available to the enemy.

The landings were a complete success. At no point was there determined resistance from the enemy and the only Allied shipping losses – one LST, three MLs, three PTs and one landing craft – were almost entirely due to mines. It was only towards the end of the month, by which time the land forces were well on the way to taking the entire coastline from Marseilles to Nice, that Coastal Forces came into direct contact with the enemy in the invasion area. Just as during the Normandy invasion, it was against human torpedoes and explosive motorboats which the Germans began to launch in large numbers. But they proved no more successful in the Mediterranean than they had in the English

Channel. With the help of air patrols, the PTs and MTBs located and destroyed most of them before they even had a chance of approaching the Operation Dragoon support ships. Even an attempt by the one-man submarines failed to cause any damage, and after a particularly disastrous sortie from their base at San Remo on the night of 25/26 September, when only two returned from a force of ten, they were not used again.

By that time, most of the MTBs and PTs had resumed their patrols in the Gulf of Genoa, hunting down the enemy convoys moving between Genoa and Spezia. Coastal Forces now operated from a new base at Leghorn on the Italian mainland, following the closing down of Calvi and Bastia, which brought them much nearer to their targets. In September, no less than seven F-lighters, one merchant ship, one corvette, and four barges were sunk, with more claimed as probables.

After these losses, the Germans considerably increased their convoy escort forces, as well as installing even heavier guns on the F-lighters, and their coastal batteries became more watchful for the marauding MTBs. These countermeasures made it much more difficult for attacks to be carried out, and, allied to the fact that weather conditions were worsening with the approach of winter, the number of successful Coastal Force actions showed a marked decline during the autumn. In October, the sixteen remaining PTs of Squadron 15 were transferred to the Royal Navy under lend/lease, thus ending their eighteen months of operations by American crews in the Mediterranean. Squadron 29 was also withdrawn, some of the boats being transferred to Russia, while the others returned to the Melville Training Centre in the United States. Only Squadron 22 remained to continue operations in the Mediterranean, carrying out patrols from St Maxime, and then, in October, from Leghorn until the last days of the war.

At about this time, Commander Allan was appointed Senior Officer, Inshore Squadron, in place of Captain N. Vincent Dickinson, who became Senior Naval Officer, Northern Adriatic. It was to the Adriatic that the centre of Coastal Force activities now shifted. The evacuation of German garrisons from the southern Dalmatian islands, which carried through until the end of September, gave the MTBs many more targets, and they were not slow to take advantage of this.

On 3 September, four MTBs of Bligh's 57th Flotilla carried out what was to become the longest single Coastal Forces patrol of the Mediterranean war. They left Brindisi at 02.45, Bligh in *MTB 662*, with *674* (Bowyer), *637* (Davidson) and *634* (Blount), to patrol the Gulf of Patras off southern Greece. The German evacuation of the Dalmatian islands was linked to their withdrawal from Greece and the Aegean islands, and it was thought that the MTBs might have a chance of intercepting some of the departing enemy craft.

The journey across to the Greek coast took over fifteen hours, but by midnight the MTBs were carrying out a reverse sweep westwards off Cape Oxia. No shipping was sighted until 00.40 when two schooners in full sail were seen to the north-west. The MTBs altered course to attack these, but moments later another two vessels, thought to be S-boats, were seen in the opposite direction.

It was decided that the schooners could be left until later and the unit altered course again to close the new targets. At a range of 150 yards all four MTBs opened fire, scoring repeated hits. The enemy craft fired back for some three minutes, then fell silent. One of them turned away to the north-east, but was chased and sunk by *MTB 634*.

Meanwhile, another small craft was seen heading towards Oxia Island. Leaving the second damaged enemy boat, the MTBs gave chase. Bligh closed and opened fire at a range of 100 yards, but his own boat was hit by return fire and flames leaped alarmingly from the port flag locker. While these were put out, with *674* standing by in case help was needed, the enemy craft sank. Then yet another appeared and this time it was *637* that gave chase. The same thing happened – when *637* started shooting, she was herself hit and set on fire. But Bligh's boat, the fire now under control, and *674* came up with guns blazing and within two minutes this enemy craft also turned over and sank.

A small caique was then spotted inshore and sunk by *662*. The sole Greek occupant was taken off alive, though wounded.

At 01.33 the MTBs reformed and returned to look for the two schooners. They were soon sighted to the east, rounding the point. Both were sunk and while *634* picked up the survivors, the other three boats went back to watch the main channel for further shipping, although none was sighted. At 05.00, the MTBs made contact with the British destroyer *Quantock*, also patrolling these waters, and transferred the sixteen German and Greek prisoners, most of whom were wounded, and the sole British casualty, Stoker Cuthbert Mayo of *662*, who had been wounded in the leg by cannon shells.

The most interesting prisoner was a German major with the Iron Cross and clusters, who was picked up by *662*; his two demands were for whisky and his friend the German naval captain. Bligh was unable to satisfy him because, as he put it later, 'the former was scarce and the latter was presumably killed.'

The MTBs arrived back at Brindisi at 01.30 the following morning, having been continuously under way for forty-seven hours, covering a total of 535 miles. Apart from the two schooners and the small caique, the other three craft sunk and one presumed sunk were unknown, but one was thought to be an Italian MS boat, one a Pil boat and one an I-lighter.

The Canadian-led 56th Flotilla, now commanded by Lieutenant Commander Cornelius Burke, also worked effectively during this period at cutting off the enemy's retreat, so that very few of the island garrisons got away unscathed. By the end of October, the southern area was completely free of German forces. And although a few isolated German garrisons remained on some of the Aegean islands, they were no longer capable of doing much harm. Rather than undertake large-scale landings to capture these islands, they were by-passed in much the same way as the Americans had done with Japanese-occupied islands in the Pacific. Allied maritime power was now restored over most of the Mediterranean. Apart from a short stretch of coast in north-west Italy, only the northern Adriatic still remained in enemy hands. It was here that Lancaster's

20th MTB Flotilla had been patrolling north of Ancona and in the Gulf of Venice, but few targets were to be found there at this time.

Also in the northern Adriatic were the remaining S-boats, now formed into the 1st Division under Kapitänleutnant Wuppermann. They concentrated their efforts on minelaying operations in the swept channels, and a number of MTBs and MLs fell victim to these during the winter of 1944/5.

Meanwhile, on the Dalmatian coast, the Coastal Forces base at Vis was moved up to the island of Ist to be closer to the withdrawing German forces. Lieutenant Commander Morgan Giles established his headquarters there, and by the beginning of November the 57th and 20th Flotillas were carrying out operations amongst the northern islands with the Partisans. These were now becoming somewhat hampered because, with the war approaching its end, they were increasingly concerned with their post-war political aims, and were fighting the rival Chetnik groups as much as they were the Germans.

In December, Coastal Forces moved yet further north, to the island of Zara, where they were joined by most of the boats of the 60th Flotilla from the Aegean. A new 28th Flotilla of Vospers also arrived at this time, of which Lieutenant Charles Jerram DSC was appointed Senior Officer.

During the first three months of 1945, coastal craft of Allan's Inshore Squadron operating from Leghorn continually harassed the German supply traffic in the Gulf of Genoa, although not all of the successes claimed in perfectly good faith at the time were later confirmed by enemy records. Nevertheless, up until mid-April, when the Squadron was disbanded, the MTBs and PTs played their part in the virtual elimination of enemy craft in these waters. These consisted largely of 'small battle units', made up of one- and two-man motor torpedo boats of the kind originally developed by the Italian Navy, as well as midget submarines, but they were even less successful than those used in the English Channel and off Southern France. The enemy fought in them with desperate determination, but they were just no match against the combined efforts of air and coastal forces.

In the Adriatic, Jerram had worked up his new 28th Flotilla in time to make an outstanding contribution during the short time left before the war ended. He began operations from Ancona early in February, and, in two patrols within six nights of each other, sank two large merchant ships and a corvette. In March the score was even higher: five F-lighters and a merchant ship. The flotilla's last successful action was on the night of 12/13 April, when three boats left Ancona to patrol off Caorle Point to the north of Venice: *410* (Lieutenant A.O. Woodhouse RNZNVR, with Jerram on board), *409* (Lieutenant C.R. Holloway) and *408* (Lieutenant R.P. Tonkin). It was a night of low cloud, slight showers, no moon and visibility very bad until it cleared slightly just before midnight to 2,500 yards.

Reaching a position 6 miles off Caorle Light at 22.01, the unit stopped and cut engines to wait. An hour later, radar contact was made with an enemy convoy approaching from about 4 miles to the north-east. The MTBs started up and headed in that direction at 8 knots. Several minutes later the contact was lost, but by this time the enemy's course and speed had been plotted and Jerram was able to fix a point of interception. Speed was increased in order that the attack should not be prolonged, in view of the rapidly lifting visibility.

It was nearly midnight when seven long dark shapes were sighted, bunched together into two main groups, with a single ship well astern. Jerram gave the order 'Flag Four' over the R/T – attack with torpedoes. He himself swung round towards the second of the two groups and fired both torpedoes at two of the enemy craft which were moving very close together and which had by then been identified as F-lighters. It was a remarkable feat of aiming for both targets were hit and sunk. The other two MTBs followed up the attack and three more F-lighters in the first group blew up and sank.

The remaining F-lighter and the escort vessel fired back at the MTBs under starshell illumination, but no damage or casualties were suffered. Having fired all torpedoes – with five hits out of six, certainly one of the highest percentages of success in any MTB attack – the unit turned and headed back to Ancona.

The last successful action by Coastal Forces in the Mediterranean came the following night when two boats of the 59th MTB Flotilla, *MTBs 670* (Hewitt) and *697* (Booth) torpedoed and sank the ex-Italian torpedo-boat *TB 45* off the Dalmatian coast. But three nights later *MTB 697*, again out on patrol in an area which was supposed to have been cleared of mines by the Partisans, suddenly struck a mine and broke in two, both halves burning furiously. The horrified crews of the two boats with her, *MTBs 658* and *633*, picked up several terribly wounded survivors, but ten of *697*'s crew were never found.

During the last days of April, unable to put to sea because of lack of fuel and supplies, the 1,500 officers and men of Wuppermann's 1st S-boat Division were ordered to prepare for fighting on land. But on the 29th, as the Partisans and British forces closed in on Trieste after capturing Venice, all the German forces in Italy surrendered unconditionally, to take effect on 2 May. It now became a matter of avoiding capture by the Partisans, who were not renowned for their consideration of the treatment of prisoners. Accordingly, on the evening of 4 May, Wuppermann put all the available diesel fuel into five of his S-boats, loaded them with 300 men each, his entire force, and set out from Trieste for the Royal Navy's base at Ancona.

The German boats arrived in the early hours of 5 May and, to an extremely surprised port commander, Wuppermann surrendered his forces. A request by him to return to Istria to pick up 3,000 German troops who were trapped and in danger of falling into Partisan hands was refused. British guards surrounded the five S-boats, and their crews and passengers. In a final ceremony, reviewed by Wuppermann, the red battle flags of the enemy boats were lowered. Then he and his men began the long journey to a naval prison camp in the North African desert, not far from the scene of so many earlier German victories.

The war in Europe was over, the once mighty German forces crushed. But there was still another enemy to be beaten in the Far East.

CHAPTER 19

Return to the Philippines

The liberation of the Solomon Islands and New Guinea by the South and South-West Pacific Forces of the United States, in which those Japanese troops who had not managed to evacuate were isolated in their island garrisons and either starved to death or surrendered, made possible the final great campaign of the war in the Pacific – the return to the Philippines, from where the Americans had been forced to retreat two and a half years earlier. Just as the PTs had been amongst the last of the US forces to fight back against overwhelming odds in the dark days of April 1942, so now they were in the van of the battle to vindicate that earlier defeat.

Before a major invasion of the Philippines could begin, with landings on Leyte by Lieutenant General Walter Krueger's Sixth Army, it was decided that a base was necessary between Mindanao and New Guinea to provide land-based air support. The strategy of leap-frogging from one island or location to another, and bypassing others, was brought into play from the very start of the Philippines campaign. There were two possible islands on which to make a landing: Halmahera or Morotai. The latter was chosen, and the Morotai Task Force under the command of Rear Admiral Daniel E. Barbey landed there on 15 September 1944. The following day Commander Bowling, commanding the Motor Torpedo Boat Squadrons of the Seventh Fleet, arrived with two tenders and forty-one PTs of Squadrons 9, 10, 18 and 33. Patrols began that night in the 12-mile strait between the two islands to prevent the numerically superior Japanese forces on Halmahera from launching a counter-attack on Morotai. These patrols continued without break until the end of the war eleven months later, when it was discovered that no less than 37,000 Japanese had been kept isolated on Halmahera and denied any chance of attacking the US air and PT bases on Morotai. During that time the PTs destroyed over fifty barges and 150 other small craft that were attempting to supply or evacuate the island, or to reinforce the small Japanese garrison on Morotai, which remained there ineffectively until the end of the war.

Even before these night patrols started on 16 September, the PTs were in action during a rescue mission earlier on in the afternoon. The pilot of one of the Navy carrier-borne fighters that had been giving support to the landing of the Morotai Task Force had been shot down during a sweep over Halmahera and had drifted in a rubber raft to within 200 yards of the enemy-occupied beach at Wasile Bay. Other planes circled the area to keep the pilot, Ensign Harold A. Thompson, in sight and to strafe the Japanese gun positions. But attempts to rescue him by Catalina flying-boat failed because of heavy anti-aircraft fire.

Hearing of the pilot's desperate situation, the crews of two PTs volunteered to go on a dangerous daylight mission to try to rescue him. They were led by Lieutenant A. Murray Preston, commander of Squadron 33, in *PT 489* (Lieutenant Wilfred B. Tatro), accompanied by *PT 363* (Lieutenant (Junior Grade) Hershel F. Boyd). From the time the boats arrived at the entrance to Wasile Bay to when they left nearly three hours later after rescuing Thompson, they were under constant heavy shellfire from the Japanese shore batteries, and only managed to avoid being hit by zig-zagging at high speed across a minefield. Miraculously no one was hurt and only superficial damage was done to the boats. For this action, Lieutenant Preston was awarded the Medal of Honour, one of only two such awards made to PT men during the entire war (the other was to Lieutenant Bulkeley for his exploits in the Philippines in 1942). Navy Crosses were awarded to Tatro and Boyd, and also to Lieutenant Donald F. Seaman and Charles D. Day, Motor Machinist Mate First Class, both of whom dived overboard from *PT 489*, swam to the raft on which Thompson was floating and towed it back to the boat.

Following the establishment of bases on Morotai, General MacArthur's original plan was to begin the Philippines operation with full-scale landings on Mindanao, the most southerly of the islands. But by mid-September carrier planes of Admiral Halsey's Third Fleet had been so successful in battering the Japanese shore defences, sinking many of their ships and destroying some two hundred of their aircraft, that Halsey suggested Mindanao could be bypassed by landing instead at Leyte, which was to be the second objective once Mindanao was seized. This plan was agreed by Admiral Nimitz, Commander-in-Chief, Pacific, and approved by MacArthur. The attack on Leyte took place on 20 October, two months earlier than originally planned, with the Seventh Fleet landing troops of the Sixth Army, while the powerful Third Fleet provided naval cover and support.

PTs arrived in Leyte Gulf on the morning of the following day, and started patrols that night. They had made the 1,200-mile voyage from Mios Woendi, New Guinea, under their own power, refuelling from the tenders which had come with them. They totalled forty-five boats from Squadrons 7 (Lieutenant Commander Robert Leeson), 12 (Lieutenant Weston C. Pullen Jr), 21 (Lieutenant Carl T. Gleason), 33 (Lieutenant A. Murray Preston) and 36 (Lieutenant Commander Francis D. Tappaan). Commander Bowling sailed with them. They saw action almost immediately, and sank seven barges and one small freighter during their first three nights at Leyte. But this was only a prelude to what was to come, when the PTs took part in one of the three naval engagements fought on the night of 24/25 October which were later designated as the Battle of Leyte Gulf, one of the great naval battles of the war.

With their inner defences breached by the Leyte landings, the Japanese were prepared for the first time since Guadalcanal to gamble on an all-out naval engagement to try to win back the initiative. Three great task forces were sent from the south, west and north to converge on Leyte Gulf. The first, comprising battleships, cruisers and destroyers, was heading through the Sulu Sea in the

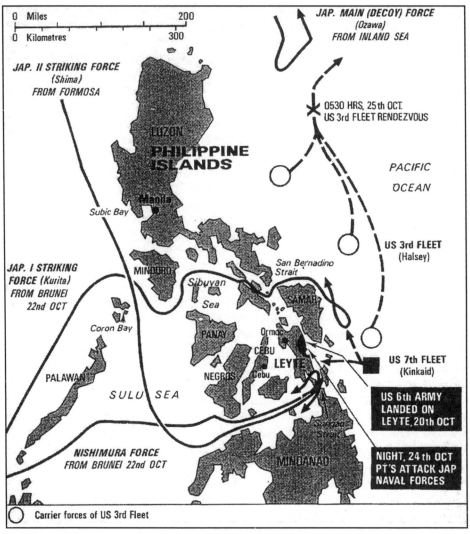

The Philippines; PTs in action in the Surigao Strait.

direction of Surigao Strait, between Leyte and Mindanao. It was in the battle against this force by ships of the Seventh Fleet that the PTs played an important part. A more powerful central Japanese force, approaching from the west, towards San Bernardino Strait, and an even larger carrier and battleship force off Cape Engano, approaching from the north, were met by ships of the Third Fleet.

The enemy force heading for Surigao Strait was divided into two groups. In the van, and under the command of Vice Admiral Shoji Nishimura, were the two battleships *Yamashiro* and *Fuso,* the heavy cruiser *Mogami,* and four destroyers. About 20 miles behind, under the command of Vice Admiral Kiyohide Shima, were the heavy cruisers *Nachi* and *Ashigara*, the light cruiser *Abukuma*, and a further four destroyers. Disposed against them were the Seventh Fleet's six old battleships, eight cruisers, twenty-five destroyers, and thirty-nine PTs. Under normal circumstances these ships would have had a greater firepower than the Japanese, but most of their ammunition had been used up during the invasion bombardment, a factor that was very much on the mind of the US commander, Rear Admiral Jesse B. Oldendorf, as the enemy came steaming through the Mindanao Sea on the night of 20/21 October. No shell could be wasted, which meant that it was vital to have accurate information as to the enemy's movements.

The American warships were strung out across the northern end of Surigao Strait, guarding the entrance to Leyte Gulf and the transport shipping there which was the enemy's major target. The PTs were dispersed in sections of three through the Strait, along the coasts of Mindanao, Leyte and Bohol, and far out into the Mindanao Sea. Their main purpose was scouting, to watch for the approach of the enemy and keep the main American force informed of his movements. It was only a secondary part of their mission to carry out actual attacks. Nevertheless, attack they did, in spite of the odds against them.

It was shortly before midnight when the ships of Admiral Nishimura's force first appeared on the radar screens of three PTs stationed in the Mindanao Sea. The weather by that time had deteriorated; it was very dark with low cloud and frequent rain squalls limiting visibility. Before the PTs could get within torpedo range, the enemy's big guns opened fire on them from a distance of 3 miles. *PT 152* (Lieutenant (Junior Grade) Joseph A. Eddin) was hit and set on fire, and one of her gunners fatally wounded. As she and the other boats retired behind smokescreens, pursued by a destroyer and two cruisers, while the two battleships sat back and continued to fire at long range, illuminating them with starshell, the concussion caused by the bursting shells put all their radios out of action. It was not until the 23-minute chase was called off by the enemy, and contact was made with another PT section, that at ten minutes past midnight the first report could be made to the main fleet on the position, course and speed of the enemy ships.

PTs stationed close to and in the middle of Surigao Strait moved in to the attack as the enemy ships approached. Many 40mm hits were scored, but the return fire from the big enemy ships was so intense that most of the torpedoes fired missed their targets. One torpedo hit on a destroyer was claimed by *PT 493* (Lieutenant (Junior Grade) Richard W. Brown). But shortly afterwards his boat was hit by 4.7-inch shells, killing two men and wounding Lieutenant Brown, his second officer and three men. The boat was beached and later sank, after the casualties and the survivors had been taken off.

Meanwhile, after the PT attacks, the enemy had come up against the main American force. First there was a succession of three coordinated destroyer torpedo attacks, then the American cruisers and battleships opened fire with devastating accuracy. The enemy were caught in a trap and utterly defeated, losing two battleships and three destroyers almost before they could open fire. The heavy cruiser and one destroyer escaped, but the cruiser was eventually sunk on the 26th by US aircraft.

The destroyer *Shigure* was thus the only ship of Admiral Nishimura's force to survive the battle. It was at this ship, coming back down Surigao Strait, that *PT 137* (Lieutenant (Junior Grade) Isadore M. Kovar) fired a torpedo at 03.35. The torpedo missed but just at that moment the second force of Admiral Shima was entering the Strait. The torpedo ploughed on through the water and struck the light cruiser *Abukuma*, damaging her so badly that her speed was reduced to 10 knots and she had to drop out of formation (she was sunk later by US bombers off Mindanao on the 26th).

The crippling of the *Abukuma* threw Admiral Shima's force off balance. When, shortly afterwards, his flagship *Nachi* was damaged in a collision with the burning *Mogami* of Admiral Nishimura's force, and realizing for the first time the extent of the destruction that had already been caused to the Japanese fleet, Shima turned and fled. During his retreat, the destroyer *Shiranuhi* was also sunk by US planes.

Lieutenant Kovar's action against *Abukuma*, for which he was awarded the Navy Cross, was the most dramatic success of the PTs that night. But even more important was their work in harassing the enemy ships during their approach and passing on accurate information to the main American force, which could then carry out their attack with the greatest precision and before their limited supply of ammunition ran out. At roughly the same time as the Battle of Surigao Strait was taking place, Rear Admiral C.A.F. Sprague's escort carriers and destroyers off Samar managed, against great odds, to hold off the enemy battleship and cruiser task force that was approaching from the west. Meanwhile, off Cape Engano, Admiral Halsey defeated the northern force. The Japanese lost four carriers, a battleship, six cruisers and four destroyers in these actions and the aircraft attacks which followed, and suffered damage to fifteen other ships. As Admiral Nimitz later reported: 'Our invasion of the Philippines was not even slowed down, and the losses sustained by the Japanese reduced their fleet from what had been at least a potential menace to mere nuisance level.'

This crushing defeat in the Battle of Leyte Gulf had its effect on the enemy. With the probability of losing the war increasing daily as the Americans poured more men and supplies onto their foothold in the Philippines, the Japanese began to launch furious air attacks on US shipping in Leyte Gulf, regardless of the cost to themselves. The Kamikaze suicide planes appeared for the first time, and it seemed that the PTs and PT tenders were being sought out as one of their main targets. With skilful handling, the boats often managed to manoeuvre out of the way of falling bombs or diving aircraft, but there was a sharp increase in the number of craft lost because of these attacks.

Meanwhile, the work of barge hunting went on, and during the weeks just prior to the US Army landings on the island of Mindoro on 15 December, the PTs began to have frequent contact with enemy destroyers for the first time in the South-West Pacific. A number of torpedo hits were made, resulting certainly in damage to the destroyers and possibly their destruction, although this was usually difficult to assess. There was no doubt, however, about the action fought on the night of 11/12 December by *PTs 492* (Lieutenant Melvin W. Haines) and

490 (Lieutenant John M. McElfresh), which was in fact the last destroyer action in the Leyte area. Lieutenant Haines led the attack on a single destroyer sighted by radar off the west coast of Leyte. His four torpedoes and two of *PT 490* were launched at 1,000 yards from the target. Two of them hit with tremendous explosions and the destroyer, later confirmed as the 1,315-ton *Uzuki*, sank immediately and before she was even aware of the presence of the PTs.

The enemy's attempt to reinforce Leyte kept the PTs in constant action, sinking many freighters, barges and other small craft. When, by the end of December, the Eighth Army had taken practically the entire island, the PTs moved up to operate from a base at Ormoc. They were Squadrons 7 (Lieutenant Roger H. Hallowell) and 12 (Lieutenant Weston C. Pullen), later relieved by Squadron 25 (Lieutenant Commander Theodore R. Stansbury). Ranging for considerable distances amongst the islands, they fought many daring actions until at the end of March 1945 the Eighth Army entered Cebu City. During that time they sank over 140 Japanese barges, over sixty other miscellaneous craft loaded with reinforcements, equipment and supplies, and destroyed six aircraft.

At Mindoro, meanwhile, the US invasion force which had landed on 15 December was accompanied by Squadrons 13 and 16, with *PTs 227* and *230*, under the operational command of Lieutenant Commander Burt Davis. They gave valuable assistance against the enemy's constant air attacks, bringing down over twenty planes during the first few days of the landing. And then, on 26 December, the news was received that an enemy task force of one battleship, one cruiser and six destroyers was approaching Mindoro. It seemed possible that the Japanese were planning to make an amphibious landing on the island to regain control of it, but in fact their intention was to bombard the American positions. The PTs were the only Allied naval forces present at that time and they set off against overwhelming odds to try to prevent an invasion should it take place. In the event, the Japanese force was driven off by the relentless attacks of US aircraft, although the PTs clashed briefly with some of the ships. And then at the last minute, as the enemy force was steaming northward, *PT 223* (Lieutenant (Junior Grade) Harry E. Griffin Jr) torpedoed and sank the 2,100-ton destroyer *Kiyoshimo*, one of the most powerful in the Japanese Navy, which had previously been damaged during the air attack.

In January, US ground forces continued their island-hopping strategy with a major assault on Luzon, the most northerly of the larger islands. The PTs once again took a foremost part in this, carrying out diversionary attacks beforehand, escorting the landing parties, and themselves landing scouts and raiders behind enemy lines, working in conjunction with guerrilla forces which were already harassing the enemy. For this purpose, Squadrons 8 (Lieutenant Robert A. Williamson), 24 (Lieutenant Stanley C. Thomas) and 25 (Lieutenant Commander Stansbury) were transferred temporarily to Task Group 77.11, returning to Leyte Gulf in February. Meanwhile, Squadrons 28 (Lieutenant Commander George A. Matteson Jr) and 36 (Lieutenant John W. Morrison Jr), under the tactical command of Lieutenant Commander Tappaan, were already operating off Luzon with the Sixth Army that had landed in Lingayan Gulf on 9 January.

By this time, with more PTs being made available as a result of the ending of the New Guinea campaign, the number of squadrons operating in the Philippines had been increased to twenty, for which many more bases had to be established. Mindoro became a principal repair and staging base, and patrols from there continued until April. The Japanese no longer dared to venture into the open sea with their small craft and much of the work of the PTs was in ferreting them out in enemy-held bays and inlets. Coron Bay, south-east of Mindoro, proved to be one of their best hunting grounds, but the PTs by no means had it all their own way. Apart from frequent air attacks, both on their bases and individually while at sea, typhoons and rainstorms had to be coped with. Bases were often reduced to seas of mud, 'making it an effort just to exist there', wrote Captain (formerly Commander) Bowling.

It was soon after the Lingayan Gulf landing that a new threat became apparent – the Japanese suicide boats which, in the manner of the Kamikaze planes, were small motorboats loaded with explosives and then driven against Allied ships. With virtually no Navy left to fight with, it was to this kind of warfare that the Japanese were reduced in the final months of their desperate and suicidal struggle. One of the main tasks of the PTs was to seek out and destroy these craft, preferably in their hideouts amongst the islands before they had a chance to be used.

With the reopening of Subic Bay as an American naval base at the end of January, the final drive began to liberate Manila. It was fitting that in February the first Allied warships to enter Manila Bay since the surrender of Corregidor in May 1942 were PTs – boats of Squadrons 21 (Lieutenant Carl T. Gleason) and 27 (Lieutenant Henry S. Taylor), patrolling south from Subic Bay. It was also fitting that following the liberation of Corregidor after a fierce twelve-day battle, General MacArthur, who had left the Rock in *PT 41* on 11 March 1942, returned to it in another PT, *373*, on 2 March 1945. Manila itself fell a day later.

During March and April, PTs continued to work with the Army in the liberation of the smaller islands of the Philippines. But the campaign had passed its peak. With sea and air superiority established by the PTs and American aircraft, the central Philippines had become a vast trap for the Japanese, from which there was no escape. Their remaining garrisons faced either surrender or annihilation. It was now that American and Australian forces turned their attention to Borneo. Danger from Japanese suicide boats was still very real and before the landings, first on the island of Tarakan in north-east Borneo on 1 May, then at Brunei Bay on the western coast on 10 June, and finally at the great oil port of Balikpapan to the south-east on 1 July, PTs were sent on ahead to sink these craft and to strafe enemy shore installations.

The final area of operations for PTs in the Pacific was to be Okinawa. But soon after the first boats arrived in August, hostilities ceased with the Japanese surrender.

At that time there were twenty-five PT squadrons in commission in the Pacific. Examination showed that the great majority of the boats were defective because of broken frames, worms and dry rot, broken keels and battle damage. And yet these were the boats, with the men who sailed in them, that had contributed so greatly to the final victory.

CHAPTER 20

Arakan

While the momentous events of 1944 were taking place in Europe and American strategy was sweeping the Japanese from the Pacific, the men of South-East Asia Command under Admiral Lord Louis Mountbatten were fighting the 'forgotten war' in which, for a time at least, there were no great victories to engage the world's attention.

Having taken control of almost the entire eastern coastline of the Indian Ocean, from Java, Sumatra, Malaya and up to Burma, the Japanese were on the doorstep of India, held back only by outnumbered British and Empire forces. Allied efforts to take the offensive from the start had been centred on Burma's Arakan coast, with the main intention of capturing the Japanese stronghold at Akyab. The first Arakan campaign started in September 1942, in which MLs based at Chittagong had comprised most of the light naval forces available to support the Fourteenth Army by offshore raids. But there were not enough of them to contribute effectively to the war on land, and by February 1943 the Allied forces were back where they started. The Japanese remained dominant in the Bay of Bengal.

In August 1943, Mountbatten was appointed as Supreme Allied Commander, South-East Asia, with the directive to originate plans for combined operations. His first intention was to make a major attack on northern Sumatra, but with preparations going ahead for the Normandy and southern France invasions, there were just not the sufficient forces available. So he turned to a lesser alternative aimed at recapturing the Andaman Islands and renewing the assault on the Arakan coast, while at the same time the Chinese would launch an offensive in northern Burma.

This plan, which was intended to take place in March 1944, was put up to the British and American Chiefs of Staff meeting in Cairo in November 1943. There followed days of argument over the policy to be followed, on whether the operation might divert strength from Europe just when it was most needed and whether the main effort against Japan should be left to the Americans in the Pacific. Eventually these were the views that prevailed, and not only did Mountbatten fail to receive reinforcements, but he was instructed to send back to Europe his entire force of landing ships that were to make the amphibious assault. He was not even able to carry out a small seaborne landing on the Mayu Peninsula, put forward as yet another alternative when the more ambitious scheme was inevitably cancelled.

The only MTBs operational at this time were two flotillas, the 16th and 17th, based at Madras and Trincomalee, and operated by the Royal Indian Navy. They comprised twenty-two Higgins boats transferred from the United States under lend/lease. From the start there had been difficulties in maintaining them, however, with few spares and equipment available, and they had deteriorated to such an extent by May 1944 that they had to be scrapped.

That left just a few MLs, manned by men of the British, Indian, Burmese and South African navies. During the first three months of 1944, these craft patrolled the Arakan coast in search of enemy supply vessels and doing what they could to support the Army's second Arakan campaign which had started the previous December. They undertook the landing of Commandos and agents behind enemy lines, in addition to other duties. But they were no substitute for proper assault landing craft, all of which had been sent back to Europe. And the targets they found were very few, for the Japanese were able to take advantage of the myriad inland waterways along the coast to hide the movement of their seaborne traffic.

In March, the Army had to turn its attention away from Arakan and the offensive against Akyab when the Japanese launched a major attempt to invade India through Assam to the north. That and the breaking of the monsoon in April put an end to most operations of coastal craft during the spring and summer.

The efforts of the Fourteenth Army in fighting on through the monsoon season, which finally turned the tide of events against the Japanese, are outside the scope of this book, but it was one of the most remarkable achievements of the war. Meanwhile, the Royal Navy's Eastern Fleet, commanded by Admiral Sir James F. Somerville since the anxious days of March 1942, but taken over by Admiral Sir Bruce Fraser in August 1944, was increasing its offensive by large-scale raids and bombardments against enemy harbours and shore installations along the entire seaboard. Carrier-borne planes were particularly successful and, together with a stepping up of the RAF's mine-laying campaign, led to the growing supremacy of British naval forces in the Indian Ocean and a tightening of the blockade of Japan.

In August 1944, Commander R.R.W. Ashby DSC, the man who had made the great trek from Hong Kong through China to Rangoon in the early days of the Far East war and who had gone on to serve with Coastal Forces both in home waters and then in the Mediterranean, was appointed Senior Officer of Arakan Coastal Forces. It was here, off the Burmese coast, that the final phase of small-boat warfare in South-East Asia was to take place.

The tasks set this force by the Commander-in-Chief East Indies were to carry out operations over 400 miles of enemy coastline as far south as the Bassein River, operating from a main base at Chittagong, by attacking enemy supply vessels, bombarding ports and coastal garrisons, taking part in landing raids and generally helping the Army fighting in the north by holding down large numbers of enemy troops in coastal defence. The craft allocated to Ashby consisted of the 36th, 37th, 49th, 55th, 56th and 57th Flotillas of Fairmile MLs, the 146th and 147th HDML Flotillas, the headquarters ship *Kedah*, the maintenance

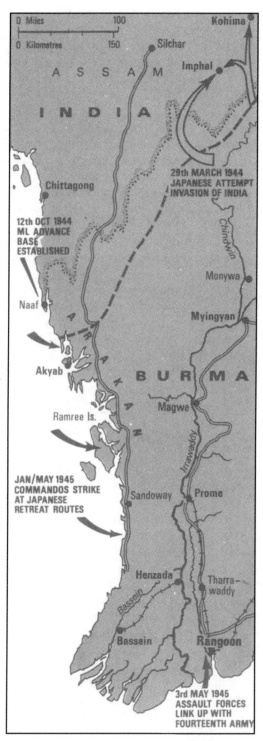

Operations in Western Burma: 1944–Spring 1945.

ship *Barracuda*, the supply and advance headquarters ship *FT 14*, and two 150-ton gasoline and water tankers.

The MLs were formidably armed with a 3-pounder forward, single Oerlikon amidships, 40mm Bofors aft, a twin Bren on the bridge, and also carried two depth charges. Many of them mounted a 3-inch mortar aft of the Oerlikon as well. To all intents they were MGBs, except for being B-class Fairmiles instead of the 'D' Type.

Operations by the main force began on 12 October, as soon as the monsoon season ended. An advance base had earlier been established at Naaf, further down the Arakan coast, from where a few MLs had carried out special duties even during the 'season'. Frequent sweeps were made along the entire coast until the end of the year, with the MLs also taking part in reconnaissance landings in Combermere Bay, Ramree and Cheduba, and Commando raids on the Mayu Peninsula. Only a few enemy craft were encountered during this period and were either destroyed or captured. But the presence of the MLs undoubtedly forced the Japanese to reduce their coastal traffic and to move supplies by other more laborious means.

In December, Coastal Forces made preparations to take part in the Army's third Arakan campaign, which was to include a major assault on Akyab in February 1945. On 27 December, however, it was learned that the Japanese were already preparing to evacuate the port. The whole plan was brought forward, without waiting for the complete assault force to be formed. But when the first Commando brigade landed on the north-western point of Akyab Island on 3 January, it was found that the Japanese had already left. The problem now was to cut off the retreating enemy forces as they made their way down the coast. This entailed a series of Commando landings at points along the Arakan coast from where they could strike inland to the coastal road which was the enemy's main escape route. And it also involved the MLs in one of the most extraordinary Coastal Force operations of the war – a hunt for enemy craft carrying parties of evacuating troops in the maze of waterways and jungle swamps that formed so much a part of the Arakan coastline.

These activities lasted until well into June, and in fact increased after the recapture of Rangoon on 3 May, when assault forces making their way up the Rangoon River joined Fourteenth Army which had fought its way down central Burma. Again the Japanese had evacuated the port some days earlier, having by now abandoned their whole position in the Irrawaddy delta. But although completely disorganized, and lacking supplies and food because of the coastal blockade, over 100,000 trained Japanese troops still remained in Burma. The MLs again played an important part in hunting them down in the inland waterways.

It was an arduous task. Not only did the Japanese fight back with suicidal tenacity, but the conditions were appalling, especially after the rains began. There was scarcely an ML that did not go aground at least a dozen times; one grounded thirty-two times in nine days. Yet another hazard was the booby traps left behind by the retreating enemy.

Typical of the operations of this time were those carried out between 14 and 18 May by a group of MLs led by Lieutenant Commander John N. Wise DSC, Senior Officer of the 13th Flotilla, and units of the 14th Flotilla whose Senior Officer was Lieutenant Brock. Both flotillas were now based at Rangoon, together with the 59th Flotilla commanded by Lieutenant Commander Campbell of the Burma RNVR and two HDML flotillas. Ashby had also moved his headquarters to there.

The first group of three MLs, 397, 437 and 367, set out on the morning of 14 May to sail up the Hlaing River, obtaining local information about Japanese movements on the way, and then make for Kokkawa village at the junction of the Kokkawa and Bawle rivers to intercept enemy craft which were thought to be using that route. When they arrived on the afternoon of the following day, villagers confirmed that the Japanese were using the Bawle River as one of their escape routes across the Irrawaddy delta. An ambush was set for that night, in which the villagers agreed to help by keeping watch from the shores and beating a gong if they sighted anything.

Nothing happened until just before dawn, when the deep sound of the gong being beaten suddenly echoed through the jungle. The MLs left their hiding places and nosed upriver to investigate. On rounding a bend, they came face to face with three Japanese landing craft. Both sides immediately opened fire and after a brisk close-range action, the landing craft were set on fire. Two sank and the troops on them were killed. The third managed to beach on the bank of the river, however, and a few Japanese scrambled ashore and got away.

The MLs suffered only minor damage. But the following night they were replaced at Kokkawa by *MLs 594, 303* and *904*, under Lieutenant Commander Wise. The same ambush arrangements were made as on the first night. After that success, the villagers had become very keen and set up even more observation posts along the river banks. They were all armed with spears and long two-handed knives, and it was considered that any Japanese getting ashore would have a 'pretty thin time', to quote one of the ML commanders.

The weather was fine, with a clear starlit sky giving good visibility, even though there was no moon. *ML 904*, commanded by Lieutenant Mervyn Fox, anchored close into a high bank to engage any enemy craft coming round the bend in the river, to be backed by subsequent crossfire from *594* and *303* which were moored further down in case the enemy came from the south. Positions were taken at 17.30. An hour later *ML 269* arrived, having been investigating reports of communal trouble in the Pyapon area. As it was too late to return that night to Rangoon, the boat was anchored well up the Kokkawa River to be kept in reserve.

At 19.50 the alarm gong sounded and at the same time engines were heard in the distance, approaching from the north. The noise became louder and thirty-five minutes later two Japanese landing craft rounded the bend in the river. They were engaged by *904*, which came up astern of them, cutting off any possible retreat, and by crossfire from *303* which was ahead of them. The first craft burst into flames but at this point the bows of *904* became firmly stuck on the shallow river bank. Seeing this, the commander of the blazing Japanese craft altered course to ram *904* and the ML was struck on the starboard side near the petrol compartment. It was only with extreme difficulty that Lieutenant Fox managed to extricate his boat, on which one man had been killed and two wounded. The enemy craft swung away and beached.

Meanwhile, the second landing craft was being engaged in crossfire from *594* and *303*. This also burst into flames – it was later found that the enemy craft were carrying fuel and ammunition instead of a full load of troops – and made an attempt to ram *594*. The ML went full astern on her anchor and was missed by only a few yards by the enemy craft, which went on to beach.

For another hour, fire was exchanged with those Japanese who had managed to get ashore. Unfortunately, some of this found its mark on Kokkawa village and the wooden houses fronting the river went up in flames. As the MLs were now silhouetted by both the blazing village and the enemy craft, they moved a quarter of a mile up the Kokkawa River. *ML 269* was brought up to cover its entrance from the Bawle River and it was from this position, two hours later, that she sighted three more enemy craft coming from the south. While *269* engaged them, *904* and *303* headed downriver to join her.

Seeing only one ML at first, the Japanese, instead of trying to escape back downriver, altered course to attack her. Owing to the narrowness of the river and the number of boats present, increased further by the arrival of *904* and *303*, arcs of fire were extremely difficult to make with any accuracy. The first enemy craft coming at close range through the line of MLs blew up after being hit repeatedly. The second suffered the same fate. The third caught fire, and, after unsuccessfully trying to ram *904*, beached on the river bank. The ammunition on board began to blow up and explosions continued for over five hours; a large patch of blazing fuel drifted upriver.

At least fifty-five Japanese were killed in these two nights' engagements. In his report, Lieutenant Commander Wise stated:

> The courage or blind animal-like tenacity with which the enemy pressed on into the heavy and concentrated fire of our ships, even after his vessels had burst into flames, was a most sickening experience to watch. In one case, one of the enemy returned to his beached vessel and, surrounded by flames, attempted to get his forward gun into action. Each boat was estimated to have carried ten plus Japanese. Of those who escaped destruction in their vessels many were shot in the river or on the banks of the river.

The only British casualties were one killed and three wounded, with minor damage to the MLs. After the action was over, the ML crews returned to what was left of the village, concerned at the damage their shells had caused. Wise's report continued: 'However, the villagers seemed to think the night's entertainment was well worth it. They assured the MLs it was perfectly all right and no one had been hurt. They set off with their spears to round up any Japanese who had got ashore.'

By the end of the month, the whole delta area was cleared of enemy craft and only a few scattered Japanese troops were left on foot. Those craft which had not been sunk had got through to the sea. Coastal Force patrols continued until mid-June, by which time all the waterways in south-west Burma had been searched to make sure no enemy craft were left. By then, with the onset of the monsoon, many of the minor waterways were becoming overgrown with a type of water hyacinth and unnavigable for MLs. Other waterways were flooding and so the Arakan Coastal Forces were withdrawn from the area, while the Army and Civil Affairs Department took over. During the period October 1944 to May 1945, the MLs had sunk thirty-one armed landing craft, six motor gunboats and sixty-six smaller craft carrying Japanese. Their own losses were one ML, *891*, which blew up after hitting a mine during the Kyaukpyu assault, killing six and wounding sixteen.

With other naval units, the MLs began to make preparations for assaults on the Malay Peninsula, but events in the Pacific were already reaching their inevitable conclusion. On 15 August, before the operation had begun, the Japanese surrendered. The flag of the Rising Sun followed the Swastika to defeat. For the first time in nearly six years the seas of the world were quiet, no longer torn by the shattering explosions of mines and bombs, the whine of plunging shells or the ominous hiss of torpedoes.

Epilogue

It is very difficult to assess accurately the results achieved by motor torpedo boats and their contribution to the Second World War. For one thing, actions invariably took place at night when visibility was poor and were fought at such high speeds that they were often over in less time than it takes to read even these brief accounts of them, making it difficult for the crews to know exactly what had happened. Claims were made in all good faith, as against those put out purely for propaganda purposes, which could not be confirmed by later examination of enemy records. Many an MTB, PT boat or *Schnellboot* came limping back to base, damaged, hours or even days overdue, after having been claimed as sunk by the opposing side. Such craft showed a remarkable ability to survive even heavy damage, especially if other boats were available to take them in tow.

A good example of this occurred early in July 1944 in the North Sea. Lieutenant D.E.J. 'Duggie' Hunt DSC, acting as Senior Officer in *MTB 245*, had led a force of six boats from Lowestoft's 22nd MTB Flotilla in an attack off Scheveningen during which two enemy trawlers and a guncoaster were torpedoed. Early on in the attack, Hunt's boat had been severely hit low down in the bows and was making water. She managed to back away stern first but was already in a sinking condition by the time another boat in the unit came up to take her in tow and was, with some justification, claimed as sunk by the German gunners. However, Hunt was particularly attached to his boat, and was determined to bring her home if at all possible, even though, on looking back now, he says he would probably have been more justified in abandoning and sinking her.

Towing by the bows proved impossible as too much water was coming in and so she was towed stern first. This kept the speed down to a few knots but even so, she was still making water. By early morning, when approaching the East Coast after being towed in this manner all the way across the North Sea, the seas were so rough that all the destroyers in the area had been called back to port. The MTB would undoubtedly have sunk had not the tow been taken over first by a 'B' Type ML and then an ocean-going tug which had been sent out specially for this purpose.

By the time the boat was approaching Felixstowe, the decks were awash and only about 9 inches of the sides were showing above water. It was at this point that she was passed by a cruiser, heading into the rough seas after the destroyers had been recalled. As his tiny craft, nearly submerged and being towed stern first, passed the large warship, Hunt could scarcely believe his ears when the cruiser suddenly 'piped the side', a form of etiquette normally reserved as a mark of respect to high-ranking senior officers. Hunt and the three members of the crew who had remained on board with him lined up to take the salute, on possibly the only occasion when a large warship had so complimented a small boat. It is now one of Hunt's most vivid recollections of the time he served in Coastal Forces. *MTB 245* eventually arrived back at base at 19.00 after being towed for more than twenty hours. After a few weeks of extensive repairs, she was ready for service again.

If the action reports themselves are not completely reliable guides to the numbers of vessels actually sunk by motor torpedo boats, then there are the official statistics published some years after the war by the major powers, although even these sometimes give an incomplete picture. Many of the vessels sunk by MTBs in the Mediterranean, for instance, were caiques and fishing craft, used by the enemy for a variety of purposes, but too small to be included separately in lists of merchant shipping losses.

Although American PT boats played such an important role in the Pacific campaigns, they were seldom directly opposed by types of craft similar to themselves, and there is little basis for comparison here between the performance of the US and Japanese navies. It was in the North Sea, English Channel and Mediterranean that the major confrontations took place between craft designed for the same specific purpose of torpedo attack – the British MTBs and the German S-boats – and it is on the record of their performances that the most realistic assessment can be made.

The strength of British Commonwealth Coastal Forces at the end of the war totalled 1,383 craft, made up as follows: MTBs 422 (including 48 still being used as MGBs); SGBs 6; MA/SBs 15; MLs (including HDMLs) 940. Losses during the war totalled 223 craft: 115 MTBs, 28 MGBs, 79 MLs and HDMLs, and 1 SGB. German and Italian warship losses credited to MTBs totalled seventy ships of 34,554 tons, including a cruiser, five torpedo boats, an armed merchant raider and a submarine; of the remainder, most were German S-boats and R-boats. Merchant shipping sunk by Coastal Forces in home waters totalled forty ships of 59,650 tons, and in the Mediterranean (with PT boats) some 100 vessels of about 70,000 tons (many being barge-type craft of small tonnage).

Including those built before the war, the Germans brought into operational service 244 S-boats and 326 R-boats. Losses totalled: S-boats, 146; R-boats, 163. (Of the 41 MAS boats captured by the Germans after Italy's surrender and used by them as S-boats, 24 were destroyed; of the remaining 103 Italian MAS boats in service during the war, 50 were destroyed, 20 scuttled and the rest either taken over by the Allies or allowed to remain in Italian hands.) British Commonwealth warship losses credited to S-boats totalled some forty ships of about 25,000 tons, including two cruisers and seven destroyers. Allied merchant shipping sunk by S-boats in all waters totalled ninety-nine ships of 229,676 tons.

With the exception of major warship losses, such as cruisers and destroyers about which there is no doubt, none of these figures can be regarded as entirely accurate. When it came to losses of minor warships of 100 tons or so, such as motor torpedo boats, small merchant ships and barges, it was sometimes impossible for either side to know for sure whether it was a torpedo or mine that had caused the destruction. Even in the number of British coastal craft actually built during the war, there are discrepancies in the totals listed by various official sources. The 'Coastal Forces Periodical Review' gives 1,568 craft (1,251 built in the United Kingdom, 143 in the United States and 174 in the British Empire); the Admiralty's *Nominal List of Ships, by Types, Built for the Royal Navy* gives a total of 1,551 craft; the *Statistical Digest of the War* published by HM Stationery Office in 1951 gives 1,604; and a Coastal Forces Monograph written in 1952 gives 1,689. The figures given here earlier of the strength of Coastal Forces at the end of the war, added to the losses suffered, come to a total of 1,606; when account is also taken of the boats which had been paid off by 1945, it would appear that something approaching 1,700 craft is the most accurate figure.

What does emerge is that the German S-boats were overall more successful against Allied merchant shipping than the MTBs were against their enemy opposite numbers, although this should be viewed against the number of targets available to both sides. British coastal convoys comprised about forty ships both ways every day, up to 10 miles long and often escorted by no more than two destroyers and a few MLs. The German convoys on the other hand usually comprised no more than half a dozen ships, invariably with more escorts than merchant vessels. It seems an unavoidable conclusion that the German S-boats should have had a much greater degree of success than they did – had the situation been reversed, British MTBs would have massacred such large, poorly escorted convoys.

The greatest successes of the S-boats against Allied shipping resulted from their mine-laying operations, just as many of the greatest enemy losses at sea were caused by the RAF's aerial mine-laying campaign (although it was some while before it was appreciated that mines were far more successful than bombs). Since mines were also laid by other types of German craft, as well as aircraft, it is impossible to credit any total number of losses to S-boats. But some idea of the proportions can be gathered from the figures in home waters during the last five months of the war, when, with few aircraft in the air, nearly all the German mines were laid by S- and R-boats. Compared with six Allied ships totalling 12,972 tons sunk by these craft by torpedo, the mines they laid caused the direct loss of twenty-five Allied ships of 75,999 tons. It may well be therefore that in achieving their greatest degree of success against the S- and R-boats, thus reducing the number of craft the Germans had available for mine laying, was here that Coastal Forces made their most important contribution to the war, even though it must be said that many of these enemy craft were also sunk by destroyers or destroyed at their bases by Allied aircraft.

Assessed against the war at sea as a whole, motor torpedo boats played a relatively small role. For example, the direct successes by torpedo of German S-boats accounted for only 1.1 per cent of the total Allied merchant ship losses of 21,570,720 tons, and mines laid by all German forces caused only 6.5 per cent of losses, as against 68.1 per cent by submarines. But the story does not end there. It was as Britain turned increasingly to a policy of amphibious warfare by combined operations that small boats came increasingly into their own, when the command of enemy coastal waters became as important as the defence of those at home. Such raids as that on St Nazaire were not only successful in their own right, and made possible by the possession of the right kind of coastal craft, but they led directly to the much larger invasions of North Africa, Sicily, Italy and finally the greatest of them all, in Normandy. All this might have been apparent in the First World War, were it not for the fact that Britain was committed so fully to the fatal continental strategy of war on land in Europe, with its far greater loss of life. Even in the Second World War there might have been a risk of such a policy again being adopted had the British Army not been forced out of Europe in the early stages.

The somewhat reluctant acceptance of a need for Coastal Forces, then its rapid expansion as this need became more fully appreciated, was one of the factors which resulted from Britain basing her overall war strategy on maritime power – hardly a new concept in the light of history, but one which in this century has seemed curiously unacceptable to Britain's leaders, and repeatedly has had to be relearned all over again. After the war, Coastal Forces suffered much the same fate as they had in 1918. The boats that had given such strenuous service were broken up or sold off, some to take up new privateering careers as gun-runners, or smuggling contraband goods, others to end their days in a more gentle manner as houseboats in sheltered inlets, where only an ex-Volunteer Reservist on holiday might suddenly come across one and recognize her for what she had been. All this was inevitable perhaps; of more concern was the cancellation of nearly all the building and research programmes then underway. Again it was left to private companies, primarily the now combined Vosper-Thornycroft Group, to continue small-boat development.

This development, in collaboration with the Admiralty, led in 1954 to the Brave class of Fast Patrol Boat, as the MTB was reclassified: a 96-foot, 50-knot craft, armed with electrically operated 40mm Bofors guns and four 21-inch torpedoes carried in side-launching chutes. Two came into service with the Royal Navy between 1954 and 1959, *Brave Borderer* and *Brave Swordsman*. In the meantime, a private venture programme by Vosper-Thornycroft had led to an even more sophisticated gas-turbine-powered FPB, mounting various types of guided missile. It was in line with the situation that existed in the 1930s that of the eighteen boats of this type in service or under construction in 1968, sixteen were for foreign navies – those of Denmark (six), Malaya (four), Libya (three), Greece (two) and Brunei (one) – and only two for the Royal Navy. At the same time, other countries, notably the United States, Russia, Italy and Sweden, have also gone ahead on FPB design and construction, including the use of hydrofoils.

The missile-firing fast patrol boat of today is a far cry from Davidson's rowing-boat with its explosive-charged pole thrust against the side of an enemy ship, or Luppis' clockwork motorboat. But the overriding importance of coastal waters in any war remains, bar a nuclear conflagration. The need to bring in supplies by sea, to transport goods and materials in coastal shipping from one part of a country to another, the offensive objectives of the blockade, the amphibious landing, the harbour raid – are all as apparent today as they were in the eighteenth century and earlier. The story of Coastal Forces in the Second World War proved this once again, if proof were needed. None of the conflicts that have taken place during the uneasy years since then have shown it to be otherwise.

Bibliography

Bagnasco, Erminio, *I MAS e Le Motorsiluranti Italiane 1906-1966*, Ufficio Storico della Marina Militaire, Rome, 1967.

British Admiralty, *Ships of the Royal Navy: Statement of Losses During the Second World War*, HM Stationery Office, London, 1947.

Brown, D., *Warship Losses of World War Two*, Arms & Armour Press, London, 1990.

Bulkeley, Captain Robert J., Jr, *At Close Quarters: PT Boats of the US Navy*, United States Naval History Division, Washington, 1962.

Cooper, Bryan, *The Battle of the Torpedo Boats*, Macdonald & Co., London, 1970.

——, *The Buccaneers*, Purnell's History of the Second World War, London, 1970.

——, *The E-Boat Threat*, Macdonald & Jane's, London, 1976.

Dallies-Labourdette, Jean Philippe, *German E-Boats in Action 1939-1945*, Histoire & Collections, Paris, 2003.

Dickens, Captain Peter, DSO MBE DSC, *Night Action*, Peter Davies, London, 1974.

Donovan, Robert J., *PT 109: John F. Kennedy in World War II*, McGraw Hill, New York, 1960.

Du Cane, Commander Peter CBE, *High Speed Small Craft*, Temple Press, London 1951.

Ferrell, Bob and Ross, Al, *Early Elco PT Boats*, PT Boat Museum, Germantown TN, USA, 1980.

Ferrell, Robert, *US Mosquito Fleet*, PT Boat Museum, Germantown TN, USA, 1977.

Fock, Harald, *Die deutschen Schnellboote 1914–1945*, Koehlers Verlagsgesellschaft, Hamburg, 2001.

Frank, Hans, *Die deutschen Schnellboote im Einsatz*, Verlag Mittler und Sohn, 2006.

Hichens, Anthony, *The Biography of Lieutenant Commander Robert Hichens DSO DSC RNVR*, Pen & Sword, Barnsley, 2007.

Hichens, Lieutenant Commander Robert Peverell DSO DSC, *We Fought Them in Gunboats*, Michael Joseph, London, 1944.

Hobday, Geoffrey, *In Harm's Way: An RNVR Officer at War 1940-1944*, Imperial War Museum, London, 1985.

Holman, Gordon, *The Little Ships*, Hodder & Stoughton, London, 1943.

Hümmelchen, Gerhard, *Die deutschen Schnellboote im zweiten Weltkreig*, Verlag Mittler und Sohn, 1996.

Johnson, Frank D., *United States PT Boats of World War II*, Blandford Press, London, 1980.

Kemnade, Friedrich, *Die Afrika-Flottille*, Motorbuch Verlag, Stuttgart, 1978.

Kent, James Foster, *E-Boat Alert*, Airlife Publishing, Shrewsbury, 1996.

Lambert, John and Ross, Al, *Allied Coastal Forces of World War II*, Conway Maritime Press, London, 1990 (vol. I), 1993 (vol. II).

Lawrence, Hal, *Victory at Sea: Tales of His Majesty's Coastal Forces*, McClelland & Stewart, Canada, 1989.

Mayen, Jan, *Alarm: Schnellboote*, Gerhard Stalling Verlag, Hamburg, 1961.

Phelan, Keiren and Brice, Martin H., *Fast Attack Craft*, Macdonald & Jane's, London, 1977.

Pope, Dudley, *Flag 4: The Battle of Coastal Forces in the Mediterranean 1939-1945*, William Kimber, London, 1954.

Preston, Anthony: *Strike Craft*, Bison Books Inc, Greenwich CT, USA, 1982.

Reynolds, Lieutenant L.C., DSC, *Gunboat 658*, William Kimber, London, 1955.

Roskill, Captain S.W., DSC, *The War at Sea 1939-1945*, HM Stationery Office, London, 1960.

Schlutz, Herbert Max, *Die deutsche Schnellbootwaffe in zweite Weltkreig*, Erlangen, 1987.

Scott, Lieutenant Commander Peter MBE DSC & Bar, *The Battle of the Narrow Seas*, Country Life, London, 1945.

Tregaskis, Richard, *John F. Kennedy and PT 109*, Random House, New York, 1962.

Volkmar, Kühn, *Schnellboote im Eisatz 1939-1945*, Stuttgart, 1978.

White, W.L., *They Were Expendable*, Harcourt Brace, New York, 1943.

Whitley, M.J., *German Coastal Forces of World War Two*, Arms & Armour Press, London, 1992.

Index

Abukuma, 199, 200
Admiral Scheer, 95
Adriatic, 192, 194; cooperating with
    partisans in, 151–63
Aegean, actions in, 137–45, 193–4
Afrika Korps, 69
Aitape, PT actions off, 125
Akers, Ens Anthony B., USN, 62, 106
Albrighton, HMS, 85–6
Aldridge, A/B Stanley, 43
Alexander, Gen, 46
Alexandria: 'human torpedo' attack
    on harbour, 70; MTB base (HMS
    Mosquito), 73
Allan, Lt (later Cdr) Robert, RNVR, 73,
    128, 132, 137, 146–8, 192
Amagiri, 110
Ancona RN base, 195
Arakan: campaigns, 203–9; Coastal
    Forces at, 204
Ardrishaig base (HMS Seahawk), 47
Ark Royal, HMS, 70
Armstrong, Capt H. T., RN, 165
Arnold, Gen, 182
Ashby, Lt (later Cdr) R.R.W., HKRNVR,
    56–8, 133, 204
Ashigara, 199
Atherstone, HMS, 94, 96–7, 102–3
Atkins, Lt Cdr Barry K., USN, 119–20
Auxiliary Patrol, 24
Azalea, 175

Baglietto boatyard, 26–7
Bailey, Lt, 133
Biley, Lt G. E. 'George', RNVR, 51
Bains, S/Lt P.P., RNVR, 173
Baker, Lt Cdr P., 182
Baker, Lt G.H., RNVR, 180
Bales, Ens Bruce, USNR, 124
Barbary, Lt H.A., RN, 153

Barbey, RAdm Daniel E., 196
Barge, S/Lt R.M., RNVR, 84, 165
Barham, HMS, 70
Bari, German air raid on, 155
Barlow, Lt Peter, RNVR, 147
Barnes, Lt Cdr Stanley M., USN, 130,
    147, 149
Barnet, Lt R.L., RN, 85
Barnett, Harry, 124
Barracuda, 206
Bate, Lt W.O.J., RCNVR, 105
Baughmann, Lt, USN, 118
Beadles, A/B Henry J., 161
Beart, Lt E.H., RNVR, 97
Beattie, Lt Cdr S.H., RN, 96–103
Beckett, A/B S.J., RN, 18
Bennett, Lt S.B., RNVR, 78
Berthon, Lt P.A., RNVR, 9, 54
Bey, Kptlt, 34
Bismarck, 95
Bligh, Lt (later Cdr) 'Tim', RNVR, 128–9,
    155–63, 192; describes Adriatic action,
    161–3
Blomfield, Lt A.C.B., RN, 149
Bloom, Victor A., 123
Blount, Lt Walter, RNVR, 158–61, 192
Bône base, N. Africa, 128
Bonnell, Lt C.E., 'Chuck', RCNVR, 12, 14
Booth, Lt, 195
Bougainville, 116
Boulogne, as S-boat base, 31
Bourke, Lt Roland, RNVR, 56
Bourne, Lt F.W., RNVR, 185–7
Bowling, Cdr Selman S., USN, 120–2,
    197, 202
Bowyer, Lt, 192
Boyd, Lt (jg) Hershel F., USNR, 197
Boyd, Lt T.W., RNVR, 97, 100
Bradford, Lt Cdr D.G., RNR, 179
Bradley, Gen, 182

Brantingham, Lt (jg) Henry J., USN, 106
Brave Borderer, 213
Brave Swordsman, 213
Breed, Lt J., RNZNVR, 138
Brest, 79, 95
Briault, Lt D.L., RNVR, 97
Britain: development of MTBs and
   MGBs in, 27–33; naval forces in
   Mediterranean, 1940, 66–7
British Power Boat Co, 9, 27–9, 31
Brock. Lt, RNVR, 207
Brocklesby, HMS, 103
Brown, Lt (jg) Richard W., USN, 199
Bulkeley, Lt (later Lt Cdr) John D., USN,
   60–5, 119–21, 174, 182
Bulkeley, Lt Cdr Robert J., Jr, USNR, 125,
   197
Burk, Lt C.A., RCNVR, 169,172
Burke, Lt Cornelius, RCNVR, 147, 193
Burt, Lt E.A., RNVR, 97
Bushnell, David, 22
Butler, Lt H.E., RNVR, 131
Butow, Konteradmiral, 41

Cairo, HMS, 74
Caldwell, Lt Earl S., USN, 37, 60
Calhoun, Ens Fred, USNR, 123
Calvert, Cdr Alien P., USN, 110
Cameron, John, 45
Camouflage, ship, 86
Campbell, HMS, 169
Campbell, Lt Cdr, Burma RNVR, 207
Campbell, Lt L.G.R.,'Boffin', RNVR, 51,
   53, 87
Campbell, Lt R., RCNVR, 137
Campbell, Sir Malcolm, 9
Campbeltown, HMS, 93–104
Camper & Nicholson boats, 33
Canterbury, Morgan, 124
Carr, Lt F.W., RNVR, 165
Carr, Lt R.A., 'Bussy', RNVR, 87
Carruthers, A/B John, 14, 20
Casteloriso base, Aegean, 137
Caulfield, Lt J.A., RNVR, 169
Chaffey, O/S N.A., RN, 21
Challis, Stoker, 144
Channel, English: operations in, 11–21,
   47, 77–92, 167; following D-Day,
   177–90; western channel, 86–7, 182;

Scharnhorst, Gneisenau and *Prinz Eugen*
   in, 79–81
Chen Chak, Adm Sir Andrew, 57
Cherbourg, 180–1
Churchill, Brig T.B.L., 156
Clark, A/B F., 45
Cleveland, HMS, 103
Clynes, Capt C.M., 141
Coastal Forces, British and
   Commonwealth, 146–50; 'Battle
   Squadron', 146–50; craft allocated
   to D-Day, 63; early boats of, 31;
   establishment early 1942, 76; formation
   of, 47; position at end of 1942, 94; post-
   war, 214; strength at end of war, 33, 211
Coastal Motor Boat (CMB), 24–5, 36
Cobb, Lt H.P., RNVR, 89
Cole, Lt Cdr Anthony, RN, 43
Cole, Lt R., RNVR, 152
Collier, Lt T.A.M., RNVR, 97
Colvin, Lt Cdr Aimer P., USN, 126
Cornflower, HMS, 56
Cornish, Lt E.A.E., RNVR, 80
Corregidor, SS, 61
Cotswold, HMS, 89
Cottesmore, HMS, 88
Courage, Cdr R.E., RN, 140
Cox, Ens, USN, 64–5, 106
CRDA boatyard, 26
Crete, operations around, 68–70
Cunningham, A/B Edwin, 84
Cunningham, Adm, 68–72, 128, 132
Curtis, Lt D.M.C., RNVR, 96, 101
Cutter, Ens Henry W., USNR, 123

Daley, CMM William, Jr, 123
Dalmatia, 154
Danielsen, Lt Per, RNN, 12, 13, 21, 55
Davidson, Capt Hunter, 23
Davidson, Lt Robert C., RNVR, 154, 158
Davis, Lt Cdr N. Burt, Jr, USNR, 122, 126,
   160, 201
Davis, Lt Cdr Richard, Jr, USN, 185
Day, MMM f/c Charles D., 197
D-Day, 176, 178
Dean, Ens Frank H., Jr, USN, 122
de Jong, J. Van Zyll, 60
DeLong, Lt Edward, USN, 61
Dennis, Lt Cdr S.H., RN, 46

Derna, German base at, 71
Destroyer, development of the, 28
De Vol, Lt Norman, USN, 135
Dickens, Adm Sir Gerald, 89
Dickens, Lt P.G.C., RN, 89–91, 165–9
Dickinson, Capt N. Vincent, 192
Dixon, Lt J.D., RNVR, 183, 189
Doenitz, Adm, 153
Dover, 11–14; base (HMS Wasp), 46
Draug, 55
Drayson, S/Lt R.Q., RNVR, 88
Dreger Harbour PT base, 125, 127
Dreyer, Lt Christopher, RN, 45, 134
Du Bose, Lt Edwin A., USNR, 132, 147
du Cane, Peter, 25
Dumpulinar, 138
Duncan, Lt G.F. 'George', RCNVR, 87
Dunkirk, evacuation of, 45–6
Dupre, Capt M.M., Jr, USN, 110

Eagle, HMS, 74
Eardley-Wilmot, Lt J.A., RN, 48
E-boats, see Schnellboote and Raümboote
E-boat Alley, 51, 89
Eddin, Lt (jg) Joseph A., USN, 199
Edgar, Cmdre C.D., 176
Edge, Lt Patrick, RNVR, 165
Eglington, HMS, 169
Eighth Army, British, 73
Eisenhower, Gen Dwight D., 128, 182
Ekins, HMS, 189
El Alamein, 73, 128
Elba, Allied capture of, 145
Elco boats, 29, 37
Electric Boat Co, 25, 37
Elford, Lt Cdr Robert, RNVR, 169
Esmonde, Lt Cdr E., RN, 80
Evensen, Lt Peter, RNVR, 127, 137
Everitt, Lt W.G., RN, 45
Ewing, Ens Rumsey, USNR, 123

Fairmile Marine Co, 31–2
Falconer, Lt H.G.R., RNVR, 97
Falkner, Lt R.I.T., RN, 48
Falmouth base, 93
Fanner, Lt Cdr G.C., RNVR, 182
Fargo, Lt Cdr Alvin W., Jr, 126
Fast Patrol Boat, post-war, 214
Felixstowe base (HMS Beehive), 43, 46, 50

Fenton, Lt L., RNVR, 97
Fesq, Lt W., RANVR, 173
Fimmen, Kptlt, 178, 190
Fletcher, A/B E., 18
Flewin, A/B, 144
F-lighters, German, 130, 146, 158, 189
Foresight, HMS, 74
Fort William base (HMS Christopher), 46, 165
Foster, Lt A.D., RNVR, 127, 185–9
Foster, Lt Mark Arnold, RNVR, 78–9, 165–7
Fowey base, 46, 50
Fox, Lt, 143
Fox, Lt Mervyn, RNVR, 208
Franklin, S/Lt H.G., RNVR, 185, 187
Fraser, Adm Sir Brace, 207
Fucili, Evo, 124
Fuller, Lt (later Lt Cdr) Tom, RCNVR, 133, 151
Fulton, Robert, 22
Fuso, 198

Gamble, Lt L.H.J., RN, 45, 78–9
Gandy, Lt Cdr G.H., RN, 56
Gay Corsair, 33
Gay Viking, 33
Gemmel, Lt Cdr K., RN, 92, 165, 184
Germany: develops S-boats and R-boats, 33–6; intervenes in Mediterranean, 70; overruns Western Europe, 42; secret weapons at sea, 181; transfers S-boats to Mediterranean, 70–1
Gibson, Lt Cdr Jack E., 125
Giles, Lt Cdr Morgan, RN, 153–5, 194
Gillings, O/S, 14, 20
Gleason, Lt Carl T., USNR, 202
Gneisenau, 78, 80, 95
Good, Lt E.S., RNVR, 150
Gordon, ACMM Thomas, 13, 20
Gort, Lord, 46
Gotelee, Lt A., RNVR, 89
Gould, Lt Stewart, RN, 15–18, 21, 45, 50, 80, 130–1
Grafton, HMS, 46
Greece, overrun by Germany, 68–9
Green, Lt A.R., RN, 96
Greene-Kelly, Lt E.T., RNVR, 133
Gregory, Allen, 124

Grey Fox, 86
Grey Goose, 86
Grey Owl, 86
Grey Seal, 86
Grey Shark, 86
Grey Wolf, 86
Griffin, Lt (jg) Henry E., Jr, USN, 201
Griffiths, Lt J.R., RN, 85
Guadalcanal, 106–11

Hadley. P/O James, 13, 21
Haines, Lt Melvin W., USNR, 200
Hall, Lt D.A., RNVR, 185
Hallowell, Lt Roger, H., USNR, 201
Halsey, Adm, 200
Halstead, HMS, 180
Hamilton-Hill, Lt E., RNR, 48
Hanson, Lt Cdr R.J., RN, 85
Harbour defence motor launch (HDML), 31
Harllee, Lt Cdr John, USN, 120
Harris, Lt Alien H., USNR, 174, 182
Harris, Lt K.E., RNVR, 185
Harrison, Stoker T.R., 19
Hart, Norman, 31
Hartley, Lt K., RNVR, 166–7
Harwich base (HMS Badger), 46
Harwood, Adm Sir Henry, 72
Hasty, HMS, 73
Henderson, Lt I.B., RNVR, 102
Hennessy, Lt R.A.M., RN, 128–9
Hewitt, Adm H.K., 191
Hewitt, Lt Eric, RNVR, 158
Hichens, Lt Cdr Robert P., RNVR, 50–4, 78, 87, 166
Hickford, S/Lt J.E., RNVR, 143–4
Higgins boats, 29, 37
Higgins Industries, 37–8
Hitler, Adolf, 79
Hobday, Lt G.M., RNVR, 156
Hodges, Gen, 182
Holloway, Lt C.R., RNVR, 194
Home, Lt J.B.R., RN, 78
Hong Kong: operations in, 56–9
Hopewell, 33
Horlock, Lt K.M., 102, 151
Hornet, HMS, 23
Howes, Lt Peter, RN, 51
Hubback, Capt G.V., RN, 74, 152

Huckins Yacht Co, 37
Huffman, George B., 60
Hughes-Hallett, Capt J., RN, 96
Humphreys, Lt J.F., RNVR. 185
Hunt, Lt D.E.J. 'Duggie', RNVR, 210
Hyde, Ens Robert, USNR, 124
Hyslop, Lt P.H., RNVR, 154, 156

Ijmuiden: MGB action off, 78; MTB actions off, 186–7
Iltis, 80
Immingham base, 50
Indomitable, HMS, 74
Ingram, Lt Cdr J.C.A., RN, 88
Irwin, Lt C.S.B., RNR, 97
Isotta Fraschini engine, 28–9
Italy: develops motor torpedo boats, 26–7; fleet in 1940, 68; invasion of, 135; success of one-man TBs, 69

Jakes, Torpedoman, 14, 20
James, ACMM Leonard, 84
Jane, A/B Richard, 83–4
Japan: coastal barges of, 110, 125; motor torpedo boats of, 39–40
Jenks, Lt Cdr R.F., RN, 97
Jermain, Lt Dennis, RN, 73, 130
Jerram, Lt C., RNVR, 133, 194
Johannsen, Kptlt, 178
Johnson, Lt Cdr Richard E., USN, 126
Jones, Stoker W.E., 19
Joy, Lt A.P.G., RNVR, 127, 134

Kamikaze suicide planes, 202
Kedah, 204
Kekewich, RAdm Piers K., 47, 165
Kelly, HMS. 42
Kelly, Lt (later Lt Cdr) Robert B., USN, 63–5, 108
Kemnade, Korvettenkpt F., 70
Kennedy, Lt John F., USNR, 110–14
Kenya, HMS, 74
Keyes, Adm, 46
Kingston, HMS, 71
Kirk, RAdm A.G., 176
Kirkpatrick, Lt Cdr J.R.H., RCNVR, 182
Kiyoshimo, 201
Knight-Lacklen, Lt, RNVR, 152
Komet, sinking of the, 88

Kosky, Lt, 41
Kovar, Lt (jg) L.M., USN, 200
Krueger, Lt Gen Walter, 196
Kuma, 65

La Combattante, 183
Ladner, Lt T.R., RCNVR, 87, 133, 147
Lancaster, Lt J. Donald, RNVR, 154
Lance, HMS, 71
Lanfear, A/B, 19, 21
Law, S/Lt (later Lt Cdr) Anthony,
    RCNVR, 79, 179
Leaf, Lt E.D.W., RNVR, 91, 172
Lee, S/Lt Philip, RNVR, 84, 165
Lees, Capt D.M., RN, 165
Leese, Gen, 46
Leeson, Lt Cdr Robert, USNR, 125, 197
Le Febure, Stephen P., 123
Le Havre, 179; Allied blockade of, 181;
    attacked by Bomber Command, 180;
    German evacuation of, 183
Leith, Lt Barry, RNVR, 15, 21
Leyte, 196: Battle of Leyte Gulf, 197–8
Lightning, HMS, 130
Lightoller, Lt F.R., RNVR, 170
Lloyd, H.L. 'Harpy', 45, 78
LST 715, 180
Lummis, Lt D., RNVR, 158, 160–1
Luppis, Giovanni, 23
Lürssen shipyard, 34–6
Lützow, 95
Lützow, K-Kpt, 170, 190
Lyme Bay, 92, 175
Lynch, Ens Robert F., USNR, 118

Mabee, Lt, RCNVR, 129
MacArthur, Gen Douglas, 60–5, 106, 197
MacArthur, Mrs, 60
Macbeth, Capt J.S.F., 141
McClure, Lt (jg) J.C., USNR, 110
McCowen, Lt Cdr D.H.E., RNVR, 180–1
McCutcheon, Teleg. H.F., 45
Macdonald, S/Lt G. J., RNZNVR, 78, 90,
    166–7, 184
McElfresh, Lt John M., USN, 201
McIlhagga, S/Lt L.B., RCNVR, 83
McIlraith, Lt Alan, RNVR, 83
Mackay, HMS, 169–71
Mackenzie, L/S Robert, 84

McLachlan, Campbell, 147
McLaughlin, Capt R.V., RN, 173–4
Maclean, Brig Fitzroy, 153
Macreath, A/B Tom, 83
Maddalena base, Sardinia, 146
Maitland, Lt (later Lt Cdr) Douglas,
    RCNVR, 133, 147–8, 158
Mallard, HMS, 172
Malta: attacked by Italy, 69; attacked by
    Luftwaffe, 71; MTB operations from,
    127
Manchester, HMS, 74
Marshall, Gen, 182
Marshall, Lt R.M., RNVR, 169
Martino, Chief Torpedoman John, 61–2
MAS boats: development of, 24; in action
    in Mediterranean, 67, 135; strength
    and losses of, 211
Mason, Stoker, 14
Master Standfast, 33
Matteson, Lt Cdr George A., Jr, USNR, 201
Maund, Cdr, RN, 45
Maurice, Capt F.H.P., RN. 165
May, Lt J, RNVR, 189
Mayo, Stoker Cuthbert, 193
Mediterranean: operations in, 66–75,
    127–36, 146–50
Midway Island, operations on and
    around, 106
Mihaitovich, Gen, 154
Mindoro, US invasion of, 201
Minshall, Lt Cdr Merlin, RNVR, 153
Mios Woendi PT base, 125
Mirbach, Kptlt, 178
Mitchell, James, 124
Mogami, 198
Montgomery, Lt Cdr Alan R., USN, 107
Moon, Adm, 182
Moore, Lt A.H., RNVR, 150
Moran, Cdre Edward J., USN, 116
Morotai Task Force, 196
Morrison, Lt John W., Jr, USNR, 201
Morrow, Lt N.C., RNVR, 185
Motor gunboats (MGBs): development
    of, 29–32; Fairmile 'C', 32; in action
    in North Sea, 106–7; purpose of, 16;
    tactics, 48–9, 77–8
Motor gunboat/Motor torpedo boats
    (MGB/MTBs): development of, 166;

Fairmile 'D', 32, 84, 129–30; Fairmile 'F', 33
Motor launches (MLs), 25, 31, 77; Fairmile 'A', 31; Fairmile 'B', 31; Special Service, 154
Motor torpedo boats (MTBs): at Dunkirk evacuation, 45; attack *Scharnhorst* and *Gneisenau*, 79; development of, 9, 27–33; establishing bases for, 46; evacuate Hong Kong, 57–8; support Eighth Army, 74–5; tactics, 13–14, 48–9, 152, 173–4
Mountbatten, VAdm (later Adm) Lord Louis, 96
Mountstevens, Lt, RNVR, 151–2
MS boats, 26–7, 142–3
Muir, Lt John G., RNVR, 129, 137
Müller, Kptlt Karl, 185
Mumma, Cdr Morton C., Jr, USN, 119, 122
Munroe, Lt Pat, USNR, 120
Mussolini, Benito, 134–5

Nachi, 199
New Georgia, US landings in, 108, 114
New Guinea campaign, 118–26
Newall, Lt L. E., RNZNVR, 130, 137
Newcastle, HMS, 72
Newhaven base, 169
Newman, Lt Col Charles, 94, 104
Newman, S/Lt, RN, 144
Nigeria, HMS, 74
Nimitz, Adm, 197
Niobe, see *Dalmatia*
Nishimura, VAdm Shoji, 198–200
Noakes, Lt Cdr C.S.D., RN, 73
Nock, S/Lt N.R., RNVR, 97
Nonsuch, 33
Normandie, 95
Normandy landings, 173–5, 178–90
North Sea, operations in, 41–55, 77–8
Norwegian MTB Flotilla (30th), operations of, 91–2, 188

O'Brien, Lt Richard, USN, 132, 135
Ohio, SS, 74
Ohlenschlagar, S/Lt V., RNVR, 166–7
Oigawa Maru, 119
Oldendorf, RAdm Jesse B., 199
Opdenhoff, Kptlt, 41–2
Operation Neptune, 176; Operation Overlord, 176; Operation Torch, 172
O'Rourke, S/Lt J. E., RCNVR, 96

Packard engine, 28–33
Page, R/O John L., 183
Papua, 118
Parkinson, Lt R., RN, 43
Parley, Lt Edward I., 123–5
Parry, RAdm W. E., 176
Partridge, US tug, 180
Patch, Lt Gen A.M., 191
Patrol Torpedo (PT) boats, US, 8; advance of bases with S.
Pacific campaign, 115; at the Battle of Leyte Gulf, 199–201; barge-hunting by, 114–15; early actions against Japanese, 60–5; evacuate Gen MacArthur from Philippines, 60; in action in Mediterranean, 66–75; in Riviera invasion, 191–5; MTB Training centre for, Rhode Island, 107, 192; prepare for D-Day, 162; Presidential Unit Citations for, 120
Patterson, Maj, 143
Peake, Lt Cdr E.C., RN, 67
Pearl Harbor: PT action in, 56, 60, 106
Perks, Lt R., RNVR, 131
Perkins, Lt J.P., RNVR, 91
Petersen, Kptlt (later F-Kpt) Rudolph, 41, 75, 175
Petrie, Cdr J., RNVR, 56
Philippines: PT actions around in early 1942, 60–5; return by the Americans to, 196–202
Phillips, S/Lt A., RNVR, 78
Pickard, Lt, 147
Pike, L/Signalman, 99
Platt, Lt T.D.L., RNR, 97, 103
Pollard, O/S J., 168
Portland base (HMS Attack), 46
Portsmouth: base (HMS Hornet), 46; Command, 173, 180
Preston, Lt A. Murray, USNR, 197
Princess Josephine Charlotte, 93
Prinz Eugen, 78, 95
Pullen, Lt Weston C., Jr. USNR, 197, 201
Pumphrey, Lt Cdr E.N., RN, 12–21, 79
Pytchley, HMS, 169–71

Quantock, HMS, 193
Queen Elizabeth, HMS, 70

Rabaul, 116
Ramseyer, Lt Cdr, RN, 143

Rangoon, MLs in action in, 58
Raümboote (R-boats), 36, 211;
    minelaying by, 81, 212; sinking of a,
    83–4
Ray, Capt, USN, 63
Reith, Lord, 47
Rendova Harbour, PT base, 108, 111
Rennell, Lt Paul T., USNR, 122
Rhodes, captured by Germans, 137
Richards, Lt G.D.K., RN, 81–3, 166
Ritchie, Lt J.D., RN, 85
Riviera invasion, the, 191–5
Rockwell, RAdm, 60
Rodier, Lt M.F., RNVR, 97
Rogers-Coltman, Lt Cdr Julian, RNVR,
    11, 21
Rommel, Gen, 69, 73
Roosevelt, Pres Franklin D., 25, 36
Ross, Ens, USN, 110–13
Round, Lt M.V., RNZNVR, 172
Russell, Lt Cdr D.M., RN, 141
Russell, Lt G.L., RNVR, 131
Ryder, Cdr Robert, RN, 93, 104

St Nazaire raid, 93–104
Saladin, Santorre Santorosa, Italian sub,
    127
Saunders, Lt (jg) Cecil C., USNR, 134
Saunders, S/Lt Richard F., RANVR, 79
Savage, A/B W.A., 101
Sayer, Cdr G.B., RN, 28
Scantlebury, Stoker, 14
Scharnhorst, 78, 80
Schlichting yard, 36
Schmidt, Edgar, 124
Schmidt, Obit, 136
Schnellboote (S-boats), 8, 34; attack
    convoy in Lyme Bay, 92; attack convoy
    in Mediterranean, 71–2; attack North
    Sea convoy, 169–72; design of, 9;
    development of, 34–6; final effort of,
    189–90; losses of, 184–5; on D-Day, 180;
    successes of, 36, 212; surrender of, 189
Schofield, A/B, 46
Schultz, Kaplt Max, 136
Schumacher, Lt (jg) Vincent E., USN,
    63–5
Scimitar, 175
Scipione Africano, 134
Scott, Lt Cdr Peter, RNVR, 54, 86, 165, 182
Scott, Lt David, RN, 153, 156

Scott-Paine Hubert, 25
Seadler, 80
Seaman, Lt Donald F., USNR, 197
Searles, Lt (jg) John M., USNR, 197
Searles, Lt (jg) Robert L., USNR, 107, 174
Segrave, Sir Henry, 9
Shaw, Lt D.A., RN, 180, 183
Shearwater, HMS, 172
Sheldrick, S/Lt (later Lt) Harwin W.,
    RNVR, 13, 20, 127
Shetlands: operations from the, 91, 189
Shigure, 200
Shima, VAdm Kiyohide, 198–200
Shinyo suicide boats, 21, 42, 202
Shiranuhi, 200
Shore, Lt the Hon. F.M.A., RNVR, 154
Sicily, invasion of, 134
Sidebottom, Lt D.C., RNVR, 81–4
Slapton Sands, 175
Smith, S/Lt G.R., RNVR, 135
Smith, Lt R.R., RNVR, 130
Smyth, Lt E.F, RNVR, 131
Snelling, Lt William, USNR, 182
Somerville, Adm Sir James F., 204
South Pacific campaign, 106–17
South-West Pacific campaign, 118–26
Sparkman and Stephens, 37
Specht, Lt Cdr (later Cdr) William C.,
    USN, 60
Sprague, RAdm C.A.F., 200
Stanley, MMR. J.J., 19, 21
Stansbury, Lt Cdr Theodore R., USNR,
    201
Stark, Adm, 182
Stayner, HMS, 185
Steam gunboats (SGBs), 33, 169
Stephens, Capt J.F., RN, 152
Stephens, Lt Cdr W.L., RN, 97
Strachey-Hawdon, A/B Trevor, 83
Strasburg, 186
Strong, Lt L.V., RNVR, 135
Sturgeon, HM Sub, 97
Sturgeon, Lt J.B., RNVR, 128, 134
Submarines, midget, 181, 183
Sutherland, Maj Gen Richard K., 62
SVAN boatyard, 26
Svenner, 178
Swift, Lt Henry M.S., USNR, 122
Swinley, Cdr R.F.B., RN, 165
Sykes, Lt R.T., RN, 180
Symi (Aegean): raid on, 140–2

Tait, A/B James, RNR, 21
Tamber, Lt Cdr, R.A., RNN, 91
Tappaan, Lt Cdr Francis D., USNR, 126, 197, 201
Tate, Lt D.G., RNVR, 20, 134
Tatro, Lt Wilfred B., USNR, 197
Taylor, Lt Cdr Le Roy, USN, 115
Taylor, Lt Henry S., USNR, 202
Taylor, Lt P.R.A., RNR, 128
Thorn, Ens. USN, 110–13
Thomas, Lt Stanley C., 201
Thompson, Ens Harold A., USNR, 196–7
Thompson, Lt James R., USNR, 122
Thompson, Lt P.A.R., RCNVR, 78
Thomson, Lt F.N., RNVR, 110
Thornborough, HMS, 183
Thornycroft Co, John I., 9, 24
Tillie, Lt A.B.K., RNVR, 97
Timmons, Henry, 124
Tirpitz, 78, 95
Tito, Marshal, 153
Tobruk, 69, 73
'Tokyo Express', 107
Tonkin, Lt R.P., RNVR, 194
Torpedo, 23: German 'human', 181, 194; Italian 'human', 70
Torpedo boat, 23–4
Trelawny, Lt I.C., RNVR, 166
Tunisian campaign, MTB supporting actions, 127, 31
Turnbull, Brig D.J.T., 141–2
Tweedie, Lt Cdr H.E.F., 97
Tynedale, HMS, 96, 101

U 375, 134
U 561, 134
Union, HM Sub, 70
USA, develops MTBs, 36–8
Uzuki, 201

Valiant, HMS, 70
Varvill, Lt R., RNVR, 149
VAS boats, 26
Venice, surrenders to S-boat, 136
Verity, Lt R.E.A., RNVR, 96
Versailles Treaty, 34
Vian, RAdm Sir Philip, 72, 176

Vienna, HMS, 155
Vimiera, HMS, 76
Vimindale, 134
Vis base, Adriatic, 151–5
von Arnim, Col Gen Jurgen, 132
Vortigern, HMS, 78
Vosper yards, 9, 28; experimental MGB from, 33
Vulcan (depot ship), 43

Wadds, Lt H.P., RNVR, 127
Wakeful, HMS, 46
Wallis, Lt N.B., RANVR, 97
Watson, Francis, 124
Weekes, Lt N.R., RNVR, 82
Weeks, O/S Harold, 83
Welman, Lt Cdr (later Cdr) A.E.P., RN, 47, 137, 155
Werf Gusto yard, 36
Weymouth base (HMS Bee), 50
White, J.S., 29
White, Lt (jg) Byron R., USNR, 110
Whitehead, Robert, 23
Wibrin, LMM John, 81
Wien, 24
Wilkes, Adm, 182
Wilkie. Lt Cdr D., RNVR, 110
William, Stephen, 170
Williamson, Lt Robert A., USNR, 201
Willingdale, A/B Victor, 83
Wise, Lt Cdr John N., RNVR, 207–8
Woodhouse, Lt A.O., RNZNVR, 194
Woods, Lt J.R., RCNVR, 156
Worcester, HMS, 169–71
Wright, Lt Cdr D.G.H., RNVR, 184
Wuppermann, Kptlt Siegfried, 46, 70, 195
Wynn, S/Lt R.C.M., RNVR, 96

Yamashiro, 198
Yarnall. Acting P/O Richard, 84
Yarrow shipbuilders, 23
York, HMS, 70
Younghusband, Cdr J.L., RN, 87
Yugoslav partisans, 151–2

Zeebrugge, 25
Zuiderzee, 43